A Turnk

An Autobiography of a Prison Officer

by

Tony Levy

Table of contents

Woodhill

Grendon & Springhill

Prologue

A turnkey: that's what the government wants; that's what the Criminal Justice Agency wants, and that's what the public thinks we are. But we are not, or rather we were not. We used to use our initiative, employ common sense, and make snap decisions, sometimes based on our gut feelings. We were decisive and were considered authoritarian but usually fair. We were the prisoners' mothers, fathers, confidants, peers and even friends. Some looked up to us; some looked down on us. We were everyday men from the streets, mainly from a forces background (although I hasten to add, I was not). We understood discipline and trained in a disciplined, regimented manner to enable us to maintain discipline and authority in very difficult conditions and situations. In other words, we were prison officers.

However, all has changed, because politics and money have got in the way. It's no wonder that our prisons have become more violent and more dangerous for both prisoners and staff. Drugs are rife, and it appears that we've not only lost the battle but also given up the fight against it. Repeated legislation has taken all the rules away that enabled us to maintain discipline. Staff are demoralised and burnt-out by repeated change, and are fed up of hearing the now monthly cry of 'budgetary cuts'.

So long as each establishment can tick all the right boxes, then the Criminal Justice Agency is content. As long as we continually prove that we're doing what we claim to be doing, all are happy and content. So long as we continue to make budget cuts, our bosses leave us alone … until it all goes wrong, and it will.

Looking back, I loved my job as a prison officer, although probably at the time I didn't realise it quite so much. I felt I was important, useful, respected. I wasn't just a cog in a wheel; I was an essential part of the mechanism that made the wheel run smoothly. How I dealt with the prisoners, the visitors and my colleagues were important. Putting on the uniform didn't make me a man; it wasn't something to hide behind, but rather something to be seen.

Over the years, however, all that has been eroded by political influences. Who now cares? Certainly not the government. Prisons are a necessary evil, but they're also a good place to make budgetary cuts. They are the underbelly of a government department, to be ostracised when anything untoward becomes public and criticised when all is well. Nobody cares how the staff or prisoners are treated. Nobody cares about the substance anymore. All they care about is what's on the outside of the tin, not what's inside. It's all a façade. All they want is turnkeys that follow the party line, don't criticise, don't think as individuals and don't speak out. I am not, and never was a turnkey, and I want to share my side of what being a prison officer was like for the vast majority of prison officers.

It is April 2008 as I'm writing this, and I've just come to the end of my 25-year career in the prison service, after taking early retirement and leaving for pastures new. I've witnessed many interesting, amusing and potentially violent incidents during my time in the service, and along the way, I've accumulated many anecdotes and amusing stories. I'd often thought that maybe I should put pen to paper and try to write about my experiences and inform the world of the reality of everyday prison life. However, like most people who've never written a book before, I didn't know where to start, how to put it all together or how to get it published. I had no idea how long it would take or what to write about specifically, and I was worried that nobody would be interested, so the project never got off the ground.

The idea was brought to the forefront of my mind, however, when one night I was watching a thriller on television.

The programme depicted a prison governor and his staff and the goings-on in the prison in a completely unrealistic light. Firstly, it showed a prison governor being decapitated. Now, despite many times wishing disasters to befall my various governors for a wide variety of reasons, I can't remember one instance in which a governor was physically harmed, let alone decapitated, especially at the hands of his own staff. The most interesting feature of the early sequences in the programme was that the governor was collected from his prison in a chauffeur-driven Jaguar. Oh, if only that were true, I can hear 146 prison governors saying! The inaccuracies and lack of realism continued apace until I simply couldn't watch any longer. It gave a wholly false picture of the modern prison service and was a gross misrepresentation of the work and attitude of prison officers in general. I don't know how these programmes can be allowed to show such blatantly inaccurate material. Having said that, the real-life prison service probably wouldn't capture the imagination of the viewing public, whereas sensationalism attracts high viewing figures.

I lay in bed later that night, my mind tracing back over the 25 years I'd spent in the prison service and the changes I'd witnessed, and I decided that maybe I should write that book after all and see if the reality of day-to-day prison life was of any interest to the public.

Several books have been written in the past, factual, fictional and semi-autobiographical, either about the prison service itself or about how certain individuals of national notoriety have spent their time in the confines of Her Majesty's establishments. I would never dispute their versions of events and also fully understand that to sell a book as a commercial venture does require some literary licence, but their perceptions bear little resemblance to my own experiences.

I spent my 25 years of service in four different establishments, all with differing regimes, as well as visiting many other prisons or working in them on what was called 'detached duty'. While I'm sure that there were, and still are, many wanton acts of violence carried out in prisons, whether by prisoners against prisoners or by prisoners against staff and vice versa, given that we currently lock up over 78,000 prisoners throughout the 146 establishments in England, Wales, and Northern Ireland.

The Scottish prison service is run as a completely separate system), the actual number of such incidents is quite small. I'm not making light of the importance or the seriousness of any incidents that do occur, but in reality, the vast majority of prison life is dull, boring routine, occasionally interspersed with short periods of serious and sometimes violent action and incidents. That said, there is no doubt that prison is becoming a more violent place - a reflection of society in general.

Certainly, if I were to tell you that prisoners were constantly running riot, shitting all over their cells, taking drugs, having sex, attempting to escape and smuggling in contraband, or that prison officers were systematically beating up prisoners, bringing in drugs and alcohol, providing any manner of illegal items, having illicit sex with prisoners and on the take, it would make for a great read or a good film, but it is far removed from my experiences and those of the vast majority of my former colleagues. I have therefore endeavoured to avoid any mention of these types of activities, except where they have particular relevance to the story.

I've witnessed and been involved in some extremely violent and potentially violent situations, and I've seen some horrendous injuries inflicted by prisoners on other prisoners, in some instances leading to the victim's death. I've seen some of my colleagues being violently attacked by prisoners and, in some cases, by prisoners' visitors. I've discovered prisoners hanging in their cells, unaware of the reasons for their actions, or having taken drug overdoses. I've been involved in dirty protests, mass sit-ins by prisoners and the aftermath of a prison riot. I've even been accused by an MP of treating Iraqi detainees inhumanely. I've been accused by some prisoners of racism, and I was subjected to disturbing threats by convicted IRA terrorists. I've been spat at by visitors, I've had my car vandalised while parked on prison premises, and I've been told by both prisoners and their visitors that they hope my family die of horrible diseases or are killed in car accidents.

Not all those involved in prisons are nice, honest, law-abiding citizens, but I can honestly say that throughout my life I've never treated any person, whether within the prison service or outside, in any manner that could be interpreted as less than professional.

I must say from the outset that during my 25-year career I have personally never witnessed any wanton acts of violence meted out by any prison officers under any circumstances. However, I wouldn't dispute that such actions do happen, given that there are approximately 36,000 members of prison service staff. There must inevitably be some amongst their numbers that have the potential to be violent or are bullies, or display criminal tendencies, or abuse the prison officer's uniform and believe that it gives them the right to behave unacceptably. I would never condone anybody that acts in this manner.

I should point out that when you join the prison service, you're required to sign the Official Secrets Act, and in my early days this required me going to a solicitor, swearing on a Bible and signing a legal document. This means that while you're a member of the prison service you're restricted in terms of what you can or cannot reveal about the service. However, by the time this book is completed, I will have retired and, so far as I'm aware, I will no longer be bound by these restrictions and can therefore relate some of the actual events that still take place every day.

Many of the incidents described in this book either happened directly to my close colleagues or me and some were related to me by other members of staff during my 25 years in the service. To protect their privacy and ensure their anonymity, I have changed their names (in the first instance only, these pseudonyms appear in inverted commas), but those involved will recognise themselves and their colleagues they worked with. I hope that nothing I've written will cause upset to any of my former colleagues or their families - I would be truly horrified if any were offended by the contents of this book.

I've used a small degree of a literary licence when relating my stories, and the exact words used during conversations may not be replicated exactly, but they are pretty much the language used as I remember it.

In conclusion, I would like to say that, compared to all the other programmes and books depicting life in Her Majesty's Prison Service, in reality, it has been for me more like a rolling episode of *Porridge* rather than *Bad Girls* or a Lynda LaPlante television play.

Chapter 1

Me, Become a Screw?!

I joined Her Majesty's Prison Service on 4 July 1983. It's funny to think that the whole of America will unwittingly celebrate my joining the service, and it's a date I'll certainly never forget.

Why did I join? What was the motivation? I certainly never grew up thinking I wanted to be a prison officer, a screw. I didn't even know what a prison looked like, except that it occupied one corner of a Monopoly board and you looked forward to going to jail so that you could throw in your 'get out of jail free' card and carry on trying to buy Park Lane or Mayfair.

I wanted to be a famous footballer, or a fireman, or train driver - but a prison officer? Don't talk daft! For a start, I'm only 5ft 7in, I weigh just 10½ stone and I would run a mile rather than get involved in a punch-up. Most of the kids in my street either joined the army or became a train drivers or policemen. Some ended up on the dole or went on to become criminals and landed up in prison, although my understanding of that was a little unclear at the time, to say the least. Their mums used to say to my mum, "Oh, Billie's gone away again," and later I would ask my mum where Bill had gone and she would tell me he'd been taken away to Borstal. I thought Borstal was a holiday camp and wanted to go there, too, until mum explained that it was where naughty boys went. So, for me, becoming a screw was never on the agenda.

I was born on 14 August 1951 in Tottenham, North London, and my family's only claim to fame was that the comedian Mike Reid lived in the same street as us and went to the same junior school as my elder sister. I had various jobs in my early days. I once worked at the Great Northern Telegraph Company of Denmark Ltd, based near Liverpool Street, London. It was there that I learned to touch-type - a very handy skill, particularly for the later stages of my career in the prison service and, of course, now for composing this book. I then managed to get into the computer industry as a trainee computer operator and progressed up the career ladder. I eventually ended up working as a driving instructor for the British School of Motoring, based in Baker Street, London. London is a really interesting place to teach people to drive and it was certainly an eventful occupation - probably worthy of a book in itself. If anybody can remember a film that came out around that time called *Confessions of a Driving Instructor*, well, that was very close to the truth.

I have to say I enjoyed my time as a driving instructor and discovered that I was rather good at teaching people. I seemed to be able to relate to my pupils in a way that I'd never believed possible. During that time I was involved in several road traffic accidents, all involving other motorists running into the back of my vehicle while I had a pupil at the wheel. Suffice to say, they were not very pleasant experiences and were certainly not good for your health.

After one particularly nasty accident, when a delivery van shunted into the back of my tuition car and wrote it off on the morning of the marriage of Prince Charles and Lady Diana, thankfully without anybody being injured, I thought: bloody hell, this job can be dangerous! I need to find a safer job, but what? The other downsides to the job, even though I enjoyed it, were poor earnings and very long hours and, as my marriage was also failing at the time, I felt I needed to reshape my life and find a more secure career.

In a last-ditch attempt to save my marriage, I took my then wife on a holiday to Majorca. In hindsight, the idea that we could salvage the relationship was rather daft, because by then we both wanted different things out of life and had irrevocably drifted apart.

As it turned out, however, this holiday was probably the best thing that could've happened to me, and it certainly changed my life. My wife and I sat miserably at the bar opposite our hotel in a very small Majorca holiday resort. This little resort is now a huge bustling holiday town called Alcudia.

The two of us we're not talking and were probably both wishing we hadn't bothered to go on holiday, when a young couple approached us and, grabbing hold of my wife, they asked if they could borrow both her and her chair. They led her to another table, where a large gathering of people was seated. They then came back and said they needed me as well, so I was also led across to their table. This group of people, all couples or partners, introduced themselves to us, and 'Steve' and 'Brenda', the original pair that had brought us over to their table, told us we'd looked so miserable that they'd decided we needed cheering up, and that was why they'd come over and grabbed us. They then informed us that they were all gathered together to take part in an arm-wrestling competition against a group of Dutch holidaymakers later in the evening and they wanted us to make up the numbers. As we'd so far not had a particularly good holiday, and probably aided and abetted by the several Cuba Libres we'd consumed earlier, we decided to join in with the general fun and games.

Many drinks later and now inside the bar, as it was past midnight (in those days all Majorcan holiday resorts had rules stating that entertainment or drinking after midnight had to be behind closed doors), the arm-wrestling competition began. I'd been drawn against this huge mountain of a Dutchman, who constantly referred to me as his "little English friend" and kept reassuring me that he wouldn't hurt me during the impending duel. I wasn't convinced of this given his size. However, I did warm to him, although I'm not sure if this was due to the amount of alcohol I'd consumed or for reasons of self-preservation. Needless to say, I lost both my arm-wrestling bouts, but by then we were all past caring anyway.

And so the seeds had been sown. The rest of our holiday always involved the group, and Steve and Brenda became both mentors and confidants. Luckily my sense of humour fitted in very well, as did some of the more hilarious adventures that I could relate to the group about my experiences as a driving instructor. Despite the difficult marital situation, the holiday became quite enjoyable, and always at the heart of it were Steve, Brenda and myself.

On our last morning, I was sitting on a sun lounger on the beach with Steve and Brenda, when Steve suddenly said he thought that with my sense of humour I would fit right into his profession. I asked what he did for a living and they both just looked at each other and fell about laughing. Steve then explained that Brenda was a policewoman - oh my God, I couldn't believe it! She just wasn't the stereotypical policewoman, considering her size (she was a large lady), her filthy laugh, her appalling bad language, her complete disregard for any rules or regulations and her competitive spirit, which seemed to give her the ability to beat the men at anything we attempted to do.

Come to think of it, she probably did act just like a policewoman! And then I thought back to some of the stories I'd told them about and the somewhat less than legal strokes I'd pulled in the past and about my experiences as a driving instructor – oh boy, was I in trouble or what! My mouth must've dropped to the floor, and they just continued to laugh Eventually, Steve told me that he was in the prison service - not officer/instructor in charge of the mailbag sewing shop. Now it was my turn to laugh. Steve, a prison officer?! Mind you, being with the two of them was like being in a never-ending *Porridge* episode, with Steve as MacKay and Brenda as Fletcher! As an aside, funnily enough, when I eventually joined the prison service and was working at my first ever prison establishment, HMP Pentonville, one of my fellow officer colleagues was just like the *Porridge* character Mr Barrowclough he acted like him, he was kind-hearted and soft-natured, and he spoke like him.

He was so similar in character that the prisoners nicknamed him Mr Barrowclough. He was a real gent and he helped me as a new-entrant prison officer (NEPO) n so many ways, and this stood me in good stead for the remainder of my career in the prison service him.

Anyway, Steve a prison officer, a screw? And his wife was a policewoman? They're both having me on! After a week of continual wind-ups, I thought this was their grand finale. I was gobsmacked to discover, however, that this was the truth. I just couldn't believe that someone with Steve's personality and fun-loving attitude to life would be a prison officer. My preconceived idea of prison officers was that they were all built like brick shithouse doors, ate babies for breakfast, possessed no sense of humour and were all egotistical, vindictive bullies. And yet here was a small, stocky, madcap-humoured loony, who drank too much laughed constantly and loved to wind people up! I was incredulous, but Steve was indeed a prison officer at HMP Maidstone in Kent and taught prisoners how to sew mailbags. He went on to tell me so many humorous stories about happenings at his place of work, of crazy colleagues and the things they'd got up to and of the wind-ups they did to each other and with the prisoner population. It was like *Porridge* in reverse!

My whole perception of prisons and the people who worked there was shattered forever.

Later, over a final beer, Steve said that he was serious about my suitability for the prison service. I'd previously told him that I was looking for another job and career path, so he said he'd let me know when the service was next recruiting new staff on a national basis. Not really thinking that anything would come of it, I told him that if any vacancies turned up I would consider joining. I still didn't know what the prison service was all about and I certainly never thought at that stage I would ever go down that route.

However, eight months later I sat an entry examination held at HMP Pentonville and was told that I and three other candidates had passed, out of a total of thirty men and five women. We four were then taken to the prison hospital and were given a perfunctory examination.

During the examination, the 'doctor' held up a vessel and said, "Can you piss into this?" I immediately replied, "Yes, but not from this distance." He turned to me, displaying absolutely no emotions at all, and retorted, "You'll fit in well here, that's for sure," an expression that was said to me many more times during my initial training.

I discovered later that the medical examiner, whom I'd assumed was a doctor as he was wearing a white coat, was just an officer who just happened to have been detailed to work in the hospital on that particular day and he possessed no medical qualifications whatsoever.

Some weeks later I was sent a letter informing me that I had to report to HMP Wandsworth in South London for a formal interview. As a North Londoner, South London seemed like a foreign country, and it was in trepidation that I made my way to HMP Wandsworth on the appointed date.

My first impression of the place from the outside was of a depressing, dreary, drab old building. There were bird droppings all over the razor wire adorning the top of the surrounding wall. The interview, which was held in what looked like a derelict building at the back of the prison, lasted about 45 minutes and involved a panel of two male interviewers, who treated me to something akin to a good cop/bad cop routine. I think the two of them had watched too many episodes of *The Sweeney*! The 'bad cop' wore a very thin tie, which honestly has no relevance to my story but it has always stuck in my memory This man kept pursuing the subject of my financial situation and he was particularly aggressive in his style of questioning.

However, I must've answered all the questions correctly, as a few weeks later I was informed that I'd been successful in my application and I was given a start date of 4 July 1983. I must admit that I still didn't quite believe that I would ever be taking up this job permanently, but I figured it would do for now.

American Independence Day and the start of a new career for me - how appropriate, I thought.

Chapter 2

Initial Training

HMP Pentonville. Well, all I knew was that Pentonville appeared on a *Monopoly* board. What I didn't know was what a depressing, dilapidated building it was. The 'Ville', as it was known, is an old Victorian building and took its first prisoners in 1842. It was designed by Captain Joshua Jebb in a prototype radial design inspired by Jeremy Bentham's panopticon (literally 'observe all') type of construction. It consists of a central hall for the staff and five wings, each with five landings, extending from it like rays of the sun, all of which are visible to staff positioned at the centre. Pentonville was originally designed to hold 520 prisoners under what was termed the 'separate system', with each inmate having his own cell measuring 13ft (4m) long x 7ft (2m) wide x 9ft (3m) high. However, by 1983 it held over 1,500 prisoners. In 1902 Pentonville took over from Newgate Prison as the establishment allowed to carry out executions. It was here that the famous hangman Albert Pierrepoint was trained and operated. The training manager, Principal Officer 'Brown', informed me on my first day that his office was the actual one used by the official hangman until the death penalty was scrapped.

So, on the morning of 4 July 1983, I entered HMP Pentonville as a prison officer under training (POUT), a title that was changed within days to new entrant prison officer (NEPO).

I wish I could remember what the weather was like on that day, but to be perfectly honest it's all a bit of a haze. I remember being ushered into a room with two other men, 'Nasher' and 'Ray', who were to be my colleagues for the next three months, at least during our initial training. Nasher was a youthful, baby-faced Northerner and seemed very self-conscious of his young looks. When he got excited or laughed his cheeks would go bright red. Ray, on the other hand, was an ex-submariner who had seen a bit of the world, and he was always relating funny yarns from his days at sea. Then there was me, an early 30-something. Neither Nasher nor I had any forces experience, which at that time made both of us a little different to the vast majority of staff, most of whom were ex-forces and particularly ex-army personnel. Furthermore, I also stood out as one of only six members of staff that were actually Londoners. The policy at that time seemed to be that if you were young and single you were sent to a London jail to work. The view was that you did not want to be there but you would work diligently and conscientiously in the hope that after two years you could get a transfer to an establishment nearer your hometown. The fact that most prison officers in the London jails were not from London meant that they were unlikely to have family members as inmates and therefore could not be influenced by any relatives or acquaintances in the local area. I was never sure if this was official prison policy, but it seemed a logical approach at the time.

We spent our first month in civilian clothing and we were given a programme to complete, which involved going around different departments and then composing a 'diary' explaining what we had seen and identifying the staff in charge and their roles. Our observations were then presented to the training principal officer (PO), Mr Brown, who highlighted in red ink everything we had got wrong - which in my case seemed to be quite a lot, looking back at the diary, which I still have in my possession. I well remember this PO once yelling in my face, "Thank God I'll be long retired or dead by the time you ever get your sorry arse promoted, Mr Levy."

One of the only other things of note that I can remember well was the first time we were given a tour of the prison. We were taken to B wing, which was known as the dossers' wing as most of these prisoners were tramps and drunks. These prisoners had a particular party piece for any strangers entering the wing in civilian clothing. They would come out of their cells and stand in front of you, then drink their own urine out of their piss buckets and declare, "Nice drop of the stuff, guv."

There were no in-cell sanitation facilities at the Ville, so all prisoners were issued with two pots, a green one for collecting fresh, clean water from the recess (toilets), and a clear, lidded container to hold their 'slops' (urine and excrement). They were allowed to obtain clean water and empty their pots (known as 'slopping out') in the morning, breakfast, lunch and supper unlock periods, at which time they would have to carry their two buckets to the nearest recess to perform their ablutions.

I learnt later at the training school that you always unlocked a landing by moving from cell to cell in the opposite direction to the recesses, so if a prisoner started walking in the wrong direction and following you it was obvious, he was intent on pouring the contents of his buckets over you. You always hoped that one of your colleagues would spot this in time to warn you, but this didn't always happen.

One of the most important lessons from this period was that all prison officers should refer to prisoners by their surnames and address each other as either Sir or Mister. Another vital piece of information was that, however hot the weather was, you should always wear your prison-issue hat and walk close to the walls when moving along the landings.

The reason for the latter became all too clear some months later when I was detailed to take a group of trainee magistrates on a tour of the establishment. I repeatedly advised one particular member of this group to follow this procedure, but he continually refused to conform and continued walking in the more exposed area; that was until a prisoner poured the contents of his slop bucket all over this unfortunate gentleman from the fifth landing above us. I'm not sure if this man went on to be a fully-fledged magistrate, but if he did, I sincerely hope he remembered what happened to him during his first tour of a prison when sentencing newly convicted criminals.

At this stage, neither my colleagues nor I had been issued with our uniforms. I still had a niggling feeling that this was not going to be my permanent career anyway, so I had a pretty light-hearted approach to the whole month of training.

I remember as part of our training programme we were assigned to the censor's office, where all prisoners' incoming and outgoing mail was logged and read by an officer before being handed to the prisoner or sent out. The officer in charge, 'John', had been in the service many years and informed us that this particular job was only given to experienced officers and that 'us sprogs' weren't likely to be allowed to work in that capacity until we had put in at least ten years' service time. Whilst we were there, John explained that he was going to call up a prisoner and hand over some photographs that had been sent to him by his wife. He explained that prisoners were only entitled to have in their possession a maximum of ten personal photographs at any one time, so if more were sent to them, they were required to exchange them on a one-for-one swap basis.

The prisoner arrived and was allowed to choose which pictures he wanted to keep. He showed us the photographs as he was making his selection, and among them were ones of a table with two full glasses, a bottle of champagne and a rose, and also of a woman, whom I could only assume was his wife, in various poses and wearing increasingly fewer clothes until the last one in which she was only wearing a man's tie and she was draped provocatively over a chair with the rose in her mouth.

The prisoner said to John, "I'll have this one for my collection," pointing to this last photograph, adding, "She's a cracking-looking bird, my missus, don't you think?"

John took the photo and studied it for a few moments.

"Yeah," he said, "but whose tie is it and who's the other drink for, you moron?"

The prisoner took the photo back, looked at it again, and then ripped it up in front of us, before storming out of the censor's office muttering, "The fucking bitch! I'll kill her when I get out!"

John also explained the two types of visits that took place at the prison and told us of the dreadful mistake he once made when sending out visiting orders (VOs), which gave prisoners' family and friends permission to visit on set dates. The Ville locked up both convicted and unconvicted prisoners and each had different rights and privileges: one visit per month and one privileged visit for convicted prisoners, usually from the wife; and a 15-minute visit every day for unconvicted ones, usually from the girlfriend. Anyway, while preparing the VOs one day, John accidentally put the same date and time on two separate VOs for the same prisoner, thus unwittingly inviting both the wife and the girlfriend to visit at the same time! When they both arrived at the table to meet their loved one and saw each other a fight broke out. The prisoner's wife was eventually restrained and escorted off the premises, but not before breaking the girlfriend's jaw and then attacking her prisoner husband. This is one obvious mistake to avoid in the future!

This was how our initial training continued for the four weeks, experiencing the workings of different departments and generally getting a feel for the place. We were never allowed to be near any prisoners on our own and were always escorted by a prison officer. We received a lot of verbal stick from the prisoners, who at that time were generally referred to as inmates until thankfully some bright-spark psychologist some years later realised that the word inmate conjured up a vision of someone being held in a mental institution

At the Ville we were told right from the start to call them prisoners anyway, so we were way ahead of the game

Poor Nasher seemed to take a lot more stick from the prisoners than either Ray or myself, but that was probably because he looked so young and innocent.

Never during this training period did I believe that I would be making this job into a full-time career; it just never seemed real. At this stage, we did not know to which prison establishment we would eventually be assigned. This would only be designated towards the end of the eight-week officer training, I suppose just in case you either failed the course or didn't want to be sent to that particular posting. This was the same with our uniforms, which would only be issued during the officer training course.

The four weeks drew to an end and we three were informed that we would be going to Officer Training School at a place called Leyhill, starting during the first week in August. There were just two establishments that carried out prison officer training at that time, the other being HMP Wakefield.

It is interesting to note that the role of the modern prison officer has a relatively short history, stretching back only 80 years or so since the dissolution of the separate system when 'warders' had restricted communication with prisoners and were forbidden from developing any kind of personal relationship. It was around this time that prison staff, by the Royal Commission, became known officially as prison officers. Of course, when the press and media chose to portray us in poor light then we were more commonly referred to as wardens or screws.

It was a well-known belief throughout the prison service at that time that Leyhill trained officers and Wakefield trained screws. We were to become officers.

Chapter 3

Officer Training School, HMP Leyhill

This was probably the most enjoyable eight weeks of my whole career. There were 112 men and eight women all starting their training on this course. Each course was assigned a number and this was OTS L.

HMP Leyhill originally opened as hutted accommodation and was formerly a wartime hospital for the USAAF (United States Army Air Force) and handed over to the prison service in 1946. Located in South Gloucestershire, Leyhill was the only minimum-security prison in the South West Area (known as Category D). Leyhill was rebuilt in the late 1970s to early 1980s and in 1986 prisoners were rehoused in new living accommodation. The two famous inmates at Leyhill are arguably Leslie Grantham, who served the final part of a sentence for murder at the prison before being released in 1977 and going on to land himself numerous roles as a TV actor, most notably as Den Watts in *EastEnders*; and T. Dan Smith, a Newcastle politician disgraced by the Poulson affair. It was Smith who encouraged Grantham to go into acting on his release.

The training centre was an old country house situated adjacent to the prison. In its grounds was a lake where only a select few people were allowed to fish, including HRH the Queen Mother and the Archbishop of Canterbury. So it was strictly out of bounds to us NEPOs.

We were designated different sections, each having a principal officer in charge and run very loosely on military lines. I was assigned to the D section and Nasher and Ray went to the F section.

The principal officer of my section was a small, wonderful Scottish man (Mr McLowthian), who taught me a great deal about how to do my job. He explained the three self-defence weapons at our disposal: our staves, our whistles and, most importantly, our mouths. He also taught me that officers should never hide behind their uniforms and think that it alone will command respect from the prisoners; it's the person behind the uniform that counts. I think the whole philosophy that I implemented throughout my career was down to this man. I learned that I should be professional at all times, whatever provocation came my way, and that I was there to set an example to the prisoners in my charge, not the other way around. He always told me that by using my sense of humour appropriately I would be able to (nearly) always defuse potentially dangerous and violent situations and this proved correct throughout my career.

After each day's training, Nasher, Ray and I, along with another lad from F section, 'Bill', would get together and visit the local pubs in Watton-at-Stone, the nearest town, or go over to the prison officers' club across the fields at HMP Leyhill. Our outing to the officers' club on our very first night got the four of us our first official bollocking of the course.

As raw recruits on our first night, as we left the house, we could see the lights of the officers' club just across the field, so took the most direct route across this well-maintained stretch of greenery to reach it, and after showing our newly issued identity cards we were allowed into the clubhouse for a well-earned beer.

I don't honestly remember much from that first night, except that when we walked into the club and saw some of our new colleagues, we noticed that all the men seemed to be on one side of the room and all the women on the other. After obtaining our beers, which incidentally were a lot cheaper than pub prices as all drinks were subsidised, we made the obvious choice and headed over to mingle with our new female colleagues.

Something that sticks in my mind is that two records seemed to be playing constantly on the jukebox, so we adopted them as our signature tunes: Wham's 'Club Tropicana' and most appropriately

Joe Cocker and Jennifer Warne's 'Up Where We Belong' from the film *An Officer and a Gentleman.*

Each section contained 20 recruits, and my section had two of the eight women in it. Each morning we had to attend a morning parade and assemble in our own sections in front of the chief officer, who was a small but very stocky man known as 'Chief Blockmore'. Nobody messed with him, as this was the man who held your future in his hands, in charge of deciding whether you were good enough to pass each phase of the course or whether you would be sent back to your previous life. It sounds a bit melodramatic, I know, but in those days the chief officer really did have all the power, and this was true for every prison establishment.

Everybody, including both the prisoners and some of the governor grades, feared the chief. The head governor of any penal establishment relied on the chief to ensure the smooth running of his prison and that is exactly what these chiefs did, believe me.

So, it was a bit of a shock when at the end of our first parade my name, together with those of my three outing buddies, was called out and we were all instructed to report to the chief officer's office immediately. What the hell had we done? After all, it was only the start of our second day there. We knocked on the chief's door, entered the office and stood in front of him in trepidation. He looked up and a verbal explosion ensued. He told us, in no uncertain terms, of our flagrant disregard for the feelings of all the hard-working members of the prison community and the prison's longstanding traditions. Who did we think we were, blatantly contravening correct procedures when attending the prison officers' club? We were all stunned. What the hell was he on about?

Our transgression was then explained in further detail. The field we had traipsed across to get to the club was the prisoners' football pitch, which they had just finished mowing. It was their pride and joy, having transformed it from an overgrown, disused field into this now pristine, beautifully manicured pitch, and it was strictly out of bounds to NEPOs such as us. One of the prisoners had spotted us and made an official complaint to the training school, and so the chief had duly shared these concerns with us, the guilty four, in his unique inimitable fashion.

Suffice to say, lesson fully learned. From then on we took the designated route to the club and faced the threat to life and limb that this involved. To get to the officers' club you had to walk down the mile-long drive from the old country house, then turn right at the junction and walk along the road for another three-quarters of a mile. This road comprised numerous blind bends and there were no pavements or street lighting, so the walk back was in total darkness. Believe me, it was so black that you really couldn't see your hand in front of your face, and I'm surprised that none of us was ever hit by passing cars, although we did have some close calls.

Several days later, whilst I was taking a comfort break in the nearest toilet, the chief came alongside me to carry out his ablutions. He looked me up and down and said, "What's your name?"

I replied, "Officer Levy, sir."

"Okay," he said. "I just wanted to put a name to the face. You walked across the cons' field, the other day and I gave you a rollicking for it, right?"

"Yes, sir," I replied. Then, thinking I should make some witty remark to excuse our misdeed, I added, "You see, although we realised that the correct way to the club was down the drive and along that very dangerous road, we thought that as the government was investing so much money to train us in the skills required to take our place as part of Her Majesty's Prison Service and serve the community, the least we could do was ensure we completed the training safely rather than waste their money by getting run over."

Without even looking up, the chief replied, "You'll fit in well in this job with that sense of humour, and you'll need it, sunshine. But don't try to bullshit me again."

With that, he finished what he was doing and walked out of the toilet, leaving me wondering whether I had made a terrible mistake in trying to be funny.

During the first few days, we were issued with our full prison uniform, which consisted of six-blue shirts, two pairs of blue trousers, one blue jacket, one Gannex raincoat (made famous by Harold Wilson, who was frequently seen wearing one when he was Prime Minister), one hat with cap badge, two epaulettes, a stave, two blue clip-on ties, waterproof leggings and a waterproof cap protector. We were also issued with best uniform jacket and trousers, which were made of really heavy barathea cloth. It weighed a ton and made you sweat buckets. We were made to try all these on to ensure that they fit and were informed that once it had been established that they were the correct size then any future issues would always be of these sizes. This practise continued for several years until the system was thankfully changed. Until then, if you put weight on it was impossible to request a different size from central supplies, so you could end up feeling very uncomfortable. Every part of the uniform seemed to fit okay except for the Gannex raincoat, which was much too long and the sleeves extended over the end of my fingers. We were inspected by the chief and I pointed out my dilemma to him. He just gave me one of his looks and said. "At least it'll keep your fingers warm until you get some gloves, which could take about ten years in this service. Just roll the sleeves up and it'll fit a treat." So that was that. I still have that raincoat today - in perfect condition, but the sleeves are still too long.

Apart from the initial first two weeks, when the whole school had to remain 'on duty', we were allowed to go home at weekends. As I mentioned earlier, my marriage was coming to an end and so, although I went home on Friday afternoons, I couldn't wait until Sunday and my return to Leyhill.

A large number of us formed into our own little group, which included most of the women, and we would all meet up in the officers' club or one of the pubs in Watton and chat about what we'd been up to over the weekend. One weekend it was my birthday and I left my home in North London earlier than usual to return to Leyhill. I felt very guilty about leaving so early, but it was my birthday and I wanted to have some laughs and a drink. On arriving at Leyhill I dumped my bag in my room and walked round to the club to meet all my colleagues. They were all waiting for me with birthday cards and drinks and I think someone had baked a cake. We had a great evening, and I knew deep down at that point that my marriage was truly over; and a short time after the course finished, it was indeed.

We were assigned a task that would take a few weeks to complete. We had been given a subject to research and at some point later in the course, we would be required to give a 20-minute presentation on it in front of the governor and the rest of the course group, with two minutes for questions at the end. My subject was 'The Battle of Trafalgar & Horatio Nelson', of all things! There was a big library in the school, but it didn't contain any books relevant to our research, so this would have to be done in our own time. I had found out that the prison governor was a keen reader of books by C.S. Forester, particularly his Horatio Hornblower series, which depicted life at sea in the British Navy during the Napoleonic Wars and the time of Admiral Nelson.

Twenty minutes seemed to me to be a bloody long time to stand up and speak in front of a class and appear knowledgeable, but with intensive research over my weekends, I managed to put my presentation together. I also discovered that Forester's Hornblower character was based on a real person, albeit a minor sailor, that actually took part in the Battle of Trafalgar. This little gem allowed me to really impress the governor during my presentation. He asked me afterwards how I found out about this and I informed him that Forester had handed a sealed envelope containing this information to his solicitors before his death, with the instruction, that it was not to be opened until a hundred years after his passing, and that it had therefore only recently come to light. He was most impressed, but I must admit that, to this day, I'm not sure if this story is true. I may have misinterpreted what I had researched, but hey, who really cared? Presentation over, thank goodness.

The course continued apace. We would spend sessions in the classroom going over procedural documents that enabled the smooth running of prison establishments, although why we had to remember the actual names and numbers of all these documents were beyond me, except for the fact that we had to conjure them up for our regular written examinations. These exams took place on Friday afternoons and their completion always seemed to send you home for the weekend in a good mood.

Our skills would be tested in simulated prison situations, such as dealing with a prisoner visit that gets out of hand or conducting a cell search, or - my favourite - searching the grounds for an escaped prisoner. We would usually be part of a team of three in these simulations, with a nominated leader and the rest of the class would then make notes of what they witnessed and afterwards, we would return to the classroom and review the exercise.

I never seemed to get picked for any of these teams and always seemed to end up playing the part of the prisoner or the crafty visitor trying to smuggle contraband into the prison. Once, when I had been given the role of an escaped prisoner on a very hot August day, I managed to circumnavigate the searching team and walked back to the classroom to await their return. It was a good hour and a half later when my classmates, bedraggled and sweating profusely, finally appeared and, on finding me asleep in the classroom, I was subjected to a load of verbal abuse. The principal officer had told them that they would have to stay out in the fields and continue searching until they found me, which had meant suffering the baking sun in a full prison uniform.

This was the daily routine, interspersed with practising as a section of how to march, with a nominated member of the class picked as leading the group. I found myself at a huge disadvantage having no military background, unlike the chap to my right, who was ex-RAF and made it look like a stroll in the park on a hot summer's days. The girl on my left 'tick-tock' marched - you know, left arm with left leg, right arm with right leg - which was most off-putting, so I spent most of these sessions smiling to myself or laughing out loud and completely disrupting the whole section's overall appearance, much to the consternation of Mr McLowthian.

On one particular day, following a heavy drinking session the previous night, I was selected to lead the marching. I was a little hung-over and my voice was so husky it felt as though I had laryngitis. Off the section went, down the drive, with me trying to shout, "Left, right, left, right, right, right," etc. Mr McLowthian approached me and started asking how I was feeling, and I completely forgot about the section still marching towards the end of the drive and the main road. All of a sudden Mr McLowthian said, "Learn a valuable lesson here, Officer Levy. If you are in charge of a prisoner work party, don't let anybody come up to you and distract you from your duties. Otherwise, like your section, they will end up on the road or trying to escape. Now do something before it's too late!"

On one occasion we were all given five minutes to think of something to talk to the class about. It could be on any subject and would be filmed so that it could be played back and reviewed by everyone. We always sat in the same position, behind desks arranged in a semicircle around the principal officer or session tutor. I was seated about halfway round the group, so I had some time to think about my subject. But, blow me, the person seated two places away from me had chosen the same topic. So when it came to my turn, I couldn't think of anything. Nothing came to mind - literally, so I began: "Most of you that know me know I've always got something to talk about. Well, today I have nothing to talk about, so I'm gonna talk about nothing. There are three types of nothing. You can have a long nothing, a medium nothing or even a short nothing. And the beauty of talking about nothing is that nobody can ask questions. I will now give you a demonstration of a short nothing."

I stopped talking and just sat there until the two minutes were up. I received rapturous applause from my classmates and a wry smile from our PO.

Occasionally we would carry out joint exercises with another section. Again, I usually ended up as an observer or as the object of the exercise. On one such occasion, three officers were selected, given role-play scripts and sent out of the room to prepare themselves. The rest of us were given the opportunity to ask questions about anything connected to the course. I asked if it was true that at some time during the course we would actually, get the opportunity to lock and unlock a cell door. We were told we would, but not yet. There were very few other questions and then the class went silent.

Mr McLowthian pointed out that the exercise was not ready to start yet and tried to prompt further questions or comments, but his efforts were met with further silence. He then said, "As there is nothing anybody wants to say or ask, nothing at all, within our midst we have an expert on the subject of nothing, and if we ask him politely Mr Levy would. I am sure, come out to the front and give us his renditions on the subject of nothing."

Talk about being put on the spot! But what could I do? I had to take up the challenge, otherwise, I would lose all my 'street cred' and be made to look a fool. No way, I thought. But, Christ, it meant doing that stupid presentation on the subject of nothing again and this time in front of two sections, two principal officers and the bloody governor! I had no choice, so I went out to the front and somehow managed to talk on the subject of nothing for over 15 minutes. Don't ask me how, or what I said because I honestly don't know.

As I walked back to my desk amid rounds of applause from the whole audience, I heard my PO say to the governor, "I win my bet. I told you he could do it." I never found out how much the bet was for or if it was a complete set-up from the beginning, but boy did my standing in the school shoot up after that.

And so the course continued, with classwork, simulated exercises, marching and lectures. I remember once, during a presentation from the POA (Prison Officers' Association), falling asleep within two minutes of the guest speaker's opening remarks. This wasn't an unusual occurrence, however, particularly when the whole school was in the main lecture room and we had partaken in a heavy night at the local watering holes.

We were taught 'mufti' training, which was a mixture of self-defence, wristlocks and judo. All PEIs (physical education instructors) shared the same sadistic tendencies and seemed to relish inflicting pain on us new recruits, so much so that some of my colleagues ended up at the casualty department of the local hospital.

One poor unfortunate was so severely injured that he had to leave the course. I learned very quickly, after being chosen as the victim of a very painful wrist-hold demonstration, that this was one session in which it was best to keep my mouth shut and maintain a low profile for the sake of self-preservation.

Thankfully, this type of training has since been completely transformed into what is now referred to as C&R (control and restraint), which comprises a series of defensive manoeuvres aimed at avoiding physical injury by immobilising an aggressor with minimum force using certain pressure points in their nervous system. These techniques are very effective, particularly with very aggressive and violent prisoners, and never result in any serious or lasting injuries, except perhaps to an individual's pride.

On a Friday morning, the whole school held a formal parade along military lines. We would form up in sections, with the elected section leader at its fore. We were always asked to make an extra effort for these weekly parades, as the governor in charge of the training school, carried out a formal inspection of each section line by line, while we all stood to attention. Before this, an officer pupil supposedly selected at random would call the whole parade to attention. His or her job was to notice when the governor, closely followed by the chief and all the section principal officers appeared at the entrance to the parade ground.

The whole parade would then come to attention and two other carefully selected officer pupils would raise the union flag onto the top of the flagpole. Each section leader would then order their section to march up towards the governor and management team, who by now was standing in front of the parade, and report that their section was 'all present and correct'.

What a load of drivel! We were not an official armed force and new officers were not selected as officers because of their military backgrounds (although this was not the case not that long before I joined the service) but supposedly based on their exemplary attitude and man-management skills, along with their ability to set a good example as peers to the prisoner populations. So I found it difficult to take the whole thing seriously, but some of the ex-military types took this parade to an extreme. Boots or shoes shined until you could see your face in them, they stood rigidly to attention, making the rest of us look like a bunch of slobs. It really makes you wonder what they made of the rest of us.

To my dismay, on the very last Friday of the course, I was selected as the officer to lead the full parade and two other officers were given the task of raising the flag. We three were called into the chief's office and given our instructions. I remember it was one of the only dull, cloudy and miserable days we had during those eight weeks. The sky was grey and there was a hint of rain in the air. The chief explained that I had been chosen to lead the parade rather than carry out the flag duties, as he didn't trust me not to play a practical joke and hang it upside down or raise a pair of ladies' underwear just for a laugh, and also the two other officers had previous military experience.

Great, I thought. I was to lead the parade - just what I wanted, to be launched into the spotlight like this! And I was probably one of the only officers who thought the whole parade thing was a load of crap!

The chief further explained to me, "As it looks like rain, if one drop of rain falls from the sky before the governor or I step foot out of the door onto the parade ground, you will dismiss the whole parade section by section and the parade will be cancelled. You understand, sunshine?" Just so that there was so misunderstanding on my part, he added that if a single raindrop fell on his head, I would be in for the biggest verbal bollocking I'd received so far.

Because of some of my previous verbal bollockings, I wasn't too pleased about being given this job on this day, especially as I genuinely had now developed a sore throat and could hardly speak let alone shout commands that would be audible to a parade of 120 new officer recruits and all the associated staff.

And so to the parade. I stood at the front terrified in case it rained, and yet in a weird way I was wishing it would rain so that

I could call the whole thing off and not have to go through with it. Why hadn't he picked somebody with military experience, who would have relished this experience, instead of me, someone that hadn't taken any of the previous seven parades seriously? But, of course, I knew why. In the prison service, you often have to carry out tasks that you do not agree with or support, but they must be done, and given my stance, it would prove interesting for them to use this as part of their assessment of my ability to do a prison officer's job, or so I thought.

I stood facing the assembled course members, looking out of the corner of my eye towards the door to check for the appearance of the governor and his entourage. Was that a spot of rain I just felt? Bloody hell, I'm sure it was. But it's only one spot. Do I call it off or not? Too late - here they bloody well come. Oh shit, the chief looks thunderously furious.

They approached me and moved to their respective positions directly behind me. I turned to face the governor and reported that the parade was ready. He nodded his head. I turned around again and squawked the order: "Parade, attention!" My voice was at the point of giving out. Oh shit, and now it's started to rain! What the hell do I do? Then it stopped again, so I carried on.

Each section leader marched up to me and gave me their section numbers. Was I supposed to keep a total of the number or just hope that all 120 were actually on the parade ground? When all had reported to me I once again turned and faced the governor and reported that all officers were present and correct. I then turned to face the parade, while the governor gave a little speech about the success of the course before proceeding with his full inspection.

The chief, following the governor on his inspection, as he passed me whispered in my ear, "Wanker, I told you to call the parade off if it rained, and I felt a spot of rain just before we entered."

The training was over. We had received our posting notices earlier in the week. I suppose leaving it until the end of the course meant that you were less likely to resign if you weren't keen on working at the designated establishment. Generally, all single officers were posted to the London prisons, which were always short of staff, although I found out later that those who underwent their officer training at Wakefield usually got posted to the big city prisons in the north of England for similar reasons. I wanted to be posted to Pentonville, as it was the nearest prison to my home, and I had been dreading being sent to Brixton, as it was in South London and would have meant a nightmare journey every day. Luckily, along with Nasher and Ray, I got the Ville. Three others were also posted with us, and Bill was one of them. He wasn't too happy about this, as he came from the West Country and was getting married after the course, so his posting meant that he would be away from his new wife until they could sort out suitable accommodation.

We were given two weeks' leave (taken off our annual leave allowance) and then had to report to our designated establishments for a further week's induction before starting as fully-fledged prison officers.

Chapter 4

Pentonville - My First Day!

I suppose my most lasting impression of the Ville will always be the stench. The whole place stank of stale tobacco, body odour and rotting human excrement. Its walls wept the smell; it got on your clothes, in your hair, and on your skin. Immediately on getting home from work, I used to take off all my clothes, put them in the wash and then take a shower. The next morning I'd put on clean, fresh clothes, but when I got in my car there was that smell again. It never goes away. Even with today's new internal sanitation facilities that smell still pervades everything; it will never go away until they knock the Ville down. That said, boy did I have some fun and games while serving at the Ville.

So, along with Nasher, Ray, Bill and two other newly qualified officers from our OTS course, I arrived to start work as a prison officer at the Ville. Having previously spent a month there, as mentioned in an earlier chapter, Nasher, Ray and I had a distinct advantage over the other three in that we knew the layout of the prison. I still didn't quite believe this was real, that it would honestly be my new career, yet here I was, parking my car in the staff car park in front of the prison.

The first thing that struck me was how many brand new cars surrounded me in the car park and how few parking spots there were along the main drive leading up to the prison's main gates. I knew that the staff mess was near one of the two barriers at the entrance to the prison. Looking from the gatekeeper's box out onto Caledonian Road, a barrier was set to the right, allowing access to the staff living quarters. Many staff were housed there but by the time I joined the service very few quarters were available for new staff. If you didn't have a family then you didn't qualify.

To the left was the main entrance barrier that led into the staff car park and the mess, located on the left-hand side. An 18ft wall surrounded the prison.

I was pleasantly surprised when several officers remembered me from that initial month at the Ville and they welcomed me back. The induction week was a bit of a bore really, as it repeated much of what Nasher, Ray and I had already learned in our training month. The initial comments from the training manager, PO Brown, made us feel completely at home: "So you three Herberts made it through training, then. Now the real stuff begins. Let's hope you can become real officers and not just wear the uniform."

That first week dragged by. The most important thing we learned was where to find the detail board, which from around 2 p.m. every afternoon. displayed your designated work for the following day and also to which wing you had been assigned and in what division you had been assigned to for your weekend duties.

Pentonville had five wings - A, B, C, D and R - and we worked on the 'V' scheme, which meant one weekend on followed by one weekend off. We worked a ten-day shift pattern: 'E' shift worked mornings only, starting at around 6 a.m. to relieve the night patrols, and finishing at one fifteen; 'M' shift worked from 7.45 a.m. to 5 p.m.; 'L' shift from 1 p.m. to 9 p.m., or later if you worked in reception, and ' an A' shift started anytime after 6 a.m. and could extend up to 11.30 p.m. if you were in the reception area.

Initially, you only worked a 39-hour week, but you could put in additional hours with overtime. Once established, I worked an average of 70 to 80 hours per week and my earnings were very good with all the overtime.

We were also issued with our set of security keys. This worked on a tally system, whereby whenever you entered the prison you placed the tally you had been given down a chute and were then issued with a set of keys bearing the corresponding tally number.

Along with the keys we were issued with a metal chain. The keys would clip onto one end of this and the other end would attach to your trouser belt in such a way that they keys could be secured in the key pocket on the front of your trousers. I still have my original chain, which I kept as a souvenir. You're actually supposed to hand these back at the end of your term of service, but after 25 years it was in such poor condition and so badly discoloured that I reckoned the government would allow me to keep it.

The one-week induction eventually drew to a close. I checked the detail board on the Friday afternoon and saw that I was detailed to D wing and due to start at 7.45 a.m. on Monday. Although that was my designated parent wing, this didn't mean that I would be detailed there exclusively and could be sent to other areas if there were staff shortages.

On Monday I arrived in good time, so I decided to go into the mess and have a cup of tea before entering the prison and starting my first shift as a prison officer. I also knew that there were some toilets in the mess, and by this time I needed them. Whilst sitting in the cubicle (these toilets were in a very clean condition for Pentonville), I heard from outside a voice saying, "Slop out, McVicar," followed by, "Freeze, arsehole". Wondering what the hell was going on, I quietly opened the door enough to see an officer looking into the mirror on the wall, with a comb in his hand. It seemed that every time he pulled his comb out of his back pocket he chanted these two phrases to his reflection in the mirror! I learned sometime later that this officer was known to all and sundry as 'Nutty Freeman'.

I walked to the gate area and announced to the officer that I was Officer Levy reporting for duty. The officer checked a list of names in front of him looked me up and down, and then over his shoulder announced to his fellow PO, who was sitting in an armchair looking completely disinterested and reading *The Daily Mirror*, "Another fucking NEPO!" This was one of the same officers that had greeted me in such a friendly way the previous week, so I wondered why he was behaving in this way. Anyway, he ticked my name off the list and then issued me with my set of keys: a cell key for opening prisoners' cells; three keys for inner and outer security gates; and a general key for all non-security doors. So, now fully equipped with these, together with my previously issued belt, whistle and stave, and dressed in my nice, new, pristine uniform, I was allowed into the prison. Incidentally, the stave was a longish stick that fitted into a special stick pocket sewn into the inside of your issue trousers. We were supposed to carry these staves with us at all times whilst on duty, as they formed part of our uniform, but I observed that most officers seemed to carry their daily newspaper in this pocket.

I entered the prison and walked along the corridor past all the administrative offices, making my way towards the main prison area and the centre gate that would allow access into the main body of the prison. God, I was feeling nervous and apprehensive - and, boy, did I want to go to the toilet again! I reached the gate, got out my keys and for the first time used them to unlock the gate and enter the main prison. I turned to the left to check the detail board just to make sure that nothing had changed, and then looked in the information book housed in an information box nearby, which contained details of any recent major issues, in case there was anything I should know about, but there wasn't. I then walked past the centre gate again to make my way to D wing and came across another box, housing the duty principal officer (PO), his senior officer (SO) and his 'gofer' (an officer was detailed to this area to do any running around the PO or SO wanted, such as fetching their tea, etc.) The principal officer is in charge of the prison for the duration of his shift (in those days there were no female officers of any rank at Pentonville).

Looking out from this box, the wings were arranged like a clock face, spanning alphabetically from A wing on the far left to D wing on the far right. R wing was attached to C wing and could only be accessed via the education block, and C wing also housed the punishment block. The centre box also contained the tannoy system, which was used to announce the start and finish of every part of the regime, such as "Unlock" for unlocking the prison doors once the centre had confirmed the prison roll, "Lead on for exercise", "Lock up for roll check", and so on.

I walked past this centre box to my wing. Bloody hell, 'my wing', I thought to myself. D wing was on five levels and, as with all the other wings, it had a stairway at each end. It was a little confusing, as the first/ground floor of the wing was known as 'the twos', the second as 'the threes', etc. This was because there was also a landing below the ground floor and this, for some strange reason, was known as 'the ones'. I knew from my induction week that on arrival on your allocated wing you had to report to the wing office. This was on 'the threes' and was where the wing PO, SO and gofer was based. As I walked up the stairs I noticed that the SO was taking down the names of the staff as they reported to him, assigning them to various landings in preparation for 'slop out' and reminding them of their morning's duty.

I approached very apprehensively and stammered, "Officer Levy reporting for duty, sir."

The SO replied, "On the twos. Just help out with meals supervision." Then, without pausing for breath, he continued, "Well, what the fuck are you waiting for, mister, an invitation get down those bloody stairs?"

I was livid, not to mention shocked, at being spoken to in that manner. Jesus, what the hell had I let myself in for? I made my way down the stairs, still angry and smarting, and on reaching the bottom I noticed a group of staff congregating around an officer near the hotplates, which comprised a series of long, gas-heated metal containers designed to keep the food warm before dishing it up. In those days political correctness had never been heard of and we 'fed' prisoners, whereas in the modern prison service we 'serve' food to them. These hotplates were great in the winter, as they helped to keep us warm, but in the summer months, they made the whole place baking hot. I realised that this officer in charge was 'holding court', relating stories and comments to his audience, and it was obvious that as a new officer I wasn't included in this group, so I just stood near the stairs and waited.

I knew that the individual wing rolls had been counted and the numbers supplied to the centre. These would then be collated to ensure that the prison roll was correct before the PO could announce prison unlock. At that point, each wing was allowed to unlock the cells and start the process of slopping out. The prisoners would have about 15-20 minutes to complete their ablutions and a junior officer would be posted at the toilet end (recess) of the landing, while a more senior officer stood at the centre end, taking prisoner applications. If you were lucky, a third member of staff would stand alongside the senior man to keep an eye on proceedings at the recess ends. The prisoners would then be locked up again until the call to serve breakfast. This would be carried out on a landing-by-landing and cell-by-cell basis, usually involving two or three officers, depending on staff availability.

The prisoners would walk down one stairway to the twos, collect their breakfast at the hotplate area and proceed along to the other stairway to make their way back to their cell. As each prisoner re-entered his cell, the officers would move along the corridor and lock them in again.

As I stood by the stairs, I thought to myself: I've done a month in this place, eight weeks at training school and another bloody week here, and everybody I met during that time was kind and considerate, yet now I'm being treated like a bloody leper! What is this all about?

My thoughts were interrupted by a prisoner ringing his cell bell, at Pentonville, all cells were equipped with a bell, and when it was pressed it rang in the wing box and caused a flag on the wall outside each cell to drop from a vertical to the horizontal position, thus enabling the staff to identify at a glance which prisoner required assistance. It also caused a resounding reaction from the PO in wing office that I heard many a time while working at the Ville: "Answer that fucking bell!"

Then I heard another voice: “Oy, you, sonny!” It was the officer holding court. Could he be addressing me? “Oy, you, sonny, answer that fucking bell!” he yelled, pointing at me. I was furious! There I was, a 30-year-old man who’d previously had his own business - not that successful, admittedly, but even so - being referred to as ‘sonny’, an appellation I’d last heard 20 years earlier from my dad! Bloody hell, I was angry!

I approached the cell and opened the spyhole following my newly acquired training skills, i.e., with the fleshy part of my thumb, to avoid the risk of any pointed object being thrust into my eye, which had happened to a few officers in the past. I said to the prisoner, “What do you want?” He replied, “A shit, guv.” Without thinking, I responded, “Well, you’ve found one. Now get off your fucking bell!”

I wasn’t very proud of myself, I must say. That wasn’t the way I’d planned to talk to the prisoners, but I was still seething. At that point, the senior of the officers detached himself from his group, approached me, put his arm around my shoulder and said, “Well done, mate. You’ll fit in well here.” And, with that, I was accepted into the fold.

This particular officer and he and I became good colleagues. He really taught me many of the skills required for me to be a fair and highly regarded member of staff. And I did manage to achieve that status, but it was only years later that I realised it.

Chapter 5

A nick in the nick

Nearly every member of staff in the prison service was given nicknames, some just names and others reflecting the character, appearance or mannerisms of the individual concerned. You must remember that this was 1983 and political correctness wasn't something that had even been thought of in the prison service at that time. Here are just a few of the ones I came across:

Cabbage Patch: As his hair looked like the Cabbage Patch dolls.

Exocet: Because, as the missile, you could see him coming, hear him coming, but could do nothing about it

Slim: Pretty obvious - due to his size

Diddly Diddly: Because he was a completely nutty Irishman, who had served in the British Army

Nobby: After the footballer, and because his surname was Clarke

The Cardboard Cut-out: Because he was always dressed so immaculately

Wing Nut: Due to his very large ears that stuck out.

Put-put: An Asian officer who always started a conversation with those words.

Sinex: Named after the nasal spray, as he was a little squirt that got up your nose.

Dinger: Because his surname was Bell.

As I was from Tottenham, was a Spurs fan and was Jewish, I quickly became known as Yiddo, which is how most Spurs football fans are known throughout the country, and I was occasionally referred to as Red Sea Pedestrian, which came from the popular Monty Python film, *Life of Brian*.

Sometimes, I was given the more derogatory, tasteless and highly offensive name of Oven Dodger, referring to my Jewish background and the gas chambers in German concentration camps during the Second World War. However, Yiddo was the name by which I was most commonly known throughout my prison officer years, and it occasionally spilt out into my life outside of the prison service, as I will relate later in the book. Apart from 'Oven Dodger', for the reasons explained, I never found these names offensive or even racially motivated; in fact, quite the opposite. They were terms of endearment and a sign that I was being accepted into the team.

Although it didn't register with me back then, but there was undoubtedly an undercurrent of racism within the prison service and I did come across members of both the prison staff and the wider openly racist prisoner community, whether between prison officer, staff towards prisoners and vice versa, or prisoners against prisoners. Over the years, racism between prisoners has become more the prominent and disturbing part of prison life, particularly with the increase in world terrorism and growing numbers of Muslims among the prisoner population. This pattern can also be seen in terms of gang culture and associated violence, particularly with the younger generation, which is increasingly evident in certain streets, estates, towns and districts outside of the prison boundaries and also in Young Offenders Prisons (YOIs), such as HMYOI Feltham.

I remember I'd only been at the Ville a short time when I realised that there was a lot of overtime available if you were in the know and on the radar of the staff who worked in the detail office, who appeared to have control over who worked what overtime. There were many mundane jobs that some staff wished to avoid, so these officers used to allocate these jobs to other staff who wanted the overtime. Although I was now living the life of a single man, at this time I was also still contributing to the mortgage for the house I'd shared with my estranged wife on top of paying for my living accommodation, so I really needed the extra money. The staff that worked a lot of overtime were referred to as 'overtime bandits', and I wanted to become a bandit.

Our basic pay was around £8,000 per year, but it was possible to earn over £20,000 by working overtime. We would receive our earnings in cash every week and had to collect our pay packets from the cashier's office when our regime allowed. This was one of the only times we had any contact with non-uniformed staff. We would be handed our money in the usual little brown envelopes, open them up, look at the wage slip and count the money out before leaving the cashier's desk, just to make sure that there were no errors. On a normal week, I would take home around £110, but with lots of overtime, I regularly used to take home £220 to £280 per week, which was really good money in 1983, believe me. Mind you, you would have to work over 70 hours per week to earn that sort of dosh, but I could afford all sorts of things on that level of earnings.

First, however, I had to get on the overtime bandwagon. I came up with what I thought would be a good idea in terms of getting noticed, formally introducing myself and being accepted onto that elusive overtime list.

It was the end of one of my very first evening shifts and as usual, all prisoners had been locked up for the night, each wing roll had been confirmed and the staff were congregating in the central area, near to the corridor gate that led out to the main gates. As mentioned earlier, that was where the PO's box was located, enabling a good view of all the wings, and from where all the tannoy announcements were made. There was a blackboard in the central area, too, which was used to inform staff of any important meetings, and so on. The staff that had completed their shifts would go to the centre and wait there until the prison rolls had been confirmed and all the night shift staff had arrived and were in place. Then the centre PO would go to the duty chief officer's office to inform him that the prison was all locked up and secure. He, in turn, would make a great play of leaving his office, walking to the centre and saying, "Break off," which would allow the staff to exit the establishment, return their keys, retrieve their tallies and go home.

That evening I was amongst the first of the staff waiting at the centre, surrounded by the general hubbub of conversation, mainly about who was going to work what overtime over the next few days and nights. We were always short of the agreed number of staff required to run the prison regime, so there was lots of overtime to be had if you were in the know. I wasn't included in any of these conversations, so I idly walked up to the blackboard rubbed out everything written on it and replaced the messages with 'YIDDO' in huge capital letters. I then just stood back. The conversations died down and by now all the staff had arrived at the centre.

I then stepped forward and announced that I was Officer Levy, better known as Yiddo and that I was interested in working any available overtime. The chief officer (aka The Cardboard Cut-out, as mentioned earlier) came out of his office, saw what had been written on the board announced break off, and then turned to me and told me to wait behind. Here we go again, I thought, expecting a bollocking.

He called me into his office, but rather than tear strips off me he just told me that he thought it was a most unorthodox way of introducing myself to the staff and he didn't approve. Mainly, however, he just wanted to warn me that working all the overtime under the sun wasn't healthy and that I should ensure I had a life outside the prison service and not focus solely on earning lots of money and then 'piss it up a wall' like a lot of the others. I realised some years later that this man, who honestly did take a lot of stick from the staff was a very kindly person whose whole life had been devoted to the prison service. It was his life and was all he had. He was so obviously talking to me from his heart at that time.

Boy, did I become popular after that! I have to report that it worked a treat and I was never short of opportunities for overtime from then on. And I worked a hell of a lot of it, too. Most evenings I was given overtime shifts, as well as on weekends, and as I was 'single' with no children I was a very popular choice for working over Christmas. This was great for me. I would work a main shift and evening shift, which usually meant starting at 6.30 a.m. and finishing at 9.00 p.m. Overtime was paid at time-and-a-half during the week and double time at weekends and on bank holidays. So I became a big bandit! and I never did 'piss it up a wall', though.

Chapter 6

A Day at Pentonville

A typical day at HMP Pentonville began at 8 a.m. when the day staff came on duty on the main 'M' shift, although some were detailed for 'early starts' or 'E' shifts, commencing at around 7 a.m. Quite often they would come even earlier so that the night staff could get away early.

On arrival at the prison, you would proceed through the gate, put your key tally down the chute in the gatehouse and then receive the corresponding keys. If you need a radio you would then turn left and make your way to the security department. You would then join the radio network using the radio call sign assigned for the duty you were on. There was a locker room to the right of the gatehouse, where staff could change into their prison uniforms and store their civilian clothes in a locker. For obvious reasons, this area was strictly out of bounds for prisoners.

You then entered the prison by way of the administration corridor. At the end of this corridor was the gate, which led into the heart of the prison and the central area where the PO's box was located and the five wings could be viewed. To the left of this box was the detail office and you would check the board to make sure that there were no changes to the duties you had been assigned when the list was first posted on the previous afternoon - for instance, due to staff sickness or a requirement for additional escort cover. There was one other box here, known locally as the 'sin bin' as it was where you were instructed to wait if you had been off sick and had just returned for duty. This was the staff information centre, where all the latest details on prison procedures and the prison policies were kept.

From here you would report to the SO standing outside the wing office on the threes, who informed you of your allocated landing and tasks for the morning. If you were amongst the first to arrive on your respective wing, you counted up the prisoners and reported the number to the wing SO

Once the prisoner count had been carried out and the numbers had been passed to the centre and confirmed as correct, you waited for those two magic words - "Slop out" - to be announced by the centre PO over the tannoy. However, it didn't always run quite that smoothly. On many occasions, the count would be wrong and instead, you would hear the announcement of "Recount" and the whole counting and reporting process would have to be repeated.

On the instruction of "Slop out," you would start unlocking each cell door, in turn, moving in a clockwise direction, with each prisoner filing away in an anti-clockwise direction rather than following behind you as they made their way towards the recess (toilet) located at the right-hand side of the landing. As explained earlier, the direction was important to avoid the danger of a prisoner deciding to retrace his steps behind you and deposit the contents of his slop bucket on you or attack you in some other way. There was no internal sanitation, so if prisoners needed the toilet during the night they would have to use a bucket in their cell and wait until morning to dispose of the waste - hence the great Pentonville smell. So at unlock time, the prisoners would take this bucket to the recess to empty it, together with another bucket for collecting freshwater. Once all the cells had been unlocked, you would take up a position of relative safety to supervise the slopping-out process.

Of the (usually) three officers on your landing, two would stand at the centre end - one taking prisoner applications and the other watching his back - and the other (usually the most junior officer, poor mug) would be positioned at the other end of the landing, right next to the main recess. This was the worst place to be detailed, with prisoners trooping past in both directions with either a full piss pot or an empty one. Also, it wasn't uncommon for the old plumbing to have problems coping with the volume of excrement from the slop buckets and private use of the toilet cubicles, resulting in leaks or, worse still, blowbacks from the toilets. You would then end up with excrement running past your feet and around your shoes. You always hoped your shoes were watertight, that's for sure. It was honestly bloody disgusting for everybody concerned - prisoners, staff and even visitors. Thank goodness slopping out has now been replaced by in-cell sanitation.

If you were unlucky enough to be posted at the recess ends, this also meant that you were first in line when the inevitable punch-up started. Either you were the first one in to try and break up the fight after raising the alarm or you were the first one to get clobbered by one of the aggressors with his bucket of crap. A great place to be detailed! You just hoped that the other officers were looking out for you while in this vulnerable position. I always tried to make sure I could see either the officer immediately below me or the one above, so in the case of an emergency I could raise the alarm on their behalf, and I always hoped they were doing the same for me.

After about 15 minutes you would then reverse the process and start locking the prisoners back in their cells. Incidentally, a common prison expression used both back then and now is, "Happiness is door-shaped," meaning that once prisoners are locked behind their doors you're in a safe environment.

At this point, you usually nipped off for a quick cup of tea or a cigarette while the prisoners' breakfast was being prepared. This was served on the ground floor of each wing around ten minutes after the post-recess lock-up.

And so to the 'serving' of breakfast, rather than the zoo-like 'feeding' the prisoners as it used to be called. Once breakfast was ready to be served and the staff had come back from their crafty cuppas or fags, the centre PO would announce over the tannoy, "Commence breakfast". Each landing on your wing would then be called down in order, one at a time. Again, the unlocking of the cells was carried out in a clockwise direction, with prisoners proceeding down the landing in the opposite direction to you and taking the stairs to the ground floor, collecting their breakfast and returning to their cells using the stairs at the other end of the landing. Once all the cells doors had been locked again, there was around a 30-minute window to allow the prisoners to eat their breakfast, so it was off for another cuppa and fag for the officers. This was followed by another slop out, lasting 15 to 20 minutes, before happiness became door-shaped once again and another cuppa and fag were in order.

Once this was completed, the staff then went off to attend to whatever the duty they had been allocated - bathhouse, education, solicitors' visits, social visits, workshops, etc. One officer would be left to unlock the prisoners and send them off to their designated pursuits.

The PEIs (physical education instructors) would collect their prisoners and take them to and back from the gym. Every movement of a prisoner going off the wing had to be recorded in the wing office and reported to the centre so that an accurate record of the location of each prisoner and the number of prisoners in each activity could be maintained and easily checked. Every activity area also kept a roll of attendees. Reporting numbers is a hugely important part of prison life, and yet it is often fraught with errors. Amazing really.

By around 11.30 a.m. the morning activity period was over and all prisoners were returned to their wing and locked in their cells while lunch was prepared. Lunchtime follows the same routine as breakfast and generally on the command of "Commence lunch" over the tannoy you would go back to the same landing unless there were staff shortage and help was needed with serving meals on other wings.

Meal times could be very volatile periods and officers had to be very aware of potential dangers. Not only were prisoners carrying a metal tray, loaded with crockery and metal cutlery (yes, in those days we issued metal knives and forks, whereas nowadays everything is made of plastic), but also they were allowed to fill their cups with boiling hot water to make tea or coffee. I have seen some horrendous injuries to both staff and prisoners as a result of boiling water being thrown at them, and if they've added sugar to their hot drinks then it sticks to you like napalm.

Usually, lunch was served in a different wing order to breakfast. It was supposed to follow a strict rota, but changes often had to be made due to prisoners arriving back late from their various morning activities. Once all the prisoners had collected their food and were back behind locked doors, a roll check was carried out again, numbers once again were submitted to the wing office and passed on to the centre for collation and confirmation. The PO always made a great ceremony out of it, walking slowly in his pristine uniform to the chief's office, and he, in turn, would make a fuss about something or other, while everyone else waited anxiously for the announcement of "Break off". Then it was off to lunch. Yippee!

The afternoon routine was pretty much the same. We would report to our respective wings, count the prisoners, report the numbers, await the tannoy announcement of "Slop out", and repeat the recess procedure. Once the prisoners were back in their cells, the staff could embark on their various allocated duties. The prisoners' afternoon would comprise an hour's exercise period, together with visits and workshops. Then it was back to their cells to await the preparation and serving of tea, following the same routine as lunchtime. Then another count would be done and numbers would again be reported to the centre to be confirmed, with the usual rigmarole of the PO's walk to the chief's office and the chief's little cameo, before everyone's favourite words, "Break off," rang out. That signalled home time, unless you were on evening duty like me, as I became an overtime bandit and worked most evenings.

To be honest, if I left work at around 5 to 5.15 p.m. it could take me upwards of two-and-a-half hours to get back to where I lived in Cheshunt in Hertfordshire due to the rush-hour traffic, whereas

a finishing time of about 8.30 p.m. following an evening shift resulted in only a 30-minute journey home, so it suited me to do the overtime on that score, even though the additional money was my main motivation.

The evening duty usually consisted of unlocking the prisoners for education, gym or sometimes association, the latter being only for a small number on a rota basis. Once they were locked up again, we went around with two large metal buckets and issued all the prisoners with a cup of tea or coffee. This was followed by a count, and once the numbers had been submitted and signed for we would then congregate around the centre, to witness the chief's party piece ritual and Shakespearean monologue of, "The roll is correct. Break off and goodnight."

One officer per wing would be designated to remain on duty until the night shift staff arrived. They would count the prisoners and confirm that the roll was correct before they took over responsibility for the wing.

So that, for me, was another day for Queen and country, not to mention my wallet and I could head off home. Night, night, prisoners. We'll be back tomorrow to do the same things at the same time as we've done today and did yesterday and the day before that, and so on since time began. It's a great job working in Her Majesty's human dustbin!

Chapter 7

A Day Trip to France

I was detailed to go on prisoner escort duty with two other officers, 'George' and 'Taff'. We were detailed to take this prisoner to Dover Magistrates' Court on a production order, which the courts give to the establishment to ensure that a prisoner is brought in front of a judge at court. Taff was to drive the green prison transit van or, as we used to call it, 'green pixie'. Daily we also used big green coaches, known throughout the service as 'green goddesses', which were fitted with horrible hard bench seats.

As the junior screw, or 'sprog', I knew I would have to be handcuffed to the prisoner throughout the journey, which wasn't a very comfortable experience when travelling in a green pixie.

On the previous evening, just before I left for home, George said to me, "Hey, Yiddo, don't forget your passport tomorrow. You'll need it." Having already checked my detail, which told me that I would be on escort duty to Dover Magistrates' Court, I assumed his comment was some sort of in-house private joke. How wrong could I be?

The next morning, bright and early, at around 6 a.m., I arrived in reception ready for my journey to Dover Magistrates' Court. No further mention was made about a passport, so I concluded it was just a wind-up. We collected our prisoner and brought him back to reception, where he was given a breakfast pack. It was too early for a sit-down breakfast, as we had to set off at 6.30 a.m. to be there for 9.30 a.m. The prisoner was searched and then handcuffed to me. We completed the relevant discharge-under-escort paperwork and then headed for our awaiting transport, the beloved green pixie.

Once onboard and seated in the correct formation, to ensure safety and security, we set off on our long and painful journey (if you sit in one of these green pixies for more than half an hour, believe me, you have pains in places you wouldn't think possible!) I couldn't tell you what the route we took. From the middle row of the pixie I remember just watching the countryside go by, and I was probably fast asleep within half an hour of us setting off.

Once, on a journey on one of the green goddesses around inner London to 'drop off' prisoners at their respective courts for trial, I'd fallen asleep by the time we'd reached the prison barrier and before we'd even joined the Caledonian Road. I'm not sure if this was a record, but it was acclaimed as such by everybody on board, including the prisoner handcuffed to me! In fact, it was the prisoner that woke me up to inform me that we were almost at the courthouse and I really ought to stir myself!

A big plus about the magistrates' court visits was that these courts were staffed (I would've said manned, but that might've been deemed sexist) by the local police and were usually either attached to a police station or located close by. This meant that once at the court, the police took your prisoner into their custody and you had nothing to do but sit around until the court appearance was over. Usually, the duty sergeant would say, "Okay, lads, off you go to the canteen. You can have a game of pool or watch TV, or the shops are just up the road. Just make sure you're back here by 3 p.m. to return your charge to prison." This was bloody great - a magic combination of overtime pay plus the day off to do what you wanted, within reason. We all loved going on these types of jobs.

I remember one such occasion when I was detailed to escort a prisoner to Grays Magistrates' Court in Essex, along with a superb officer who was a sort of mentor to me. He was from Bermondsey and some years later his son became the World Snooker Champion. He was a great bloke and a wonderful escort partner. What he didn't know about the job and how to handle prisoners wasn't worth knowing. Anyway, we got there and handed over our prisoner. The sergeant said, "Just wait over there." So we sat down on a bench and waited.

After about an hour my colleague said to the sergeant, "Sarge, is there a problem, as we've just been sat around waiting for ages?"

"Yes," replied the sergeant. "Last week two of you guys came here, handed the prisoner over and were instructed to be back around 3 p.m., and they came back absolutely pissed, so from now on you can wait there until your guy's finished in court and then you can bugger off back to Brixton with your prisoner."

"Hang on," said my colleague, "we're not from Brixton, we're from the Ville - you know, Pentonville."

The sergeant suddenly changed his tune. "Oh, sorry about that, lads. I thought you were from Brixton and I won't let those piss artists out of here from now on. Anyway, if you want a full breakfast the canteen's on the fourth floor, or there's the …."

Normal service had been resumed.

Anyway, back to Dover Magistrates' Court. When we entered the court we were greeted by the sergeant, the handcuffs were removed and we handed our prisoner over to the police for their safe custody. Happy that our prisoner had all that he required, the sergeant said, "Okay, lads, it's a nice day, so off you go. The beach is about ten minutes away, or there's the town centre just up the road. Don't knock the arse out of it and don't come back pissed, and don't be later than 3.30 'cause we pack up then. Have a nice time. See yas later."

That was that. It was 9.45 a.m. and we'd got the rest of the day off. These escort duties really are the dog's bollocks.

You learn very quickly that when undertaking any activity outside the prison you always take a civvies jacket with you to slip on over your uniform. This day was no exception. So we put on our civvies and walked out into the Dover sunshine.

"Right then, what we gonna do?" said I. George answered, "Right, you've got your passport, so let's get in the van and get down to the docks. We should just make the 10.30 ferry."

"The 10.30 ferry? What the fuck are you talking about? What fucking ferry?" I said.

"The ferry over to France for a booze cruise," replied George. "I told you to bring your passport. They won't let us on without it."

I was dumbstruck. I'd thought all the passport talk was a joke and hadn't taken it with me. Going over to France when we're supposed to be working? Having a day off once we've got rid of our prisoners is one thing, I thought, but a trip over to France is taking the piss.

"You are joking, aren't you?" I queried.

"The fuck I am!" came the response. "We're going over and getting some booze and tobacco. If you didn't bring your passport then you'll just have to amuse yourself for the rest of the day and we'll see you back at the court by 3.15," said George. And, with that, he and my other colleague got in the pixie and drove off.

So there I was, left in Dover on my own for the day. What the hell was I going to do to fill the time? Oh well, I thought, the sergeant had said the beach wasn't that far, so I'll just go down there and have a sunbathe and eat my lunch. What else could I do?

By 3.15 p.m., as arranged, I was back at the Magistrates' Court awaiting my colleagues' return, having had a very pleasant day down on the beach. Sure enough, a few minutes later they appeared.

“Right,” said George, “let’s get cuffed up, then back on the road and head for home.”

I was once again cuffed up to the prisoner, who, noticing my red glow, said to me, “Bloody hell, guv, you’ve been sunning yourself, ain’t you?” “Yeah. Thought I’d take advantage of the lovely weather. Went down the beach and sat in the sun,” I replied.

“All right, don’t rub it in. I got committed to Crown Court while you were out sunning it,” he said. “I’m probably looking at seven years at least if I’m found guilty.”

We said our goodbyes to the sergeant and thanked him for allowing us the time off, before walking out of the court into the secure compound and up to our pixie. George opened the sliding doors to let me and the prisoner in.

“Bloody hell!” I exclaimed. “What the fuck’s all that?”

The van was filled with crates of beer, boxes of wine and packs of cigarettes.

“Just get in the fucking van quick, Tony, will ya!” grunted George.

The prisoner and I just about managed to squeeze into the van and ended up almost perched on the boxes and crates.

“Bloody hell, George, what are you gonna do with all this booze when we get back to the Ville?” I asked.

“Don’t worry ’bout that. We’ll unload it before we take laddo back in,” said George.

If I wasn't worried before, I certainly am now, I thought. What the hell does he mean? Unload the stuff? Where? And without anyone seeing us?

Not only was the journey back more uncomfortable than the outward-bound one, but also I was now really worried. Christ, I've only been in the job a short while and now I'm into this lark, I thought to myself. So much for my career! We're gonna get the sack for sure if the chief finds out. And I had nothing to do with it. I'll be guilty by association. I can wave goodbye to my job. Thanks very much, George.

We arrived back at Pentonville and approached the barrier. George indicated to the officer on duty that we were going to drive up to the prison quarters, so he needed to open the other barrier. Oh my God, I thought, he's gonna unload this fucking van within sight of the prison - into one of the quarters, no less! What the hell am I going to do?

The van pulled up and then reversed up to one of the prison quarters (housing accommodation usually for officers with families, as explained in an earlier chapter). George jumped out and opened the garage door. He then opened the back of the pixie and, together with Taff, started to unload the van. I remained seated in the van.

"Come on," said George, "jump out and give us a hand, will ya?"

"How the hell am I gonna do that, George? I'm cuffed up, remember." "Oh yeah," he replied. He then turned to the prisoner and said, "Okay, sunshine, if I take you off the cuffs and you help unload, I'll make sure there's a beer in it for you. What d'ya say?"

"I'll do it for two beers," the prisoner replied.

"Okay then, it's a deal," said George.

And, with that, George uncuffed the prisoner and we both started helping to unload the van and take the stuff into the garage.

I was still panicking, convinced that we'd get caught. We were only just outside the wall, in an area overlooked by D wing. Bloody hell, I thought, all it'll take is for one officer to look out of the window! How the hell did I get myself into this?

When we'd finished, George cuffed me and the prisoner together again and we hopped back in the van. We then drove back down towards the barrier, turned left through the other barrier and made our way along the drive and up to the prison gates. Taff sounded the horn and we were allowed back into the prison complex. Once back in the reception area, we handed our prisoner over to the reception staff so that he could be officially readmitted and returned to his cell. George had promised him that he would see him later with his reward.

And that was that. It was all over. The prisoner was back where he should be, George had got his booze, and nobody seemed to have any idea what had happened. I suspected that maybe this was a fairly common occurrence, but thankfully one that I was never involved in again.

I learned later from George that he did indeed get the prisoner two bottles of beer, which he must've enjoyed as he kept quiet about the whole affair. I must admit, however, that over the next few weeks I kept expecting to be called into the chief's office or the governor's office for a bollocking. Thankfully, the call never came and I never heard another thing about that day trip to France.

Chapter 8

Paul Childs, Here I Come!

Working long hours, because most of our earnings came from overtime, did take its toll on many staff.

A survey carried out at that time by a national organisation found that the job of a prison officer was one of the most stressful occupations and that life expectancy following retirement was on average just nine months. Bloody hell, that didn't seem very long! In contrast, the average factory worker's post-retirement life expectancy was 15 years, a doctor's 14 years and a politician's 18 years. I assume that this was based on a retirement age of 65, whereas our contract at that time gave us the option to take early retirement at 55.

The survey had to take into account the type of stress experienced by prison officers. The job entailed a constant need to remain vigilant, interspersed with long periods of boring routine, followed by short bursts of high-adrenalin activities. Being an officer meant that you were always on alert for the sound of an emergency alarm bell, indicating that an incident was taking place, and you never knew the nature of the crisis until you arrived at the scene. It could be a fight, an assault, a hostage situation, a barricade or even a death. The bell would sound and staff would respond by running (or, in official parlance, 'attending as soon as possible', as if you were to say you'd run to the scene it invalidated your insurance claim) to the centre where you would be directed to the site of the incident. In the rush to attend an incident it wasn't unknown for staff to injure their colleagues in the process. It was the same if you ever heard a prison officer's emergency whistle. On average, these types of emergencies occurred around four times a day, but there could be up to seven or eight of these incidents on some days.

So you can imagine how this daily scenario affected a prison officer's stress levels: one minute you'd be carrying out some mundane task and the next you'd be rushing to the scene of an incident, unaware of what you'd face when you arrived. It was very stressful, I can tell you.

The survey also considered the number of hours that most prison officers worked on average every week. Nearly all big city prisons were short of staff and were overcrowded (not much has changed there then), and the only way these prisons could operate any sort of effective regime was to rely on staff working overtime, so most worked long hours; in fact, I can only really remember half a dozen officers at Pentonville that never did any overtime.

Despite the high levels of stress that came with long shifts, they became an essential part of life. You adjusted your lifestyle to match your overtime-based earnings and came to rely on that level of pay. If you took a holiday you only received your basic pay, which was pretty meagre, and you worked a week in hand. So you would come back after your break, work the week, go and collect your pay packet and then realise just how little you earned on basic pay, especially if you were an overtime bandit like I was.

If you were injured at work you received no compensatory pay award, just your usual basic pay. No adjustment was made to your earnings should you suffer an injury that incapacitated you from working. However, an insurance company called Paul Childs was used throughout the prison service and offered some sort of compensation in these circumstances. Paul Childs was a saviour to many staff and most staff signed up to them. This insurance company, for a small weekly outlay, offered a deal that covered you in the event of your sustaining an injury at work and being off work for more than two weeks, which amounted to a payout that equated to your average overtime earnings. Great! By a strange coincidence, many staff sustained a serious injury during an incident just before they were due to go on annual leave, thus meaning that they took their holiday on full pay - yet another 'Spanish' practice!

I remember one particular day when I was detailed D4 landing duty at the recess end. Oh great, I thought - first punch-up of the day and I'm right in the firing line! I swear that bloody SO has got it in for me! Why couldn't he put me at the other end? My worst fears came true. A heated argument erupted in the recess between two huge prisoners. I quickly looked upstairs to see if any other officers had heard the commotion, and then quickly down to the landing below. Dammit! No other officers were in earshot. I fumbled for my whistle to raise the alarm but - as usual in an emergency - the thing got stuck in my pocket. By this time the conflict had turned into a full-on fight situation. So, without thinking, I stepped between the two antagonists, put my hands over my head and said, “The first, one to hit me sends me off to the Bahamas for two weeks courtesy of Paul Childs.” This stopped them in their tracks and one of them said to me, “Mr Levy, you’re fucking mad!” And, with that, it was all over; both walked away once again the best of friends.

Was that plain stupid or extremely innovative? I honestly don’t know, but I would never recommend doing something that risky. But that’s what adrenalin and the power of Paul Childs can do to you!

I remember another instance when a prisoner had been placed on a disciplinary charge by a member of staff and the hearing had been arranged, following official timescale of the procedures. Once placed on a charge, a strict time limit was imposed between the prisoner receiving the paperwork explaining why he’d been placed on report and the actual date of the hearing. A special room, known as the adjudication room was set up in C wing for this purpose. C wing housed the segregation unit, or ‘block’ as it was known, where any prisoners facing disciplinary adjudication would spend their confinement (rule 48) in specially designated cells or in some instances for their own protection (rule 43).

The governor would be seated at one end of the room behind a desk, separated from the prisoner by another desk placed lengthwise, forming a T shape, to ensure that the prisoner was set well back and couldn’t lean over the desk and grab the governor. The prisoner would stand at the narrow end of the desk with officers stationed on either side and facing him - so close to the prisoner, in fact, that their nose tips almost touched. Along with the governor would be the senior officer in charge of the block, together with the officer or member of staff who'd laid the charge. Also, the prisoner was entitled to request the presence of any witnesses he wished to call to speak in his defence. He could also call on a 'Mackenzie man', who was somebody that could speak on behalf of the accused but was not involved in the actual incident.

The governor would start the proceedings, which were similar to those carried out in a court of law. First, he would ask the prisoner to confirm his name and prison number to ensure that he had the correct prisoner in front of him. It wasn't uncommon for these types of charges to be thrown out by the adjudicating governor due to errors in the paperwork, such as a wrong or misspelt prisoner name, wrong prisoner number, or a charge worded incorrectly.

In this particular case, the prisoner gave his name and number and then said, "Guv, they've got the wrong bloke 'ere."

The governor continued regardless, stating that the prisoner would get a chance to give his version of events. He proceeded to read out the charge, asking the prisoner how he wished to plead.

Again, the prisoner said, "Guv, this is a case of mistaken identity." "Yes," said the governor. "As I said, you will get your chance to tell us what happened. How do you plead?"

"Not guilty," said the prisoner. "I'm trying to tell you they've got the wrong bloke."

The governor, now growing impatient, responded, "If you don't shut up and let me get this over with, you won't get the chance to explain to me why you think we've got the wrong prisoner. Now shut the fuck up and let's continue."

With that, the prisoner looked straight at me - not very difficult, seeing as we were standing virtually eyeball to eyeball - and just shrugged his shoulders. I was struggling to suppress my laughter and remain rigidly to attention. There was nowhere else to look but directly at the prisoner's face. Catching the eye of the other officer didn't help either, as he was in the same state as me and was practically willing the prisoner to open his mouth again.

The charging officer read out his evidence and then the governor looked at the prisoner and said, "Is there anything you wish to explain about the officer's report?"

"Yes," replied the prisoner. "It's like this, guv. It's a clear case of mistaken identity."

The governor responded, "What do you mean? Do you deny that you were acting in the manner described by the charging officer in his statement?"

"No," said the prisoner, "but when all your screws came charging into my pad they were shouting, 'Paul Childs, here we come,' and like I've been trying to explain to you, my name is not Paul fucking Childs!" At this point, I almost collapsed with laughter, the governor's face turned purple, the SO sitting next to him looked up to heaven for some divine intervention, the charging officer's face went white, my escort partner looked as if he was going to kill the prisoner and the prisoner just looked at me and winked.

The governor then adjourned the hearing, and my colleague and I escorted the prisoner back to a holding cell to await the governor's assessment of the situation. The governor then called us all into the adjudication room and explained that, although indeed he felt that the prisoner was guilty of the charge, his reference to 'Paul Childs' had raised serious doubts as to whether the adjudication could proceed due to the manner in which the staff had entered the prisoner's cell. Although the governor didn't elaborate, he more than suspected that some of the staff involved had ulterior motives and had participated in the incident so that they could claim they'd sustained an injury and be awarded sick leave on full pay, courtesy of the Paul Childs scheme. I hate to say it, but this was probably very near to the truth. I have no doubt the prisoner was fully aware of what he was saying and that by 'stitching up' the officer he'd get off the charge, and I can't blame him for that.

I remember an officer once explaining to me that he was due to go on holiday the next day and was concerned about the poor pay he would receive on returning to work - unless, that is, he sustained an injury during his shift that day and ended up on sick leave, in which case he could make a Paul Childs claim. Lo and behold, later that day there was indeed an incident and this particular officer was injured and was signed off sick. As this officer was going off duty he winked at me and said, "I'll see you in two weeks. I'm off to sunny Spain for my holidays!"

There were repercussions to the adjudication incident. Thereafter, staff were very careful about shouting out 'Paul Childs' when charging into an incident or mentioning the scheme in prisoners' hearings. Several years later the scheme collapsed when 'Fresh Start' came in and the overtime in its then form was stopped. Oh well, all good things come to an end.

Chapter 9

The Prison Officers' Club

My first experience of going to the prison officers' club at the Ville will always stick in my mind. Eager to be accepted into the team, and with my home life deteriorating rapidly, I accepted an invitation to go there one evening after work.

Unlike the episode in *Porridge*, when Mr Mackay went to the officers' club and it was portrayed as a lonely, practically deserted, dreary bar, the prison officers' club at Pentonville was a fairly new, vibrant, busy and successful place. It was a fairly new building, courtesy of an IRA car bomb exploding outside the old clubhouse, which had to be demolished as a result. The new one was built into the rear wall of the prison and could be accessed by walking along the Caledonian Road onto the back road (I can't remember the name of it) or via the outside perimeter road, which was flanked on one side by the prison wall and the other side by the staff living quarters. At the end of this road was a wicker gate that led out to the street and if you turned right you then approached the entrance to the club. Thankfully, this road was marked with double yellow lines - not that I ever remember seeing any traffic wardens or police around the area.

From the central reception area, where the toilet facilities were located, on the left, there was a very spacious hall with a stage, where functions were held regularly, and on the right was the bar area.

All prison officers, whether serving or retired, became automatic members of all clubs throughout the country. If you were visiting any of the other prison officers' establishments, however, you always needed to produce your prison ID card. Prison officers were allowed to take non-service guests into the club, but only prison officer members were allowed to purchase drinks, although I think these rules have now changed.

It was with some trepidation that I entered the club for the first time, as I honestly didn't know what to expect. I'd changed into a pair of jeans and a T-shirt and I was very surprised to see several colleagues still dressed in their prison uniforms propping up the bar. They'd rushed straight there after being given the 'break off' from work, although I did notice one colleague that had finished work four hours earlier still sitting there. There was, as I found out, a huge drinking culture in those days. Many officers who lived in the quarters would go to the club for their lunch and then return there straight from work and spend the whole night drinking. As for me, I was used to a more cultured approach to socialising - enjoying mixed company, going to dinner parties and talking and laughing about all sorts of subjects, but never work. Unfortunately, right from my first venture into the officers' club, I realised that this would rarely be the case here.

There were about 20 people in the club, mostly gathered around the bar. In the centre, there was a pool table and around the opposite wall to the bar were comfy settees and tables and chairs. A couple of officers were playing pool with a young lad who played very well. He was so good at the game that at one time the officers barred him from playing because nobody else could manage to win a game. That youngster went on to become a World Snooker Champion.

There was only one woman in the clubhouse and she was serving behind the bar. I was signed up as a member of the club and joined my colleagues at the bar.

It almost certainly wasn't my scene. The conversation revolved around work, work and more work: individual or prisoners, incidents that had happened and just general small talk about prison life; nobody spoke about football, the weather, eating out, or cars. So I didn't find the conversations very stimulating and ended up listening to my colleagues without really taking anything in.

Eventually, I struck up a conversation with an elderly gentleman sitting to my left, who turned out to be an old retired officer. He told me that he lived on his own and that he, too, used to be an overtime bandit like me. He explained that, due to the long working hours, he'd never established any kind of social life outside the service and his marriage had broken down, so on retirement, all he had left was the prison officers' club. He would arrive at the club when it opened - around 11 a.m. as far as I could tell - and would just sit at the bar until it closed, at around midnight. This was his life. He offered me a sobering piece of advice:

"Don't waste your life like me, working all the hours under the sun and then just pissing it up a wall. Make sure you have a life outside the service, 'cause when it's over the service will dump you without a care in the world. Look at me. This is all I have. This is my life. Don't waste yours."

I was so touched by his honesty. He must've seen it all before many times, and yet the others in the clubhouse seemed to treat him with contempt - that old codger you just had to put up with. One officer said to me, "Don't listen to that old fart. He just likes to wallow in his own self-pity. For fuck's sake, just buy him a drink and then tell him to piss off." I couldn't do that. I continued to speak to this gentleman for most of the evening, although I only had one pint of shandy and then drank Coca-Cola for the rest of the time, as I had to drive back home. I left the club at around 11 p.m. and had to be back at work by 7 a.m. I just don't know how some of them managed to drink the way they did and still turn up for work each shift.

My experience in the club, and especially speaking to the retired former officer had a profound impact on me in terms of the drinking culture and prison officer clubs that lasted for the rest of my career. I very rarely went to the clubs and I certainly never drank alcohol whilst on duty (unlike many of my former colleagues). Occasionally I went to social events held in various clubs; in fact, that's how I met my future wife - buts that's a different chapter.

I left the club that evening and went home deep in thought about my future in the service and the prison officer's club.

A couple of days later I was informed that on Saturdays the club was much better, as the wives and girlfriends attended and it was a good social evening and a great way to get to know colleagues' families. I can't remember why, but I attended one of these functions along with my estranged wife. I think taking her was a way of showing her my new life, in the hope that she might like what she saw. Anyway, whatever the reason, we decided to go to the club the following Saturday.

The clubhouse was noisy, bustling and full of smoke, not unlike any other pubs on a Saturday night. Incidentally, in those days I was a smoker, too, so the smoky atmosphere didn't bother me. What did irk me, however, was the behaviour of the families, especially the children. Many families seemed to have dogs with them, which was a bit of a surprise, and these canines, together with the children, were allowed to run around unsupervised and totally out of control. We sat on one of the comfortable settees and spent our time there fending off kids who wanted to jump around the seating and climb all over us as if we weren't there, hotly pursued by their dogs. It was a complete nightmare for both my wife and myself and a combination of the noise, the smoke, the unruly kids and the manic dogs were too much. Enough was enough. I decided there and then that if this was what prison officers' clubs were all about then they could keep them! Good luck to my colleagues that liked that sort of thing, but it certainly wasn't my scene.

I really can't remember any of the families I was introduced to that night, but I do recall noticing, as the evening wore on and my patience was wearing thinner by the minute, that some staff were still dressed in their uniforms and some parties were getting very drunk, partly because drinks prices were subsidised and cheap.

I remember one mum leaning over to me, just after I'd avoided a trampling from her child for the umpteenth time, and saying, "Innit great here? You can just bring your kids and leave 'em to it." I thought to myself, erm, if you don't stop your fucking kid and dog climbing all over me I'm gonna punch your lights out, but managed to put it slightly more politely by responding, "But don't you think you could stop your child and the dog from clambering all over me and my wife?"

She retorted, "Why you got a fucking problem with it, or don't you like my kids?"

At that point, my evening's entertainment was completed and we decided to leave. If this was what the club was all about then it certainly was not my scene. Again, this evening had cemented my opinion of the officers' club. Don't get me wrong, lots of staff really enjoyed the social activities provided by the clubs and in one way they probably led to much of the real camaraderie needed among staff when working in the prison environment, but it just wasn't for me. After that first experience, I rarely visited Pentonville Officers' Club, unless it was for a special occasion, such as a retirement party or a charity function in the hall. Perversely, such events tended to be great nights out, but these were in the minority.

When I look back to those days now, I realise just how much the drinking culture pervaded the whole of the prison service. Whether it was due to the stress of the job, the type of people recruited into the service or an established way of fostering a real sense of camaraderie I honestly don't know, but there were some very heavy drinkers and probably potential alcoholics working in the service, and throughout my career, I continued to come across colleagues with real drinking problems. I can remember one officer that used travel to work on his bicycle each day, who was regularly seen swigging back a can of beer while cycling along Caledonian Road and he admitted to being able to down three cans before starting work even at 6 am early shifts.

On the way from the main gate entrance into Pentonville, located on the left just past the officers' mess, was a Portakabin that acted as a rank-specific mess for the POs and SOs, where they could eat their lunch and mix as an elite group during lunch or tea periods. I'd been informed that ordinary officers weren't allowed to enter their exclusive domain and that I'd probably never reach the required rank anyway. It was only after some time at Pentonville that I discovered the truth about this Portakabin.

One afternoon I was asked to go and fetch 'Principal Officer Z' from the POs' mess, as he was needed back on the wing urgently. With some great trepidation, I entered the hallowed Portakabin and was confronted with around a dozen POs and SOs lounging in comfy chairs and snoring their guts out, each with their shoes pinned under the chair legs. This strange shoe-clamping practice was due to the antics of a practical joker in the past, who had taken great delight in stealing the shoes of his colleagues while they were asleep. I can understand why they took off their shoes, as most days you could be on your feet for up to 14 hours a day.

I approached PO Z and, gently pushing his arm, whispered, "Sir, you're required back on the wing." I received no reply. Pushing harder, I said, "Sir, you're required on the wing urgently."

He grunted and opened his eyes. "Wassa time?" he groaned in my general direction.

"Sir, it's 2.20," I replied.

He and several others roused themselves, all complaining about being woken up by a sprog. "The fucking prison better be burning down for you to wake me this early, you fucking prick," growled the PO.

"Yes, I believe the number one governor is asking for you," I answered.

"The number one fucking governor asking for me? Who the fuck does he think he is? He knows full well I always have my afternoon kip at this time, the prick!"

With that, he got up, threw on his shoes and staggered out of the cabin, almost dragging me back up the drive and into the prison while emitting a tirade of expletives that seemed to be aimed directly at me. I was petrified! I honestly thought this PO was honestly going to attack me for daring to rouse him from his routine post-lunch nap. I learned very quickly that they were all there to sleep off their lunchtime drinking session.

However, for me, the biggest surprise was POs' and SOs' sheer contempt and lack of respect for the governor and what appeared to be the general acceptance of staff drinking alcohol at work and to such an extent that they needed to sleep it off in the afternoon or, worse still, went back into work still half-cut.

I always believed that it was my responsibility to set a good example to the prisoners and that my behaviour as a prison officer should be, as far as possible, above reproach. If I stank of alcohol or attempted to work under the effects of alcohol, how could I look a prisoner in the eye and tell them to follow my example and show them the correct way to behave? I always tried to encourage new staff that came under my care to adopt the same attitude, as it held me in good stead throughout my career.

I remember another time when I was detailed to be part of one of the daily escorts, transferring prisoners to other prisons or delivering them to the courts, and it included a particular favourite among prison officers - the ILCC (Inner London Crown Courts). We would work out the route beforehand to ensure that the last drop-off was at one of the Crown Courts, as we could get a cooked breakfast there before returning to the prison. At this time officers from HMP Brixton staffed all the Crown Courts in London and Brixton officers probably had the worst reputation for drinking among prison staff in the whole of the south-east of England. One of the Brixton staff was always allocated kitchen duty and his main job was to ensure that the staff had a cooked breakfast and dinner. The staff working in the Crown Courts received extra pay for this duty, so it was a coveted position for those that worked at HMP Brixton. You always jumped at the chance of duties that took you outside the prison for as many hours as possible, as you could then manage to avoid a lot of the mundane prison work.

On this particular occasion, however, we had to deliver a prisoner to HMP Wormwood Scrubs, quite near to Pentonville, which meant that it would have to be the last drop-off and we wouldn't be able to get a cooked breakfast on this trip. Wormwood Scrubs was similar to Pentonville in that it was an old Victorian prison, with the same smells and slopping-out system, but it took more high-security prisoners such as, at that time, many of the IRA terrorists.

Our escort comprised six officers, with a PO in charge. As usual, one of the officers were detailed to report to reception earlier than the rest, so that he could sort out all the property, property cards and everything else that had to accompany the prisoner. If the prisoner was due to be taken to Crown Court, he would generally be a remand prisoner, which meant that he might not be coming back to Pentonville and therefore all his possessions had to go with him. This officer would also sort out the cuffing order. If two prisoners were going to the same court they would be handcuffed together, both to reduce the number of officers required on the escort and to ensure that any attempted escape could be thwarted effectively. This scenario honestly happened while I was on escort duty some years later, in the middle of the Strand behind the London Palladium. Once the officer had completed all the necessary paperwork, the more senior member of staff - usually an SO - would take charge of the escort, but on this occasion, it was a PO. I was detailed to be cuffed up to the prisoner we were taking to the Scrubs.

It was around 10.30 a.m. when we arrived at the Scrubs, after a very nice tour of London in our green goddess. These dark green coaches were a common sight every day as they travelled from court to court and prison to prison throughout London. In fact, during the coal miners' strike some years later they were regularly seen filled with policemen, as they travelled around the various mines to hold back the striking miners' picket lines and they also featured in the 2000 film *Billy Elliot*. We drove into the prison and were escorted by a prison officer to the reception area, where the prisoner was uncuffed from me and handed over to Scrubs staff.

Our PO, obviously knowing many of the staff there, then said, "Any chance me and the boys could grab a quick drink?"

"Yes," said the PO in charge of the reception area, accompanied by a wink. "The canteen here is closed, but if you go back to your coach I'll get somebody to open the club so you can have a drink."

I must've been thick or something because I thought, they're going to a lot of trouble just to get us a cup of tea. Anyway, we got back on the coach exited the prison and parked up next to the Officers' Club, which was open. One of the two men behind the counter said, "What can I get you, gents?"

So I said, "A cuppa tea with milk and two sugars, please." Everyone started laughing.

"No," said the PO, "a proper drink, you moron."

I was dumbstruck. Not only was alcohol being served at 10.30 in the morning, but also the two men working in this club, located outside the prison, were prisoners!

We remained in the club until almost noon, at which point the PO said, "Right, we need to get back to the Ville for lunch and a pint." I'd only drunk two Coca-colas, but the PO had consumed four pints of beer and a double Scotch.

This, then, appeared to be the culture and the norm, but I became very anti-drinking while on duty and never touched a drop throughout my career, even when attending farewell lunches. If I couldn't avoid going to these dos, then I'd only ever drink Coca-cola.

Chapter 10

My First Christmas in Prison

My first Christmas in prison coincided with the first of my only two sets of 'nights' at the Ville. As NEPOs we were told that when it was our turn for night shifts on the duty rota, we would be obligated to work this detail, but after the first set, we could give future night shift work to any other officer that wished to take it on. This was a reciprocal arrangement and we would have to do the work that they'd been detailed originally to do.

In the same way that there was a core of overtime bandits keen to work extended hours, there was also a night bandits rota. Some people loved working nights, as it meant you never had to deal with prisoners face-to-face, so there were always plenty of officers readily available to take over these shifts. Night shifts came around about every 12 weeks and lasted for seven nights, starting on a Monday, and once that week was over you got a full week off. This was because the hours you worked on nights (around 77 hours) equated to two weeks' work.

I have to say that from the outset I hated working nights. My philosophy was always that if God had wanted us to work nights he would have made it light so we could see what we were doing. It upset my whole body system: I couldn't sleep during the day; working and eating during the night left me with an upset stomach within the first two nights, and I found it difficult to keep awake or alert. So by the end of a week of that routine, I was thoroughly knackered. But I had no option but to do this first set over Christmas, meaning that I wouldn't be able to eat a big Christmas dinner or see my family for very long.

Nights started at 9 p.m. and you worked through until 7 a.m., with the day (or early) shift arriving at around 6.30 a.m. for a 7 a.m. start to allow for a smooth changeover after the prison roll call had been confirmed. The rest of the staff came on duty at 7.45 a.m. and you then went off for your breakfast in the officers' mess. You were allowed about half an hour for this and it was a paid break (these sorts of perks were often later referred to as 'Spanish practices'). When you started your set of nights you would have already worked the Monday morning and finished at lunchtime. Then you could go home and get some sleep before you reported back to work. Again, you would arrive half an hour before your shift was due to start.

On your first night, you would be detailed to one of the wings. There would be just one officer per wing, plus a 'sleep in' medical officer. The latter would be an officer that had been trained to a competent level in order to look after any prisoners being held as in-patients in the prison hospital. Most of these prisoners were certainly a little mentally unstable (I'm using literary licence here), or were suffering from epilepsy or just generally incapable of looking after themselves due to being down-and-outs - 'dossers', as we called them. This 'sleep in' officer was locked in the hospital and would sleep all night unless he was required to administer any medication. He was also there in case any prisoners in the main prison wings needed medical assistance, but generally, the prison officers would simply give the prisoner some paracetamol liquid and tell them to report sick in the morning. So much for 'duty of care'.

Once you'd been detailed your wing for the duration of the night shift, you would be given a 'pegging map'. This consisted of a list of places (known as pegging points) that you had to be at a pre-designated time. When you got to the pegging point you would enter a key into the box and this would register on a computer to confirm that you had completed the pegging. This pegging routine had to be carried out within a 15-minute window and had to be repeated every hour apart from one, which you were entitled to miss and deem it as your lunch break. You then had to sign a form stating what time you completed the pegging, and the chief officer would check these sheets against a computer printout each day. We always reckoned that he was just seeing if he could catch us out for not doing our jobs or for sleeping on the job.

On my first night, I had to complete the routine on my own. It could be quite scary walking around the prison alone at night, the dead silence punctuated only by occasional sleeping noises or the ticking of the heating and water pipes. All the lights would be switched off except for the odd nightlight, but most of these didn't seem to work. Anyway, I was walking along B wing's ground-level landing when I noticed a solid black patch on the floor. I paused and just thought that the old flooring must've been repaired during the day. Then suddenly the black patch started moving towards me. What the fuck ...?! I rushed to the nearest light switch in a panic. As I flicked the switch the black patch disappeared as hundreds of cockroaches dissipated in all directions to get away from the light. I'd never felt so stunned and frightened! I never walked along a dark landing again without putting the lights on first, I can tell you that! My goodness, I could hardly bear to imagine what it was like for the prisoners in the cells. Did they crawl all over them, along with the bed bugs? Bloody hell!

After the first night, you were teamed up with another officer and from around 11 p.m. the two of you would complete the pegging for the whole prison. You had to walk pretty quickly to get around all the pegging points within the designated time, but doing it this way allowed the remaining staff to get some sleep. This was not permitted practice but had become the custom. It was probably why the chief officer used to check those computer printouts so carefully - he knew!

As it was Christmas week, we'd all chipped in to pay for a meal on Christmas Eve night. We'd decided to forego some of our sleep time and instead, enjoy some Christmas fare. We'd drawn lots previously to see who would carry out all the pegging during the night so that the rest of us could enjoy our meal and have a little nap, and luckily I wasn't on pegging duty.

At that time at the Ville, there was a 'last chance hostel' within the prison. This consisted of a block housing prisoners who would go out to work each day and return for the night. It was designed to encourage them to reintegrate back into society and develop the necessary work ethos. However, all but two of these prisoners had been given 'home leave' over the festive season.

They were all due for release from prison in the near future and home leave could be granted under the existing rules at the time. The two that were left were the permanent members of the hostel. They were serving long sentences and were not on the scheme, but had been selected as the cook and cleaner for this hostel.

The PO in charge of the night shift had made arrangements for us to unlock these two prisoners so that they could prepare the boardroom for our Christmas meal, their reward being a couple of bottles of beer and any leftovers. So, at the designated time of 11.45 p.m., we all gathered in the boardroom. The lads had done us proud: linen tablecloth, candles, glasses and wine. We had a lovely meal, but my unlucky colleagues had to keep disappearing to carry out the pegging duties. Officer 'Gwynne' produced a bottle of port for us to enjoy after the meal. Apparently, it was his favourite tipple and the two of us managed to finish the bottle between us. The meal finished around 2 a.m. and we then got a little sleep until the morning staff relieved us.

So there we were, working nights, having this great slap-up meal, getting pissed, having a kip and, better still, getting paid for it! What a great job, I thought. Why didn't I join the service ten years earlier?

It was now Christmas morning and I'd finished work, so now all I had to do was drive home. Bloody hell, I still feel pissed, I thought. Maybe that bottle of port wasn't such a good idea after all. I'd offered to give a colleague a lift home and we were both still drunk. Plain stupid.

We'd got as far as The Angel Islington when - bloody hell - we pulled up at a set of traffic lights next to a police car. To be honest, at that early hour on a Christmas morning, there were very few other cars on the road. I looked across to the police car and the female officer in the passenger seat waved to me to open my window, Christ, I hope she won't be able to smell the alcohol from there! I opened my window, scared to death that we were going to get caught. She leaned out of the window. I held my breath. Then she blew a whoopee whistle in my direction and shouted, "Merry Christmas!" while her colleague pulled away and went straight through the still red traffic lights!

"Bloody hell!" I said to my colleague. "They're more pissed than us!" We continued our journey and arrived home safely, whereupon I took myself straight to bed for some much-needed sleep.

Chapter 11

Facing Death for the First Time

The death of a prisoner isn't the most pleasant of incidents to be faced with and until you're faced with it, you cannot anticipate how you'll react when it happens -and happen it does, and in an increasing number, particularly among those in Young Offenders Institutions (YOIs), formerly known as Borstals.

I remember coming across my first dead body as if it were yesterday. It will always stick in my mind, and not really because of the horror of actually being the person that made the gruesome discovery.

I'd agreed to come in very early, around 6 a.m., to relieve one of the night shift staff, who needed to get away early. This sort of changeover flexibility was allowed, both on nights and days, so long as the wing numbers had been reported correctly. It was a handy arrangement, as it often enabled the night officers to miss the morning rush hour and the day shift staff could get home or to the club or pub earlier.

When I arrived, immediately the officer I was relieving early said, "Oh great, ace. I've already counted and the roll is correct."

I think I responded with something like, "Oh good, but I'll still do a count myself just to satisfy my own mind, cheers," and off I went to carry out the count and confirm the numbers.

Rather naughtily, and unbeknown to me, this officer told the PO in charge that I'd officially relieved him and he was free to leave the establishment and get off on his holiday.

Meanwhile, I was up on the fives counting the prisoners. It's a task that's not always easy to do, as it can sometimes be difficult to see inside the cell clearly through the spyhole, for instance, if a prisoner has covered it up or if it's dark inside due to malfunctioning nightlights or the spyhole glass has been damaged. Anyway, I persevered with my count, walking along the landing and pushing open each spyhole. "One, two, three, four, five, six, seven," I counted. Then, continuing from cell to cell, "Eight, nine …" Wait a minute … nine? Oh shit! Oh, fuck! Did I see what I thought I'd seen? No, it can't be! Damn, it fucking well is! He's bloody hanging! Fuck! What do I do?

I immediately informed the night orderly officer, the PO in charge of the prison, and he told me to wait there and he would send another officer up to unlock the cell. You weren't allowed to open up a cell door at night on your own, and this still the rules today.

My colleague arrived and informed me that medical assistance had been requested. Although I'd never seen a deceased person before, I knew by looking at this man that he was dead. He'd tied a sheet around his neck, stood on a chair, attached the other end of the sheet to the bars on his window, and then somehow managed to kick the chair away. Once we'd gained entry to the cell, I stood on the chair and supported the body over my shoulder while my colleague cut the prisoner down.

In today's world, in such an instance you would be required to cut the ligature in such a way that the knot could be preserved as evidence for a coroner's court hearing, but back then you just cut the damn thing.

As I took the full weight of the body, there was what I thought sounded like a loud fart.

"You dirty bastard," I said to my colleague. "Have a bit of respect." He answered, "It wasn't me that farted."

Shit, I thought, well it wasn't me, so who the fuck was it? Oh no, he's still alive! Quick, where's that bloody medic?

At this point, the medical officer arrived and we laid the prisoner down on the floor of the cell. The medic examined him and confirmed that he was indeed dead, and then explained that we would have to call a doctor to verify the death and complete the relevant paperwork.

"Well, who the fuck farted then?" I said.

"You dippo," retorted the medic. "You've obviously never heard that a cadaver makes that sort of noise when all the bodily fluids are moved, have you? It's a common occurrence."

Thank goodness for that at least, I thought.

The body was moved to the hospital wing and I had the wonderful task of finishing the wing count and then sitting down to complete all the relevant paperwork: an incident report, followed by another report, followed by yet another report, and so on. By now I'd completely forgotten about the officer I'd relieved what seemed like a hundred years ago. But then I started thinking. He'd made his escape and buggered off before I'd finished my count. He must've known about this, I thought, he simply must've. He must have seen the body and thought, this is gonna delay me going on holiday, so I'll let some other bastards pick up the tab. I was livid. I was so angry I just wanted to grab hold of him and kill him with my own bare hands. The bastard! Leaving me to sort out his problem! You just didn't do that sort of thing to your mates, did you?

Paperwork completed and still fuming, I was relieved by the day staff who'd just arrived, so I was able to go and have a break. On this particular shift, you came in early, had a break for breakfast in the mess, then came back on duty for the rest of the shift. You also got paid what was termed CDCs (continuous duty credits), meaning that such breaks were paid ones. I really loved this shift - normally, anyway.

I was just leaving the centre when the chief officer called me in. “Is this your first dead ’un Mr Levy?” he asked.

“Yes,” I replied.

“How do you feel then?” he inquired.

“Bloody angry, chief, but I’ll be all right,” I responded.

I couldn’t tell the chief what had happened and grass my colleague up but, by Christ, I intended to get my own back on him somehow at some time for what he’d done to me.

The chief looked at me and said, “That’s good then. Now go along and have your breakfast, and tell the mess it’s on my account.” “Yes, chief, and thank you,” I replied.

And that was that. There was no counselling, no debrief, no offer of taking time out, nothing. It was a case of ‘You’ve found your first-ever dead body hanging in a cell. Oh, good for you. Now go and have a full English breakfast and get back to work as soon as you can.’ That’s really caring for your staff and looking after them, isn’t it? But that was how it was back then.

So, having discovered my first dead body, I’d been inducted into a very exclusive band of prison staff. I’ve since come across other prisoners who’d successfully committed suicide, but this first experience will always be the one I remember in great detail.

I did have to attend an inquest, which would be a story in itself except that I really can't recall much about it. Let's just say that it wasn't one of the most pleasurable experiences I've had. Also, I did eventually get my revenge on my so-called colleague, but I'm not going to reveal the specifics as it would identify this person. Suffice to say, we were never friends after this incident and I certainly never again offered to relieve him.

Chapter 12

Funeral at Harrow on the Hill

On one occasion I was detailed to funeral escort duty, along with a senior officer and another officer. A prisoner's brother had died in Spain in unusual circumstances and, although the investigation was still ongoing over there, the body had been released. The funeral service would be taking place at Harrow on the Hill, followed by the burial near Wembley.

Taking a prisoner to a funeral service and burial wasn't an unusual occurrence, but it was one of those duties that you either enjoyed or hated. I fell into the latter category. Attending a funeral was wearing enough when a member of my own family had died, with all the crying and sadness that the day can bring, so I certainly didn't relish the thought of having to attend the funeral of a total stranger accompanied by a serving prisoner. On top of witnessing the sadness of the prisoner and those attending, such a funeral presents a huge security worry, as logistically it's a difficult event to manage, so it can be quite stressful.

Certain well-known notoriety revolved around this funeral and the family involved, who were all well-known, established criminal gang in the area. The first inkling we got of just how big the day would be was when the local police in the area of the church where the ceremony was due to be held contacted the prison to say that they would be there in force to ensure that the funeral went smoothly. Yeah, good excuse. No doubt they wanted to see who turned up and whether any of the attendees were wanted by the police.

This particular prisoner was on remand and it was a little more unusual for remand prisoners to be allowed to leave the prison under escort. Permission could only be granted by a very high government authority (possibly the Home Secretary's office) in conjunction with the agreement of the local police authorities.

Anyway, I reported to reception on the due date and the senior officer(who used to joke that he didn't like me, as he supported Arsenal and me supported Spurs) detailed me, as the junior officer, to be cuffed up to the prisoner. However, I had an ace up my sleeve, especially as I'd now found out that not only would the local police be there in force but also special armed police. Bloody hell, I thought, this lot has nothing to do with the Krays, does it?

I said to the senior officer, "SO, you do realise that I can't go onto the actual burial grounds and stand by the graveside, don't you?" "Why the fuck not?" retorted the SO.

"Well, in my religion you're not allowed to set foot on burial ground unless a close member of your family, like your mother, father or sibling, has died," I replied.

He looked at me closely, trying to work out whether I was joking or not. As I'd managed to keep a deadpan expression, he assumed that I was telling the truth. "Bloody hell, I can't get another member of staff to take your place at this late stage." He then turned to the other officer assigned to escort duty and said, "You'll have to be cuffed up to the prisoner then. Yiddo will just have to back you up and keep close to you, especially when we get to the church. He'll sit right behind you and stop anybody getting too near. You hear that, Yiddo?"

"Certainly, but what about at the actual funeral site? I can't go onto that area either," I replied.

I think he was getting a little suspicious by now, but was unsure whether to challenge me on it. Although what I was saying was factual in terms of the Jewish faith, I wasn't certain if this precluded me from going to a Christian funeral or not. “We’ll just have to cross that bridge when we get to it,” the SO responded. “I’ll get our driver to act as extra cover. I know he’s an OSG (operational support grade, therefore not allowed direct contact with prisoners), but he’s allowed to deal with members of the public so he can help. But, bloody hell, fancy detailing you to this job without finding out about your suitability. Bloody typical of detail. I’ll have a word with them when we get back.”

My colleague reluctantly had to be cuffed up to the prisoner, who was dressed in a very smart black suit, which had been sent in for him especially for the occasion. We wore civilian jackets over our prison uniforms to try to make us look less conspicuous in the crowd. What a joke! The bloody cuffs would give it away for a start, not to mention the fact that four of us would be standing so close together at all times and would look as if we were joined by an invisible umbilical cord!

We loaded up into the pixie and set off to the church at Harrow on the Hill for the funeral service. We were among the last to arrive, and as soon as we got out of the van we were engulfed by loads of grieving relatives and friends, many of them young attractive females and all wanting to hug and kiss our prisoner. It was obvious that he and his brother must’ve been very popular with the girls before one died and he was remanded in custody. It was a bit embarrassing really and not a little worrying.

Our prisoner’s father approached us and said to the SO, “Thanks for bringing my boy. I know he can’t come off the cuffs, but you won’t get any trouble from anybody here today, mate, you have my word.” Well, thanks for that, I thought, but I’ll still be glad when this is all over.

As we moved forward to enter the church, a man that looked every bit like a plain-clothes policeman came up to us. “Don’t worry,” he assured the SO, “we’ve posted armed police at every strategic vantage point, so if it kicks off we’ve got it covered.” Now ain’t this just great, I thought. I'm now on the set of an episode of *The Sweeney* and any minute Dennis Waterman and John Thaw are gonna come speeding around the corner in their Ford Granada, jump out and say, "You're nicked." He also informed us that a helicopter would be tracking the funeral cortège as it made its way to the cemetery.

The prisoner, cuffed to my colleague and with me right behind, was led to the front of the church by the vicar. They sat in the first pew and I sat directly behind, surrounded by the close family and several of the girls. I must say they were a nice distraction, but a distraction nonetheless. However, all went off smoothly. I've never been as glad to get out of a church as I was on this occasion, and it had nothing to do with my religion.

The mother asked if her son could travel in the first funeral car. I thought to myself, what bloody planet is she on? Yeah, of course, he can get in the car still cuffed to the officer, with me and the SO, and mum and dad et al! I don't think so. The SO explained to her that this would not be

possible, as we were only authorised to transport the prisoner in the prison vehicle. Thankfully, she understood. Everyone piled into their respective vehicles and formed a convoy - the hearse, the family's limo, our green pixie, another limo, a police car, then the rest of the mourners, followed by more police cars - and off we went, accompanied by the sound of the helicopter.

We arrived at the cemetery and all the cars parked up in the allocated parking area. We got out and started to walk towards the actual burial plot, at which point I looked at the SO, indicating that this was as far as I could go. He instructed me to stay where I was and just keep a watch, and the OSG driver took my place. So I stood by a tree and lit a crafty fag while keeping an eye on proceedings. I watched as the party at the graveside knelt at the foot of the coffin. And, bloody hell, my colleague was kneeling, too. Then I realised why - well, you can't stand if the person you're cuffed to is kneeling, can you? The coffin was then lowered into the hole and they started throwing handfuls of soil onto it. Thank goodness, I'm not at the graveside, I thought.

And that was that - all over. As we were walking back to the car park, once again the mother approached us.

"We're all going back to the house for drinks and some sandwiches. Would you be able to come?"

The SO tried his best to look sympathetic and apologetic. "Unfortunately, it would be against the conditions of the temporary licence, so we cannot," he explained.

She seemed very upset by this but had no choice but to accept the situation.

We piled into the van and sped back to Pentonville as fast as the pixie would take us. Once back at the Ville, we handed our prisoner over to the reception staff and the SO suggested we all went for a cup of tea in the back room of the reception.

While we were all sitting there with our cuppas, the SO said, "Thank fuck that's over with - I don't ever want to do one of those again! That's some family - it was like a who's who of all the local London villains! No wonder the police were there in force." He then added as an afterthought, "And if I find you were having me on about the graveside business, I'll have your guts for the rest of your career."

Thank goodness I remembered that crap about not being allowed on the actual burial site. You know, sometimes it pays to be Jewish.

Chapter 13

A Day at the Races

Whoopee! An organised staff day out to Newmarket Races! I'd never attended a horse race meeting before; in fact, I'd never even been to a betting office to place a bet. However, I had spent many hours standing outside various betting shops waiting for my dad to come out, having lost all his money again. They always struck me as dirty, dingy, seedy places, full of smoke and angry men. Thankfully, they've changed dramatically over the years, but my early memories remain.

I've never really been a gambler at all. Okay, I play the National Lottery and used to do the football pools, and I've been to the odd casino, but I'd never really enjoyed losing money - must be my Jewish roots. So I gave myself a budget for this day at the races. This was the amount I was prepared to lose and I wouldn't let myself spend any more than that.

I was excited to be going to the races. I had no idea what to expect, even though I'd seen horse racing on the telly before. I hadn't had much choice, as if my dad wasn't at the betting office he'd be glued to the telly on a Saturday afternoon watching the horse racing. But to be honest, it seemed bloody boring to me, dragging on for a whole afternoon, but to go to a live course must be much better, I reckoned.

The day before our trip I went to see one of the catering officers in the kitchen area, a small, wiry man who'd been recommended as the man-in-the-know when it came to horse racing and tips. He explained that he was going to Newmarket the next day, too, and said:

"Look, Tony, I'll give you the winner of the first race to give you some stake money to play with, then you're on your own. Here's a tip though: get near one of the course bookies and see which horses are taking most of the bets. Just before the off, you'll see their prices coming down quickly, especially the ones that start at around twenty to one. Go to the tote there and then and place your money on that one. But make sure you do it before the odds get lower than five to one, otherwise, it ain't worth the win money. The timing is very tight, but it'll give you a few winners." He told me the name of a horse to back in the first race and said that I should back it to win rather than back it each way. He said that after that I should back each way, but for the life of me, I can't remember most of the reasoning behind his advice.

So many thoughts were running through my head. How can he know this horse is gonna win? And if I put too much on it and it doesn't, then that's it; I'll have no stake money left to back any more horses. So I was in a dilemma. Should I spend more money initially and go beyond the limit I'd set myself? But if I did that and the horse didn't win, then I'd end up losing more money than I could afford. So maybe I should put a small stake on this tip. Then again, if I did that and the horse won, then I wouldn't win enough stake money for the rest of the day's races. Bloody hell, this gambling lark ain't easy, is it? I'll have to think about it until tomorrow. One thing was for sure: I'd never make a gambler!

We met at the club at 6 a.m. and had a cup of tea. Once everyone had assembled we boarded our coach and headed off for our day at Newmarket races.

I sat near the back and noticed four of my colleagues starting a card school. One of them was a notorious gambler, and he would often come into the mess early in the morning just to play the slot machines. Unlike pubs, the slot machines in the mess and officers club all had huge jackpots of £100 - a fair amount for those times. This particular officer was playing the machine one morning and won the jackpot - a nice start to the day. His day got even better when he moved to another machine and promptly won an additional £50. At lunchtime, as usual, he went to the club for a pie and a pint and played the slot machines there. Amazingly, he won another jackpot of £100, so by midday, he'd become £250 better off - not a bad day's work.

The card school kept going throughout our journey to Newmarket. Just as we arrived at the car park I asked my gambling colleague how he'd done. He replied that he was down to £150. So in that short amount of the journey he'd lost a staggering £150 - almost a week's overtime pay.

Complete madness!

When we'd disembarked and entered the racing ground, I was amazed at how different it was being there live compared with how you perceive it to be on television. For a start, from the TV coverage, it always seemed as if the horses were paraded around the ground for ages before the jockeys mounted them and the race began, but in reality, it was quite a short period. Why did it seem so long when watching on television?

I'd eventually decided to put all but ten quid on my expert's tip. I queued up at the tote window, placed my bet, received my betting slip and went off to watch the race. We'd managed to get a viewing spot near to the finishing post, and at Newmarket, it was possible to lean forward from this position and see the start of the race in the far distance. I don't remember the length of the first race, and wouldn't know a furlong if it jumped up and smacked me in the face, but the horses did seem an awfully long way away from us. The race order was given over a tannoy and, just like on the television, the commentator's voice got more animated as the race progressed to the end.

As luck would have it, or maybe my tipster honestly did know his stuff, my horse romped home. I had forty quid on it at seven to one and won £280. What a great start! I decided to put my original stake money to one side and just play with my winnings on the rest of the races. Boy, was I going to enjoy the rest of the day now, knowing I wasn't going to lose anything but the bookies' money! Thanks, mate, you certainly did give me the winner.

I think there were six races in all and I was betting each way at around fifty quid a bet. By following the advice given, I had a couple more winners. It was very exciting stuff, going down to stand near 'Sid's Turf' and watching the tick-tack man by the bookies' board doing all sorts of weird things with his arms and touching his head and shoulders and seeing the horses' odds changing rapidly on the board. Knowing I wasn't using my own stake money made it so much more fun too, in the same way, that answering questions and putting money on the line in quiz shows on TV is so much easier as a detached viewer rather than as an under-pressure contestant with a lot to lose.

The day went much too quickly and before too long we were all on the coach heading back to the Ville. I asked my gambling friend how he'd got on and he told me he was down by another £500. I thought, sod that for a game of soldiers! He must have more money than sense! No wonder he's not married anymore, I thought to myself.

Once we'd arrived back at the Ville we all went into the club for a nightcap. Once again I asked my gambling friend how he'd done in the card school that had taken place on the return journey. "I had to borrow a couple of hundred from 'nick' and I lost another £300, so not a very good day for me," came the reply. Not a very good day?! Well, what an understatement! So after his winning start to the day on the slot machines, he'd managed to lose nearly £1,000! Bloody hell! Then, to cap it all, he asked me to lend him five quid, which I did, so he could go and play the fruit machine. And guess what? He copped the jackpot again - with my bloody money! I didn't have the heart to claim half of his winnings for myself; after all, he'd had a 'not very good day'.

Chapter 14

The Tea Rooms

The tea room wasn't exactly a room but rather a converted cell with all the fittings and fixtures removed and seating placed along the wall and a fridge and kettle supplied. Tea rooms were dotted around the prison at various strategic points and you quickly learnt the location of your nearest one. There were always other places where you could get a cup of tea and have a fag and a sit-down away from the prisoners. Reception 'out the back' was one such place and the censor office another. But the main tea rooms were located on D1 landing, and there was another non-cell converted tea room on B wing on the three's landing, tucked away in a corner, and also one next to the segregation SO's office and one in R wing, which held remand prisoners. Looking back, I seem to recall that only A wing didn't have its own tea room; at least I can't remember one there.

In those days specially selected prisoners ran all the tea rooms and they were known, obviously enough, as tea boys. It was their job to provide for the requests of any members of staff using the tea room, which was supplied with tea, coffee, milk, sugar and occasionally some biscuits. Sometimes there would also be a toaster in the room and bread, butter and jam would be available, all at a cost. It was the tea boys' job to collect the money from the officers, and the regular members of staff that ran the tea rooms would provide a kitty to ensure that they were adequately stocked, with one officer usually put in overall control of the financial aspect.

Getting a job as a wing tea boy was a perk that many prisoners would strive to get, as working with officers was regarded as a plum job that gave them a lot of kudos among the rest of the prisoner population. Once awarded that position, they became privy to lots of inside information, unintentionally given, which helped them to maintain a prime slot in the prison pecking order. The tea rooms were the social hub of everyday life for officers working in the prison, and only uniformed members of staff were allowed access to them. POs and SOs had their separate facilities, and the PO of each wing usually had a designated prisoner as a personal cleaner and tea boy. It seems strange to call these prisoners 'tea boys', as many of them over the years that I was at the Ville were older than me.

I remember one particular man at Pentonville who was the B wing tea boy, and amongst his offences was ticket touting at major sporting events. When I first came across him I vaguely recognised him but couldn't work out from where. All became clear, however, when he told me that his ticket touting pitch was outside the Spurs ground in Tottenham and that he worked for a notorious local ticket tout known as 'Stan Flashman'. Stan supplied tickets for almost every sporting event in London at the time, and he lived in a huge house in an area of North London called Totteridge.

On the day of his release from custody this prisoner said to me, "Guv, you always bin fair to me. If ever you wanna ticket for the Spurs, it's yours for face value anytime."

I never thought any more of it, but years later I was in a fairly well-known local night club in Tottenham called the 'Coolbury Club'. If Spurs had played at home on a Saturday, quite often many of the players would go to the club that evening. It was a very popular venue and I had many good nights there over the years. I'd known the owner, a little Irishman called 'Vinnie' since I was old enough to go into pubs. Originally, he'd owned one of the most popular pubs in the area, 'The British Queen', where I spent many of my formative years failing to chat up beautiful women and also the not-so-beautiful ones. When he opened the club he got all his regulars to sign up as members, so it soon became the in-place to be.

I was standing at the bar on a very dull midweek night with a colleague from work when all of a sudden Vinnie came up to me carrying a tray with a bottle of champagne and two glasses. "Bloody hell, Vinnie. You've realised at last how much I've spent in here and now you're gonna thank me," I said.

"Feck off, Tony," responded Vinnie in his best Irish accent. "Since when have you ever known me to give anybody freebies in here? It's from that geezer over in the corner, the one with the stunning blonde next to him."

I looked over and I didn't know this geezer from Adam. The girl with him was stunningly attractive though. She was about 5ft 7in, had very long blonde hair and was wearing a very short skirt, and she had a very nice pair of legs to match - not that I noticed, of course. In my defence, being observant is part of a prison officer's job - and I was very observant where it came to a good-looking woman.

"Well, I don't know who he is," I told Vinnie as I took the tray from him. I then walked over to my benefactor. "Hi," I said, looking first at the girl and then at him. She was even more attractive closeup. "I'm sorry, but I don't know who you are, so why are you sending me champagne?"

"Guv, it's me," said the man, and then gave me his name. It still didn't ring any bells with me. "Don't you remember?" he asked. "I was your tea boy on B wing some time back. I always said I could get you the tickets at face value anytime, but you never came for one, so when I saw you I said to 'Stella' [the blonde girl], 'That's one of my old bosses from when I was inside. He was always fair to me, so I'm gonna buy him a drink'."

Now, of course, I recognised him. I don't know why, but he just seemed much bigger in normal clothes. If he hadn't introduced himself I would never have realised that this was my former tea boy. I explained that I couldn't accept his gift, but would be happy to share it publicly among the four of us, which we did. It turned out that Stella was his fiancée.

On many occasions, I'd sat in a tea room on my own and had a cuppa, and with nobody else around the tea, boy would tell me what was going on down on the wing. Information gleaned in this way was invaluable for the smooth running of the establishment, but the tea boy practice has sadly gone now.

In the main, the tea room was the meeting place for staff. I remember arriving back at the prison following the daily ILCC escort run one morning with about five other officers. It was about 10.30 a.m. and the SO in charge of the escort duty said to us, "Righto, lads, we'll stop in reception for a cuppa before reporting back to the centre." While we were taking our break, over the tannoy system I heard, "Officer Levy, report to the centre immediately." Oh fucking hell, I thought, how did they know I was back? What have I done now?

I left the reception and headed off to report to the centre. On duty was my favourite PO, who'd always been fair to me and offered me lots of advice in the past, so I had a lot of respect for him.

This PO said to me, "Now then, young Mr L," - he always called me 'young Mr L', but to this day I've never really understood why - "where have you been? You're supposed to report back to the centre when you return from an escort, you know that, don't you?"

"Yes, sir," I responded.

He then proceeded to give me an almighty bollocking and finished by saying, "Now go down to D1, have your cup of tea and wait for me to call you. I'll have a job for you in a minute."

"Yes, sir," I replied, and then added, "But can I just ask, why did you call me up if you knew we were back from the ILCC? You must know how many of us were in reception, so why single me out for a bollocking?"

He said to me, "Look, young Mr L, I expect that behaviour from them, but you, you're different, you're always conscientious and a professional and they're all beyond hope and I don't want you falling into their bad ways. Report to me and you'll be sent off for a cuppa, but try to skive and I'll be on you like a ton of bricks. Do you understand?"

"Yes, sir," I replied, this time feeling ten feet high. Bloody hell, he thinks I'm good and just doesn't want me to stray down the same road as some of the others. Well, bugger me!

The tea room was also the place where officers swapped shifts, made their social life arrangements, discussed football, the weather, their latest girlfriends, and also, more importantly, wound down after an alarm bell situation. It was used as an unofficial debriefing room. Many a time after an incident we would go down to a tea room and talk through what had happened. A typical conversation would go along the following lines:

"Fucking hell, I was shitting myself! When I got there and saw all that claret it fair turned me stomach over."

"Yeah, me too. That's when you discover that adrenalin's not brown!" "What, you? But you must've done this sort of thing hundreds of times."

"I still shit myself when it happens."

"Well, I was buzzing. Couldn't wait to get there and join in."

Do you mean that? Then you're fucking mad! How can you want to get involved in a punch-up?"

"Nah, I say let 'em fight, and then when they're knackered step in and remove them nice and safely."

This helped you to calm down and get yourself back together to enable you to continue doing this crazy job.

So that was the impact of the tea rooms. Sadly, like so many other aspects of prison life back then, they're gone forever.

Chapter 15

The Annual Hedgehog Hunt on Hampstead Heath

All working environments are filled with characters that enjoy a good wind-up and most are just harmless bits of fun. It's all part of the way we learn to cope with the pressure and stress of being at work; in such people-centred jobs, you tend to develop a good sense of humour very quickly. I'm sure the fire service, ambulance service and police force all have similar individuals within their midst and the prison service are no exception. It acts as a defensive mechanism to cope with some of the human tragedies you witness daily and also helps to relieve the periods of boredom in the day-to-day routine of prison life. Staff can often also find it difficult not to take the prison with them when they go home at the end of their shifts.

I must say that some of these wind-ups border on the brilliant. I remember one such occasion well. I'd been at the Ville for some time and was beginning to be accepted into the fold by many of my colleagues, although to be fair some of my peers wouldn't speak to me for at least another three years or so until I had 'served my time' and got some 'shit under my nails'.

Anyway, I was sitting in D wing's tea room enjoying a cuppa when 'Les' walked in. Les was a small, wiry man with a great sense of humour. He was a good officer and one that I looked to for guidance whenever I needed it. He loved a good wind-up and was known throughout the prison as the prime suspect behind all the major wind-ups that took place.

To give you an example, I'd only been at the Ville a short while when Les came up to me and asked if my officer's hat contained a 'wee'. Not knowing what a 'wee' was, I replied that I wasn't sure. So Les told me to give him my hat and he would check, as some of the newer hats didn't contain this 'wee'. So like a mug I handed over my hat, at which point Les took out the metal band that kept the top of the hat in shape and promptly threw my hat across the room as though it were a frisbee while shouting, "W(h)ee!" He then looked at me as I stood there totally perplexed and said, "There you go, son, now it's got its wee back."

Les had the most distorted and messy hat in the prison, in great contrast to the ex-forces guardsmen whose hats were always immaculate and had the peaks slashed and then sewn back in so they still looked as if they were on parade at Buckingham Palace. The chief officer was always tearing a strip off Les for carrying his hat under his arm with his hand in his pocket. Looking back I'm finding it difficult to recall ever seeing Les wearing his hat at any time during my time at the Ville. But he was a true character.

Thanks to Les, and his quick wit when I once got stopped by the chief officer, who shouted at me, "Mr Levy, put your hat on if God hadn't meant you to wear your hat he wouldn't have invented your head."

Remembering a trick that Les had used on someone else once when faced with a similar situation, I responded, "If that's the case, chief, why then, when you put your hand in your pocket, is the space created between your arm and your body a perfect fit for your hat to rest in?"

Anyway, back to the original story. There were a couple of other officers in the tea room at the time, including a brand new NEPO just back from completing his initial training at the training school. I can't remember his name, but it was obvious that he was desperate to be included in the 'team'. He would hang on every word that was spoken by his colleagues and you could see in his expression how he took in every last detail about carrying out his duties. Les, addressing nobody in particular, said, "Are you coming next week?"

Nobody answered. So he asked again, "Are you coming next week? It's that time of year again."

At this point another officer piped up, "It's not that time already, is it?" Les replied, "Yes, it's always around this time of year."

By this time I'd cottoned on to what was happening, as had the officer that had responded, so I said, "You're on. Usual arrangements?" "Yup, we'll meet as usual at Jack Straw's," said Les.

The conversation continued in the same pattern until the new officer took the bait and asked Les the question we'd all been waiting for: "Is this event open to all of us?"

Les must've been over the moon at this point, but his face never gave anything away and he continued, "Yes and we're always looking for new staff to join in. It's a great way to get to know us all and become part of the team."

The new officer then asked, "What's it all about then?" He was hooked.

In response, Les explained to our new colleague, as straight-faced as ever, "It's the annual hedgehog hunt on Hampstead heath. We do it every year. It's to help the local authorities find out how many hedgehogs are living there. We meet at Jack Straw's Castle, the pub at the top of Hampstead Heath just before you reach the pond and Hampstead village. Do you know it?"

"Not really," came the reply.

Les gave him directions on how to get there and then continued, "You must bring scruffy clothes to wear, as you'll get very muddy chasing the hedgehogs all over the heath. Once you've caught one you have to check whether it's already been tagged. If not, you put a tag on it and make a note. We get paid 50 pence per new tag. It's a mucky job, but when we've finished we all go back to Jack Straw's for a pint and a curry. Are you okay with that?"

“Of course,” replied our suckered colleague, eager to be accepted by the team. “What time do we start?”

Les said, “We usually meet around twelve on a Sunday. And just to make sure we know who’s joining in, officially like, we have a sort of uniform. Do you have a white roll-neck jumper and a pair of Levi jeans and boots that you could wear?”

"Yes," said the officer. "I'm really looking forward to this." And so was Les, not to mention the rest of us!

Jack Straw's Castle was a notoriously well-known meeting place for many of the gay London population, who frequented that area of Hampstead. You could always identify the gay males, as during this period they all seemed to wear white roll-neck jumpers and Levi jeans. It was quite an in-joke at the time, hence the outfit that the new officer had been requested to wear. Poor bloke!

And so, on the designated Sunday, our new officer went to Hampstead Heath for the fictitious annual hedgehog hunt, only to find that he was the only officer there!

The following morning he walked into the tea room on D wing, where Les and I were having a cup of tea.

"Oy, you bastards!" he said. "You fucking wind-up bastards! I suppose you think it was funny?"

"Yes," replied Les, "it certainly was. I was watching you from a safe distance, and it was brilliant. After the first five, I lost count of the number of blokes that tried to pick you up!"

"That's not the half of it!" our new colleague replied angrily. "I took my girlfriend with me, or should I say ex-girlfriend thanks to you." "Why's she your ex-girlfriend then?" I enquired.

Well," he said, "with all these gay blokes trying to chat me up, no matter what I said to her she really wouldn't believe that I'm straight and so she jacked me in. She told me everybody in London knew that Jack Straw's was full of gays wearing white roll-necks, and nobody in their right mind would wear white to go frolicking around Hampstead Heath in the mud, so I must've dressed like that to attract gays. She wouldn't believe I didn't know"

I replied, "But why did you take your girlfriend with you anyway?"

"Cause like a prick I thought it was genuine and I wanted her to see how well, I was being accepted into the team to impress her," he answered. "Well," I said, "if that's how shallow she is, then you haven't lost a girlfriend but a potential narrow-minded bore."

At this point, his demeanour changed and he started to see the funny side of it and accepted it in good humour. Soon we were all laughing, including the prisoner tea boy.

Our new colleague looked at Les and commented, "I must admit it was a bloody good wind-up - and there was one bloke I was starting to fancy." Funnily enough, although I can't remember this officer's name, I do recall that he got married a couple of years later to an old girlfriend from school and they had a couple of children. I was invited to the wedding, so the whole experience didn't do him any lasting harm. Not surprisingly, he was quickly accepted into the fold after this event.

That's the way it was at Pentonville. Wind-ups helped you to develop a thick skin and a good sense of humour and strengthened the camaraderie between members of the teams.

Chapter 16

Holloway Prison Officers' Club

HMP Holloway was originally a grim fortress prison in North London's Parkhurst Road. Originally constructed by the City of London and opened in 1852 as a mixed prison, it became all-female in 1902. It served a large area of the southeast and was the largest female prison both in the UK and throughout Western Europe. Throughout the service and beyond, it was always known as 'Tampax Towers' - I really can't imagine why!

I had to go to Holloway prison for a training course whilst working at Pentonville. This was no real hardship, as it was located at the end of the Caledonian Road and was a bit nearer to home. I'd never been to the prison before but had seen the arched entrance gate on television. Although this was an impressive and imposing piece of architecture, it served no real purpose and was simply a gatehouse façade that had been retained as an architectural feature when the prison was rebuilt between 1971 and 1985 on the same site.

I approached the actual entrance of the prison, showed my identity badge and Home Office pass and said to the female officer at the gate, "Officer Levy here, on a training course from HMP Pentonville." I noticed that she was a fairly attractive woman and remember being surprised at that, although I don't know why. I suppose at that time you only found male officers in male establishments and female officers in female ones, so it was an unusual experience. Thankfully, those days have changed for the better.

"All right, love," said the duty officer. "You look fit. They'll like you. Just wait in the room over there until everyone's here and then I'll get someone to take you to the training room."

Look fit? What's she on about? I know I'm pretty slim and I try to keep fit, but I didn't think it showed that much. It's amazing how a comment can work on your ego, so I went into the waiting room feeling a bit special.

On entering the room I noticed my mate Nasher, from my initial training period. It might seem strange, but due to the different shift patterns we rarely came across each other at work, so I was pleasantly surprised and pleased to see a familiar face. Despite having a great time on my initial training course, I honestly don't like going on courses, especially arriving on that first day, feeling nervous, not knowing anybody and worrying about making a fool of myself.

"Nasher!" I said. "Thank goodness, a familiar face. How's it going?" Nasher replied, "Great, Yiddo. Pleased to see you, too. I tell you what, though, that bird on the front desk's a bit of alright. She even said I looked fit. What do you reckon to her then?"

I thought to myself, oh well, ego back to normal then, and responded, "I bet she says that to everyone that comes here today." Sure enough, when we had our first comfort break (still being politically correct) we all confirmed that she'd said the same to all of us. After about 15 minutes of waiting, the full complement for our training programme had arrived. Another female officer opened the door and beckoned us to follow her. This officer was about 6ft tall and was built like the proverbial 'brick shithouse door'. My God, she was big! I certainly wouldn't want to argue with her at the checkout in Tesco, that's for sure. I immediately nicknamed her 'the Amazonian'. She led us into the prison itself and through all these corridors. As we were all prison officers, we were taken on the quickest route through the residential wings and past female prisoners, which wouldn't have been permitted had we have been members of the public.

On approaching the first group of women, nearly all of whom were smoking (they were allowed to at that time), one turned to us and lifted her top up, revealing her breasts to us all, and then looked straight at Nasher and said, "Want a blow job then, sonny? I bet you ain't seen tits like these before."

This seemed to set all the other women off, and another female prisoner then dropped her trousers and knickers and started to play with herself, saying to the group, "Who wants it first then?"

Fucking hell, it was like being in a porn shop! They all either showed us their breasts or their lower half while making lewd comments by using hand signs. Our Amazonian officer completely ignored them as she sailed serenely through the middle. As for we men - talk about being reduced to quivering wrecks! I was so glad when we reached the other end of the corridor. I said to our Amazonian, "Jeez is it like that all the time here?"

"Nah," she replied, "sometimes they go really over the top,"

Over the top? Bloody hell, I thought, apart from actually carrying out the act of having sex I honestly don't know how much more over the top they could be.

We finally arrived at our training venue after several further encounters of a similar nature. Baby-faced Nasher was bright red by this time. "Bloody hell, I can't walk through that lot again," he said. "Did you see that one that went to grab my balls? It frightened the fucking life out of me!"

Another course participant said, "What about that one with the huge knockers? She tried to rub them on my head!"

Trying to remain nonchalant, I commented, "I bet the Amazonian took us that way on purpose, as a sort of initiation test. I just hope we don't have to go back that way. Give me our murderers and bank robbers anytime! Those bloody women scared the shit out of me!"

At lunchtime, our Amazonian escort came back to see if we wanted to go to the officers' mess for lunch, so we asked if it meant walking through the wings again.

She replied, "Of course. What are you men scared of - a few women who were just showing off to you or what?"

Not one to show fear, I said straight away, "Yeah, I need to go to the mess and have something to eat, so I'll run the gauntlet."

At this, several others piped up, too, and in the end, we all went to the mess. We needn't have feared, however, as this time all the prisoners were locked up behind their cell doors enjoying their own lunch. I wish I could say I knew in advance that this would be the case but on this occasion, I really didn't even think of that. I can't even remember what the officers' mess was like, so it must've left a good impression.

The course finished at 4 p.m. and, sure enough, we had to run the gauntlet again to go back to the gate, with similar heckling ringing in our ears:

"Who wants a hand job - five Rizla?"

"You look hot – wanna give me a length of your hosepipe, darlin' – three snouts.

"Hey sonny, you want me to break you in?"

"Look at that tiddler, throw im back."

"Blimey, I got more balls than him."

“Oy, sonny, does your mum know you’re wearing your dad’s trousers?” “Fuckin’ ’ell, better send ’im over ’ere. I’ll get ’im outta ’is long pants, haha.”

In reality, it wasn’t that long a walk back, but it sure seemed it. I was used to insults from male prisoners. I’d been called a wanker and had prisoners say that they hoped my family got cancer and that sort of thing, but it just washed over me. What we got from the female prisoners, however, was of such a personal, intimate nature that it was hard to take, even though the staff there just ignored it. A few years later male officers were allowed to work in female establishments, but I couldn’t have worked in that environment. The behaviour of female prisoners seemed so much worse than that of their male counterparts, and it scared the shit out of me. If some of the stories I’ve heard are true, then certain male colleagues really did take up the offers of sex from female prisoners.

I can’t remember what the course was about, but on the third day it was cancelled due to staff shortages back at Pentonville, and boy was I so glad it was? I never went back inside Holloway prison, or along that dreaded wing, during the remainder of my career, although I did go there on escorts from time to time.

Within the grounds, on the back perimeter of the prison, was the officers’ club, which was a popular venue on a Friday or Saturday night, as they usually held a disco. You would often find colleagues from other London prisons there, as well as members of the Metropolitan Police, so it was a good meeting place for colleagues from a wide range of establishments. One common theme in conversations about Holloway was the number of lesbians that appeared to work there. Whether this was true or not I don’t know but in all my 25 years in the service, working in four different establishments, I only came across three homosexual officers but did encounter many lesbian officers once mixed-sex staff were allowed, some of whom worked alongside their partners.

Maybe the disparity occurred because male officers were probably less open in terms of revealing their homosexual tendencies. Let me make it clear at this point that I've never made a distinction between homosexual, heterosexual, male or female officers. The most important thing to me has always been whether they could do the job or not, irrespective of their sexuality.

When you first arrived at the Holloway club, you rang the bell at the entrance and announced who you were before being allowed in. You then made your way up the stairs to the main area, where there was a signing-in desk. You could take a non-member of the prison service with you as a guest, although the rule at that time throughout all prison officers' clubs was that only members could purchase drinks at the bar.

One night I was with some colleagues from the Ville and on approaching the bar I recognised one of the officers behind it serving drinks. 'Eric' who was an interesting character and had a reputation as one of the all-time greats. It was said about Eric that he should be placed in a glass cage, left in the centre and only allowed out in the case of an alarm bell emergency, as he was a real nutter. He had big, staring eyes, and some of the stories told about him were legendary. He was a very volatile character and his mood could change very quickly without warning. I'd heard he was an ex-alcoholic, but I'm not sure if that was true. There are many stories I could relate about Eric, but I won't unless he's directly involved in my story.

I remember one time when Eric and I were on C4 landing unlocking the cells. I think it was after lunch, to allow the prisoners to slop out. He was at one end of the landing and I, the junior screw, was at the other, when suddenly he disappeared, leaving me with all the prisoners out at the same time. This was a definite no-no, as leaving a colleague on their own while the prisoners were all out and about presented a real danger. Fortunately, just as the time came to lock up the prisoners again a colleague from another landing arrived to assist me. As we finished, 'Eric' reappeared. I decided to approach him about the situation. I knew I was the junior officer but, bloody hell, you just don't abandon your colleague in that way.

“Oy, what the fuck do you think you’re playing at?” I yelled in his direction as we approached each other.

I could see my other colleague approaching from the opposite direction, and another colleague noticed my dilemma and came toward me from behind Eric, and he was shaking his head violently and wagging his finger from side to side as if to warn me not to say anything or Eric would blow a fuse and go for me. But I was in full flow and I wasn’t about to back down. I continued, “I may be the junior, but I do know that you never leave a colleague like you have just done, you wanker. Who the fuck d’ya think you are?”

All the officers on the landings above and below mine stopped in their tracks and watched as if they were expecting some sort of punch-up between us as did the my two fellow officer on the landing. Bloody hell, if that had happened Eric would’ve killed me.

Instead, Eric looked at me with a big grin on his face and said, “Yiddo, you’ve got some balls. You’re not frightened to speak your mind and I like that. I’m sorry. I won’t ever do that again to you, and next time you’re in the club I’ll buy you a pint.” And, with that, he slapped his arm around my shoulder and we walked off to the tea room together.

That was Eric, and he kept to his promise. I ordered my drink at the Holloway club bar and Eric winked at me and didn’t take my money for it. I took my drink over to the slot machines, where my colleagues had congregated and asked, “What’s the score with the girls then? Are any of them available?”

‘Keith’ replied, “Just be careful, Yiddo. You never know who’s with who here.”

“What do you mean?” I asked.

"Let's just say, before you try to chat one up make sure what side they're batting for first," said Keith.

Sometime later I was playing on a slot machine and my colleagues had wandered off somewhere - probably to the disco next to the bar to eye up the talent. As the machine was paying out a small win for me, an attractive woman came over.

"I hope you're not gonna walk out of the club with all our money," she said.

"Nah," I replied. "Knowing me, I'll put it all back within a few minutes."

We then started chatting. I'm not sure whether it was the beer or not, but this girl seemed one of the most attractive ones in the club. A lot of the others were still in uniform, so maybe that was why. Anyway, I was just beginning to think I'd pulled when this huge hand patted me on my shoulder. It was the Amazonian officer from the course. "oy she's wiv me, so fuck off, nipper," she said.

And fuck off I did, with pleasure and rather swiftly. Bloody hell, there was no way I was gonna argue with her - she'd give Arnie Schwarzenegger a good run for his money and would've knocked ten bells out of him if he'd treated her to the line, "Hasta la vista, baby."

"Sorry," I stammered. I then rushed next door to seek out my mates. When I found them they were all laughing?

"What's so funny then?" I asked.

"You," replied Keith. "We watched you trying to pull that bird and knew what was coming. They do that to every new male officer they see. I think they get off on it. Never mind, mate, it's happened to all of us."

I remember on another occasion being at the club one midweek evening, and I was staying overnight with a fairly new 'jack the lad' officer. I got on with him very well and we remained in contact right up until I retired.

Anyway, we were just having a quiet drink. He'd been chatting up a female officer, who was accompanied by her pet dog, and 'Jack' was trying very hard to get a date with her.

She turned to my friend and said, "Before I agree to go out on a date with you, can I ask you whether you like dogs?"

I'd been sitting there like a gooseberry for so long that I think they'd forgotten I was there, so quick as a flash, I said, "I can answer that for him. Compared to some of the dogs he's been out with, you ain't half bad." Suffice to say, he didn't succeed in arranging a date with her!

Over the subsequent years, we had some really good laughs together at nightclubs, especially the Coolbury Club in Tottenham, but I won't go into those stories here. So that was the Holloway club. I had some great nights out there and met some fantastic people who are still friends today. I even remember going back there with a group from HMYOI The Mount. We went with a female PO there, who'd previously worked at Holloway, and she'd suggested going there for our Christmas drink. We had a great time, as I recall. The club had its own very unique atmosphere, with the mixture of males and females, heterosexual and homosexual, and nights out there was always an eye-opener.

Chapter 17

Ronnie Who? You're Joking!

Some years later I was on holiday in what was then the small holiday resort of Benalmádena on the Costa del Sol. It's now a huge, sprawling resort, but at that time it was a quaint little fishing village away from the big resorts of Fuengirola, Torremolinos and Marbella.

'Ray' had mentioned in passing that he wanted to go on a holiday, but he didn't have anybody to go with. I think at the time he'd just split up with his girlfriend, so I offered to accompany him. He said to me, "But Yiddo, what about your wife? Won't she mind?" "Ray," I replied, "we finally split up six months ago and haven't been together since."

"Bloody hell, Tony, you never said. How come you've kept that quiet for the last six months?"

I explained that, as far as I was concerned, it was a private matter and I always tried to keep my personal life separate from my work life.

"But, blimey mate, you should've said something sooner. We could've met up and swapped stories about our failed relationships and got horribly drunk together," he said.

"That's why I didn't say anything. Who the hell wants to get drunk with you?" I responded. But, of course, whilst on holiday we did get horribly drunk quite a few times together.

So we agreed we'd apply for leave at the same time and go off on holiday. We'd been offered the use of a colleague's holiday apartment in Benalmádena. 'Jock', who owned the apartment, had said it was a nice, quiet resort, well away from the more popular ones, so there was little chance that we'd bump into any ex-prisoners or other staff. This suited both of us, as we'd been doing a lot of overtime and needed the rest to recharge our batteries.

And it was just as relaxing as we'd hoped. We had a few pleasant days of lazing in the sun on the wonderful beach, having a few drinks at the numerous bars along the main beachfront road, eating whenever we wanted and shaking off the rigid routine of prison life that we were used to. It was bliss.

One day we were walking along the main road adjacent to the beach when we heard a shout of "Oy, Yiddo!" We looked in the general direction of the source of the loud, booming voice and saw one of our colleagues, 'Joe Forecastle', standing in a bar and waving us over, so we joined him for a drink. "Joe," I said, "I thought you'd used up all your leave, so how come you're here on holiday? How did you wangle some more leave?"

"Easy, mate," he replied. "You remember that alarm bell the other day?" "Yes," I said.

"Well, I was on the other end of that alarm bell, and you know what? The bloody prisoner attacked me and I broke my finger on his nose, so I'm actually on sick leave courtesy of Paul Childs, but I thought I'd better bring the family with me in case of a relapse," he explained with a wink.

We ended up spending the rest of the day with 'Joe' and his family, getting very drunk and relating stories of the prison service and what we'd experienced. Joe explained that he'd been to Benalmádena many times and loved it. He asked if we'd been up to the bar at Mijas yet and we told him we were planning to go there in the next few days. So Joe said, "Well, don't forget to say hello to my mate Ronnie when you're up there. He's from our part of the world, y'know."

Joe was a great bloke to know at work. Being a fellow Londoner, I understood some of the slang he used, and it was good to have him around when there was an incident at work. He had real confidence about him and when he spoke to the prisoners, they always seemed to respond to him; they never seemed to hold a grudge against him, even if he'd had to use rough tactics to deal with a violent incident. But whenever he answered an alarm bell, he always seemed to be the unlucky one that got hurt!

Jock had told us before we left the Ville to go up to the mountainside village of Mijas and meet up with a friend of his who owned a bar there. He said that his friend would probably let us kip on the floor overnight rather than have us go back down the coast to our apartment and that way both of us would be able to have a good drink. He also said that his friend was an ex-member of the Metropolitan Police and that other Londoners frequented his bar, so we'd be able to have a good old chat about how the city had changed over the years.

So we hired a car and drove the few miles inland up the mountain to the village of Mijas. We found the bar easily and introduced ourselves to the landlord, 'Syd'. He was over the moon not only that Jock had recommended that we visit him, but also that we were both Londoners and from the same area that he hailed from. He insisted that we should have a proper drink and stay the night. I certainly didn't fancy the drive back down the mountain in the dark and if it meant that we could have a good old drink and get some kip I was all for it. 'Syd', the owner, told us that his wife would get us some food and that later a mate of his called Ronnie would be along. Ronnie was also from London and up here he had his own business called The Office. It sounded as if we'd all have a really good night.

Sometime during the evening, Ronnie arrived with a few mates. We were all introduced and he seemed like a nice enough bloke. The drinks flowed and the atmosphere was great: good food, good drinks and good company. Somebody produced a camera and a photo session ensued: Ray and I with our new friend Syd; Syd's wife and me; Ray kissing Syd; Syd kissing Ronnie … the usual sort of thing. And, bloody hell, we certainly shipped some booze that night.

The next day, with really sore heads and after a full English breakfast cooked by Syd's wife - Gawd bless her - we bade farewell and headed back to Benalmádena.

The rest of the holiday passed much too quickly and before we knew it we were once again on duty at Pentonville, back to those smells and the life of working long hours in those horrible conditions.

Sometime afterwards Ray and I were in one of the wing tea rooms talking to our colleagues about our holiday and Ray produced the holiday photos to show everyone. Bloody hell, I thought as I looked at them, who the hell's that ugly bird I'm snogging? I don't remember her, or that other one with really tasty, nice legs. I wish I'd been sober enough to remember who they are.

Ray then produced his pièce de résistance: Ray, Ronnie and me with our arms around each other. A picture of perfect holiday harmony with drinking buddies!

"Bloody hell, you two! Don't you know who that is in the photo?" remarked one of our colleagues.

"Yeah," I said, 'that's us with our new best mate Ronnie."

"No, you pair of pricks, that's you with one of the most wanted criminals in the country! That's Ronnie Knight! Didn't you read in the papers that he'd buggered off to the Costa del Crime and was living up in Mijas?"

Ray and I looked at each other horrified. "Fucking hell!"

I honestly never knew. I mean, I knew he was wanted, but I'd never seen a photo of him so I'd no idea what he looked like. As far as I know, Ray got rid of the evidence very quickly and I've never seen the photos since thank goodness.

There was one other chap in the bar that night whose name now escapes me, who also turned out to have notoriety in the criminal world. I was watching a programme called *The Cook Report* on the television, featuring Australian crime investigator Roger Cook. This particular episode was all about the so-called Costa del Crime and part of the investigation focused on Ronnie Knight. I was keen to watch this programme as I was worried that we might've been caught on camera! Thankfully, nothing about us appeared.

Roger Cook then went on to interview this other chap at his villa, and I recognised him. Oh hell, I thought, that's the geezer that was in the bar with Ronnie Knight that night up at Mijas, so I've now got photos of me with two bloody wanted criminals!

I remember, as the programme progressed, this chap attempted to hit Roger Cook and ended up chasing him and his camera crew along the road while shouting, "Get that fucking camera outta my face!" Funny that, 'cause he wasn't so camera shy up at the bar in Mijas!

Some years later it was reported that this man had been shot to death whilst at his villa in Mijas.

Chapter 18

Me, a Racist!

Once I was called up in front of the governor for a disciplinary hearing. I'd been accused of making a racist remark to a prisoner, swearing at him and writing on his prison-issue shirt.

During your career as a serving prison officer, you can expect to be accused of all sorts of inappropriate behaviour towards prisoners and, as the years progressed, these accusations and complaints grew out of all proportion. It became an occupational hazard. The main reason for this was a change in guidelines appertaining to prisoners' rights and behaviour.

Some time ago, following our prison discipline code of conduct, a prisoner could be placed on an adjudication charge for misbehaviour. He would then be brought in front of the governor to respond to the charge made against him and could call any number of witnesses for his defence. This could be a serious business, as an adjudication award against a prisoner could result in his losing remission and therefore spending longer in prison. In some cases, he could appeal for the loss of remission to be rescinded, and if his behaviour over a certain period improved he would get his lost days back. This procedure acted as a small weapon in terms of keeping prisoners' behaviour within acceptable guidelines.

Nowadays, however, prisoners are allowed to call a solicitor to represent them in an internal disciplinary case brought by an officer against a prisoner. As a result, officers often don't bother to place a prisoner on a charge even if they are caught red-handed; it just isn't worth the hassle of almost having to go to court to prove that a prisoner broke the code of conduct, the code is legislated by government legislation and not by the prison service.

Originally, this code of conduct contained a clause appertaining to the charge of "making any false or malicious complaints against staff, prisoners, or any visiting members of the public". However, in their infinite wisdom, the Home Office dropped this particular disciplinary charge from the code. This effectively opened the door for prisoners to manufacture false and malicious claims without fear of repercussions. These baseless complaints often resulted in ruined service careers for the members of staff concerned.

Anyway, I was given notice of the complaint against me and was horrified to find myself the target of such an accusation. I'd simply been doing my job. The alarm bell went off to signal that an incident was taking place and, as my presence wasn't required, along with several of my colleagues I started getting all the other prisoners back in their cells and locked away to prevent it from turning into a spectator sport or sparking an all-out riot.

What you didn't want to happen, as sadly seems all too common these days is for 1,500 unlocked prisoners to be standing watching 20 officers apprehending and trying to restrain a violent prisoner. They can easily get whipped up into a frenzy themselves and it can snowball quickly into a very serious situation and this is exactly how some cases of gross indiscipline and riots have kicked off in the past. It really didn't matter in such a volatile situation whether you put half a dozen prisoners behind one door or just lock a prisoner up in an empty office, so long as they're out of the way as quickly as possible.

I saw this particular prisoner loitering and told him to go to his cell for lock-up, but he simply ignored my instruction. I then opened an office door near to where he was standing and told him to get behind that door. Again, he ignored me. At this point, I, too, could've raised the alarm, or after the current incident, I could've placed this prisoner on a governor's report for refusing a direct order. However, there was too much going on, the situation was urgent and I needed to be forceful. So I turned to him and said, "Fuck off back to your cell now, you bastard!"

He responded, “I’ll fucking well report you for that.”

I never really thought much more about it. As far as I was concerned it was just another minor incident during the main event. However on the day of the hearing I called only one witness - a prisoner who was located on D2 and was the number one cleaner for the landing.

This prisoner, ‘Mr B’, was from an ethnic background, his family had come to the UK from Jamaica many years previously. I’d asked this prisoner if he would be willing to appear as a witness for me, half expecting him to refuse; after all, he was a prisoner and I was a screw. So I was quite surprised when he agreed, saying, “That fucking bastard’s had it coming to him for some while now, so what better way than to support you against him. He’ll understand then what being a nigger is all about.” I wasn’t entirely sure what he meant, but I presumed that my accuser had alienated himself from several of the other black prisoners on the wing and they’d had enough of him as well.

The hearing was held in the boardroom, and the governor read out the complaint against me while my accuser sat on the opposite side of the table. “Well,” said the governor, “you’ve heard the complaint. You’re accused of telling ‘prisoner Q’, ‘Fuck off back to your cell, you black bastard’. What have you got to say about it?

“Governor,” I responded, “I told ‘prisoner Q’, ‘Fuck off back to your cell, you bastard’, but I never mentioned the word black.”

“Why did you use that language?” he asked.

I explained, “I had politely requested the prisoner to kindly return to his cellular accommodation forthwith, but he seemed not to understand. So I then asked him to return to his cell immediately, and he again refused to return. Being a bit of a behavioural expert and thinking on my feet, Governor, I thought I would use the street language of southeast London, where this prisoner hails from, and 'Fuck off back to your cell, you bastard' worked."

"So why, Officer Levy, did you call this prisoner a bastard?" said the governor.

"That's easy, Governor. If you check this prisoner's core record you will find that he was indeed born out of wedlock. Thus I believe the technical term I used in this circumstance would correctly identify him as a bastard," I said, with a straight face.

I could see that the governor wasn't seeing the funny side of my story, so at this point, I asked if I could call a witness to verify my story before answering any other matters. The governor agreed, and I told him the name of my witness. "But he's a prisoner," said the governor.

"Yes, and he's also black," I responded.

My witness arrived and he gave his evidence of what he witnessed, which completely corroborated my side of events, therefore the governor had no alternative but to accept it. However, he didn't want to let the matter drop entirely. He then asked me why I'd written my name on the front of the prisoner's shirt. Again, I had a perfectly good explanation.

"It was like this, Governor," I said. "The prisoner said he would be making a complaint about me swearing at him and calling him a bastard, so I told him my name was Officer Levy and spelt it out for him. I asked him if he had a pen or pencil, and he said he didn't, therefore I took my chinagraph (a specially designed pen for writing on a shiny surface such as a wall chart) out of my top pocket and, as I didn't have a piece of paper handy, I wrote my name on the front of his shirt to ensure he wouldn't forget my name when making his complaint."

I honestly wished I'd had a camera handy at that point because the governor's face went from pink to apoplectic purple in a matter of seconds. He quickly regained his composure and concluded the hearing.

"I find the complaint against Officer Levy to be unfounded," the governor announced. He then looked at the prisoner and said directly to him, "In fact, Officer Levy should have placed you on report for disobeying an order, but he gave you the benefit of the doubt, and then you attempt to discredit him, so I'm going to award you a week's loss of earnings for wasting our time. Dismissed."

The governor had the power to award the prisoner this punishment, as this was still part of the code of conduct rules at that time and prisoners could be and were punished for making false or malicious complaints, and in this case, that rule applied.

The prisoner was taken back to his cell, and as I was preparing to leave the governor asked me to stay behind. Once everybody else had left the room he said to me, "You're a lucky so-and-so and a bloody quick-thinking one at that. If I didn't know any better and it had been some other member of staff standing before me I might well have believed the prisoner, but not in your case. I've seen how you work with the prisoners and I know you're not racist, but you must be very careful in this game, Tony, because they will always try to set us against each other. Don't give them that opportunity. Now get back to work."

I left that room fully relieved that the accusation against me hadn't been upheld.

Chapter 19

Pentonville Football Team

A group of us decided to reform the Pentonville football team and enter the regional inter-prison football cup competition. The football team had disbanded some years previously, but one day in the tea room one of my colleagues asked in general if anybody was interested in starting it up again. I immediately said yes, as I loved football and played regularly until becoming a prison officer and finding that working every other weekend made playing Sunday League football a bit difficult. Several of us used to play once a week at lunchtimes in the gymnasium, so there was already a nucleus for the team.

We touted the idea around and collected names, and within a short while we'd drummed up enough interest to form a team. Our goalie 'Teflon', or Jesus as he was sometimes known (non-stick and didn't like crosses), became the secretary and we thought it would be a great hoot if I, being Jewish, became the treasurer and fund-raiser. Undeniably, there were others involved, but again the old memory is fading as to their identities and roles.

My first task was to sort out some kit. As there had been a team previously, I approached our PE department to see if they still had the old kit. They handed me four footballs and some old shirts, shorts and socks, none of which were in very good condition, and it was clear that all of it would need replacing very soon.

Teflon organised some friendly matches against other prison officer teams, but we were hoping to enter a team in a local midweek league. However, Pentonville didn't have a football pitch, which made playing matches at home rather difficult.

We approached the local authorities, who informed us that a local pitch was available but that it was AstroTurf rather than grass. Seeing as it was just around the corner from the prison, however, we decided to rent it from the local council. At the time, several professional football clubs, such as Queens Park Rangers, were experimenting with this new kind of AstroTurf surface and several councils changed to the stuff as it was much easier to maintain than grass. It was hardly surprising really, as not having to do regular grass-cutting must've saved them thousands of pounds per year. I then wrote to several local companies, explaining that we needed kit for our football team, but I received no replies and felt quite downhearted about this.

I can't honestly remember many details about the teams we played or how we performed, but we did play several matches in the inter-prison cup competitions and trained once a week on our 'home pitch'. Bloody hell, AstroTurf burns are really painful! Whoever invented that stuff should've been shot, and it should've come with a health warning! I'll explain why later.

Our priorities, however, were kit and money. I decided that the best way to raise funds we would charge all members of the team a signing-on fee, plus a small fee on match days and training days. I also booked a date in the club to hold a disco and planned to raise funds by having a raffle.

Why the hell I said I would do all this I'll never know, but I suppose at the time I'd nothing else to do in my spare time. I didn't have a girlfriend and wasn't looking for one. I was working long hours and loads of overtime, which really didn't make for a great social life anyway. Whatever the reason, I was determined to see it through. I'm the sort of bloke who, once committed to something, will put every effort into making it happen and also doing it better than anyone else could. That's just me.

I started visiting sports shops in my local area and wrote to several professional football teams asking if they could offer us either any old kit or some signed memorabilia for us to raffle off to raise funds for the team.

I was pleasantly surprised by the response of one shop in Enfield Town, Briggs Sports, who said they would donate two footballs. They also told me about a special event being held to commemorate the opening of the New Tottenham Hotspur Corporate Hospitality Stand, and suggested that it would be a good opportunity to approach the club for signed pictures and stuff for a raffle. Various local suppliers would be there selling football kits at competitively low prices, too, so there might be a chance to Be able to obtain a brand new kit fairly cheaply. Hey, this is going much better now, I thought to myself.

Teflon and I decided we'd both go along to Spurs' special night and see what sort of football kits were available and at what cost. Meanwhile, I got on with organising the disco at the club, got the tickets printed and bought some books of raffle tickets - cloakroom tickets, in reality, but isn't that what everybody uses? I managed to obtain several raffle prizes from local businesses, among them a gallon bottle Bell's whisky. I would've liked that prize for me, but decided not to buy any tickets for myself seeing as I was the organiser. I can't remember what we charged for tickets, but they were cheaper if bought in advance rather than on night. We got some good stuff from Spurs - autographed footballs and shirts and lots of pictures, so we ended up with enough donations for about 15 prizes. Spurs also gave us a couple of footballs for the team to use.

The actual night was a roaring success and the club was full. I got my friend 'Eric' to act as doorman and bouncer, and I sat on the door with him collecting money from those that hadn't bought tickets in advance. Two of the team's wives were going around the club selling raffle tickets and they approached Eric and me. He bought five pounds' worth, but I declined, explaining that I was worried people might think it was a fix if the organiser won anything. One of them said, "Oh, don't be so silly, Tony. You've worked so hard to make this a success that nobody will begrudge you winning a prize."

That made sense to me, so I ended up buying five pounds' worth, too.

The evening wore on and eventually, the raffle draw was held. "Tony, you'd better come into the hall as you've won a raffle prize," said somebody over my shoulder.

"Tell them to draw again and let somebody else win it," I replied.

"Tony," they said more forcefully, "it's your prize, so come and get it. They all think it's only fair."

So I reluctantly walked into the hall. Bloody hell, it was packed. I couldn't remember the last time Pentonville club had been this crowded. It had been a huge success. Anyway, I wondered, what's this prize I've won? Not the curling tongs, I hope - my hair's falling out. I wouldn't mind the holiday voucher, though. No, it was none of those. I couldn't believe it. I'd only gone and won the gallon of whisky! It almost felt like a fiddle, but it wasn't; I'd won it fair and square. It had turned out to be a great night and this was the icing on the cake.

The football team's committee got together to review our fund-raising efforts, and due to the great success of the evening, we'd got enough money to purchase a brand new kit and all the accessories we'd need, plus money left over to help towards our pitch fees and entry fees to the various competitions we could now enter.

Teflon and I went along to the Spurs ground, which was a real treat for me being a Spurs supporter, and I managed to get a sneaky tour of the new corporate stand. Talk about watching football in luxury! These plush boxes had everything in them, including comfy armchairs, a minibar and TV screens. I was a bit puzzled by the latter and wondered why anyone would need TVs while watching a live match, and then I realised it was because they provide instant replays. To me, all these modern facilities and luxurious comfort weren't what watching live matches were all about. You couldn't experience the atmosphere or feel the passion from behind a plate-glass window. No, you could keep your corporate hospitality and associated luxuries and give me the terraces any day.

The suppliers of kits were there in force and we eventually negotiated a good deal with my new friends from Briggs Sports for a brand new kit. Now we could be a real football team. Even if we were crap and lost every time we played, at least we'd look the part.

Funnily enough, when I got my transfer and went to The Mount, Teflon who had also transferred there, and I started up their football team, too, and bought the new football kit from the same supplier, Briggs Sports. We got it at cost price, provided we agreed to display their name as sponsors on the shorts. It's a funny old game.

I remember playing one match on a Sunday at Hollesley Bay, which may sound like a holiday club but is actually an open prison. Hollesley Bay began in 1887 as a Colonial College, training those intending to emigrate. Then in 1938, the Prison Commission acquired Hollesley Bay to train young offenders in the Borstal system. In 1983 Youth Custody replaced the Borstal system and in October 1988, when the CJA (Criminal Justice Agency) came into force, Hollesley Bay became a YOI.

In 1982 Warren Hill opened to accommodate Category C young offenders in a closed environment alongside Hollesley Bay open prison. Then in April 2002, though retaining some shared services, Hollesley Bay and Warren Hill became separate establishments, the open complex retaining the name Hollesley Bay. The establishment provides different regimes for adult Category D offenders - life sentence prisoners at the end of their custodial time and young offenders.

It was a long coach journey from Pentonville to Hollesley Bay, but the monotony of our trip was lightened by a double-page article in the *Sunday Times* about a prison officer, 'Officer X', and the struggles and terrible ordeals he'd faced whilst serving at HMP Pentonville after he'd left the SAS. It gave us all a great laugh, as the feature was all about none other than 'Eric' and several parts of the story were just that - stories. It certainly helped to pass the time, but boy was it full of crap!

I don't remember much about the match. The only things of note were that afterwards we went to their clubhouse for the usual offer of a meal and a drink and when we eventually boarded our coach for the journey back to Pentonville we first had to get local tractor to tow us out of the field we were parked in.

The idiot driver had taken the coach up to the pitch area so that he could watch the match and get his head down; unfortunately, he managed to get the wheels down, too - in several inches of mud! To make matters worse, when we all boarded the coach it sank even further. The journey back took nearly twice as long as the journey there, mainly due to the number of times the driver had to stop to allow us a comfort break – it was pretty obvious we'd had a little too much beer. I do remember at one point the driver said he couldn't stop and so good old 'Eric' opened the coach door and urinated all along the A12.

One time when we were playing a midweek match on the AstroTurf, I attempted a sliding tackle, which was a bloody silly thing to do on that surface but my competitiveness took over. For my troubles, I received a burn mark on my left buttock and a graze on my left knee, even though I was wearing tracksuit bottoms, which we all did to reduce the burn effect when we fell on the surface. It stung a bit, but I didn't think anything more of it.

In an attempt to get fitter, I and a colleague had started going to the gym and having a run at lunchtimes. We used to run along the Caledonian Road as far as Regent's Canal, then along the Regents

Park canal towpath past the famous bird aviary (designed by Antony Armstrong-Jones, the Earl of Snowden, who at the time was Princess Margaret's husband), at which point we turned around and came back. It was a nice little run and easily manageable in our lunch break.

The next day, after our match, we set out for our run as usual. It was a sunny, warm day as I remember, but along the route back my left knee started to hurt, and by the time we arrived back at the Ville I was in real pain. We showered and changed back into our uniforms, and I noticed my knee was a bit red and swollen. I decided to pop over to the prison hospital and get some painkillers before I went on exercise yard duty. Each prison had its own hospital unit and staff could go there for any day-to-day minor problems such as a bad headache, but more serious matters would have to be dealt with by your local GP or the local hospital. After obtaining the painkillers I went off to my duties on the exercise yard.

On exercise duty, I was detailed to stand by the alarm bell which was on a slightly raised platform, which enabled the assigned officer to observe the whole area more clearly. While I was standing there my knee started to throb, and the more it throbbed the dizzier I felt. Bloody hell, I thought to myself, I feel rough. One of the prisoners stopped in front of me and said, "Guv, you okay? You look like you're gonna faint." I bloody well felt like I was as well! What the hell's happening? I struggled through the rest of that hour and decided I ought to go back to the hospital and get them to take a look at my knee. When the exercise period thankfully ended, I approached the SO. "SO, I'm gonna have to go over to the hospital. I'm in agony. My knee is killing me," I said.

"I'm a trained first-aider," he responded. "Roll your trouser leg up and let's have a look.

I tried to oblige, but my knee was so sore that I couldn't get the trouser leg over it without causing excruciating pain, and by now my knee was bright red and very swollen.

"Bloody hell," said the S O when he saw it, "you'd better get over to the hospital and let them take a look."

I limped over to the hospital, feeling very unwell and in a lot of pain. The took one look at it and told me to go immediately to the nearest hospital A&E department. So I reported to the detail office and told them I was going off sick. By this time I was feeling decidedly groggy and light-headed. I managed to get my uniform trousers off and put on a pair of shorts, but my knee was about twice the size it should've been and I was in agony. Somehow, I managed to drive to the nearest A&E facility to where I lived, at Chase Farm Hospital. Following examination, I was admitted. My leg was put in a sling and I was put on a penicillin drip, the diagnosis being septic bursitis caused by the friction burn from the AstroTurf, which had become infected and had been aggravated further by running the next day. I've got to say I'd never experienced pain like that before. I was kept in hospital on the drip for a week and was then allowed out on crutches for another week. All in all, I wasn't back at work for a month.

I recall another midweek match on the AstroTurf when we were playing under floodlights. I remembered challenging for the ball and then everything after that went a bit fuzzy. I was sitting on the ground thinking, who the hell's blood is that all over the ground? Oh shit, it's mine! But where's it all coming from? My nose? And why aren't my legs working?

A colleague of mine leant over me and said, "Hey, Yiddo, you know that ed (evening duty) you're doing tomorrow night - do you still want it, 'cause if not I'll do it?"

Charming, I thought. So much for compassion.

I got up and felt like shit. My head hurt and my nose was almost certainly broken - when you've broken your nose before you know when it's happened again. I made it back to the prison club, where we always went after a match for a curry or stroganoff or something rustled up by one of the wives. I remember letting somebody drive my car, which was pretty unusual. At the time I had a Peugeot 205Gti, which I'd bought brand new, and it was my pride and joy. So I must've been bad to let anyone else take the wheel. The next thing I remembered was waking up in the hospital the next day. I'd suffered a concussion and had passed out, so a colleague had driven me to the hospital.

I told you that AstroTurf was bloody lethal, didn't I?!

Chapter 20

Going Away and Moving On

There comes a time in everybody's career when they know it's time to move on, and I'd felt I'd reached that stage. There were many changes on the way, not just locally at Pentonville but nationally throughout the prison service. The much-vaunted 'fresh start' was now imminent, which meant the ending of the so-called 'Spanish practices' of unlimited overtime and CDCs. Now it would be 'time off in lieu' and a much better pay structure with more predictable hours of attendance.

Besides, I also felt it was time for me to stand up and be counted. I thought about all the times I'd sat quietly at the back of meetings or received instructions from senior officers and principal officers and feeling that I could do their job better. I realised that now it was time for me to put my money where my mouth was. Either I sought promotion and proved I could do better than those in the next rank, or I stopped griping and just got on with my current job. Never one to be a shrinking violet, I wanted the chance to prove myself as a manager of men.

I'd already taken the senior officers' promotion exam, but we all tended to regard it as just as an excuse for a day (and night) out in London and the exam wasn't exactly taken seriously by most of us. After all, taking into account all my overtime I was earning more than the senior officers, principal officers and many of the governor grades already, so why go for the promotion? So, along with my colleagues, I would go to the central London venue intending to fail the promotion exam and get on with the important part of the day: who could get pissed quickest and pull a bird.

Another factor that influenced my thoughts of moving on was the daily commute from Hertfordshire to London, which was beginning to wear me down and would only get worse with the introduction of the new changes.

It used to take me about half an hour to drive to work in the mornings, leaving at 6.30 a.m. and having my breakfast in the mess at the Ville before starting work. Working overtime in the evening, as was usual, meant that I left work at about 8.30 p.m. and could be home by 9 p.m. If the overtime was stopped, as was planned, I would end up leaving work at 5 p.m. and get caught up in the London rush hour, meaning that I'd probably arrive home at 7.30 p.m. at the earliest. Much as the case in my previous career as a driving instructor it wasn't an inviting prospect.

So my thoughts were turning to obtaining the promotion and moving on to another establishment, but where?

All thoughts of moving were temporarily put on hold, however, due to an old football injury to my right knee, which had started giving me problems. I'd been placed on a waiting list for an arthroscopy operation and the date of the operation had now arrived.

The operation wasn't considered serious and I was told that they would drill three holes in a triangle around my kneecap and would laser any floating bone or cartilage they found and generally clean up any debris. Simple, I thought. I shouldn't be off work for long, thank goodness. I couldn't afford to lose all that lovely overtime.

I went into the Central Middlesex hospital on a Sunday evening, which turned out to be a notorious night in a sad way. It was the very same night of the Broadwater Farm riots in Tottenham, during which PC Keith Blakelock was murdered. I had parked my car at my parents' house, which was within walking distance of the scene of the riots, and I remember being so concerned about it that I telephoned my mum and dad and, rather than ask if they were all right, I asked about the riots. I wanted my dad to check if my car was still okay.

I didn't expect to be off work for long and was so confident about this that in advance I'd made firm arrangments to do some overtime on the Wednesday following my operation.

What the doctors didn't tell me until after the operation, however, was that I would be on crutches for a few weeks, as they'd carried out more extensive surgery than originally planned. And as a consequence, I wasn't allowed to go back to work for four weeks. In those days, if you were off sick you had to produce a note from your doctor to say you were fit for work before the prison would allow you to return.

During this period of incapacitation, a colleague of mine suggested that what I really needed was a holiday for a couple of weeks so that I could recuperate properly. He told me he wouldn't mind coming with me, as I would probably need some help getting around while I was on crutches. We'd both done a lot of overtime, so we had the funds available, and we were both single blokes. He'd just split up from his girlfriend and I was living apart from my wife, although still technically married. My wife and I knew we weren't going to get back together again, but we'd remained friends and had said that we would get divorced if ever one of us found another serious partner and wanted to remarry.

So I thought, yeah, why not? A nice holiday, a few drinks, meet a few girls have a few laughs. It sounded great. But where could we go that was still nice and warm in November? Our first choice was the Canary Islands, which would be warm enough to sunbathe, but we couldn't find anything suitable. The Greek Islands would be too cold, as would mainland Spain and we didn't want a long-haul journey to our destination, so eventually, we opted for the beautiful island of Madeira.

If you've never been to Madeira, it's worth a trip. It has a subtropical climate and is warm and lush, and the people are extremely friendly. It also has historical links to the UK. Set on a hillside just outside the capital of Funchal was the Reids Hotel, made famous for the serving of cream teas - oh, very British, don't you know. It had also attracted the world notoriety as the place Sir Winston Churchill went for a holiday to recuperate from his illnesses during the Second World War, and where he completed some of his most well-known paintings while sitting on the hotel's sun terrace, overlooking the Atlantic Ocean.

That particular hotel was unfortunately fully booked, but we managed to get rooms at the Savoy Hotel - not the same chain as the one in London, in fact far from it, but at least it was four-star. It was a nice hotel, but as there were no real beaches in Madeira the only place you could sunbathe was on the lido terrace, which all hotels seemed to have. To get to the Savoy's lido you had to descend the cliff face by lift to reach what looked like a flattened piece of rock surrounding a natural-looking seawater swimming pool. The water was bloody freezing, as the water came straight in off the Atlantic, but at least the terrace got the sun all day and the bar stayed open until dark.

We had a great time at this place and met lots of lovely people. We became very friendly with a couple and their daughter, who came from Belfast and told us many hair-raising stories about the troubles over there and the frequent bomb blasts and violence on the streets. It didn't seem a nice place to be living, that's for sure. Their daughter, 'Gemma', was an attractive girl around her late twenties to early thirties. We spent many hours together during their stay and I struck up a good friendship with her. She helped me exercise my bad leg on many occasions during the dark evenings. She visited me back in London over the next year and we remained friends for some time, but because of the distance and the troubles in Belfast, it made it too difficult to sustain a lasting relationship. But a holiday romance was good for my recuperation. 'Nuff said except the week that 'Gemma' and her family were staying at the Savoy came to an end all too quickly, unfortunately.

We also made friends with a chap who was the local timeshare boss. We met in a bar one day and, after several drinks while trying very unsuccessfully to sell us a timeshare, we realised that we enjoyed each other's company. He took me and my mate around the non-tourist bars of Funchal, one of which was located up in the old, very bohemian quarter. It was unusual for tourists to go there and the locals that filled it were extremely friendly towards us, especially when they found out what we did for a living and that we came from London. Several Scotches and Cokes into the evening, one of the locals picked up a mandolin and an impromptu jamming session began, with people producing musical instruments from who knows where, and it turned into a really great evening. Later on, probably around two or three in the morning, several young, attractive British girls arrived. We rather obviously made a beeline for them -after all, we British like to stick together when in a foreign country, don't we? And the fact that they were all very attractive made no difference to our desire to be friendly, I can assure you. They told us that they were employed at the top hotel on the Island (I think this was the Hilton, but I'm not sure). They were the floor-show dancers and recommended going to the hotel for a good night out: a meal, followed by watching the cabaret and ending the evening in the casino. So we did just that and had a great night. The girls made sure that we had front-row tables, and I must say their dancing was fantastic, with those incredibly long legs of theirs. We bumped into the girls on several occasions during our stay, and a few times on their days off they came over to our hotel and spent the day sunbathing around the pool and drinking with us. This was turning out to be a good holiday.

Considering that, when I got off the plane at Funchal, I was on crutches, it was amazing that by the third day I'd reduced this support to a walking stick and by the end of the first week I'd dispensed with the stick as well. It was probably the exercise I had with 'Gemma' that got me off the crutches and stick so quickly! My leg was recovering fast, which was just as well, as Madeira isn't flat. I sent a postcard back to the lads at the Ville, just saying, "You're there, we're here, tough".

Remembrance Sunday fell within the second week of the holiday, and strangely enough, it was one of the few days of bad weather, with rain pouring down on and off all morning. I was surprised to find out that there was a huge ex-pat population there, going back for many years, and Remembrance Sunday was an important festival in Funchal.

We watched the parade of ex-forces personnel and the laying of wreaths at the memorial statue in the centre of the town and then headed back to the hotel. En-route it started to rain quite heavily and, as it was still warm, we were both dressed only in T-shirts and shorts, so my mate suggested that we pop into a bar until the rain stopped. I readily agreed, as by then my bad leg was hurting like hell. I thought maybe I'd been overdoing it a little bit, so resting up in a bar seemed a good idea.

There were two other English people in the bar, a couple in their mid-forties, so we got talking. 'Lyn' and 'Dave' were publicans who were taking a well-earned holiday, or so they told us. Their pub was in a village called Bovingdon, which was near Hemel Hempstead in Hertfordshire. We had one hell of a drinking session that afternoon, eventually returning to our hotel after agreeing that we'd all go to the cabaret night where the girls were dancing and then go on to the casino to see how our luck went. As I said earlier, we had a great night there, even though I was the only one that won any money, £50, at the casino.

During the last week of our holiday, we met up with this couple on several occasions and we became good friends. But the holiday was quickly over, so we met up with the girls and with Lyn and Dave for the final time before reluctantly returning home and going back to our work routine at the Ville.

Fully fit and back at work, my attention once again turned to a move on from the Ville, but the same question kept coming up: what prison did I want to go to? I knew I didn't want to move to another London prison, but there were no prisons near my home, so where could I go? The solution came in an unexpected but pleasant way!

We kept in touch with Lyn and Dave after our holiday and visited them at their pub in the Village. On one such occasion, they arranged some overnight accommodation for us in a local house in a street called Apple Cottages. I mention this because when I transferred to my next establishment, HMYOI The Mount in Bovingdon, Hertfordshire, I bought a house in that very street.

I was having breakfast in the pub when Lyn said to me, "Did you know that they're building a new prison up the road from here?"

"No," I replied.

Dave said that the construction phase was well advanced and almost completed, so he suggested, "If you want we can have a stroll up there and take a look at the place before you go back home."

I couldn't see why not, so we went to this new prison, The Mount, and had a look around. I was impressed with such a new prison after spending over five years at Pentonville and this visit set my minding working as to whether this new prison was the answer I was seeking. What a great new challenge - a new prison, new staff and a chance of promotion. Yeah, I'm gonna go for it, I decided.

As this was a new prison and the service was short of staff (so what's new?) there was an open 'trawl', as the service calls it, for existing staff that might be interested in transferring to The Mount. Fundamentally, anybody could apply for positions at the new prison and in most cases, they would be accepted.

And so there it was. Several weeks later, and after five good years with great memories, I was saying my goodbyes at Pentonville and was off to The Mount.

Do you believe in fate? I didn't until then, but get this. I fancied a new challenge and a move to a different prison but didn't know where to go. I had to go into hospital for an operation, so ended up recuperating on an unplanned holiday. I met and became friends with a couple, Lyn and Dave, who were publicans in a small village. I visited them and found out that a new prison was being built in their village. I stayed in a house on the same street that my new home would be when I moved to my new job. And, to cap it all, once at the new prison I met the woman that I would eventually, marry and live happily ever after with and live in my new house in Apple Cottages.

Well, if that's not fate then I don't know what is!

Chapter 21

The Mount and Temporary Promotion

The newly constructed The Mount prison in Bovingdon, Hertfordshire, was at the end of a long drive and stood on the site of a former USAAF base. The Americans had handed the base back to the British Government as they had no further use for it. It had been used by several film companies, as the runway was still intact as well as some of the original outbuildings. Several war films about the RAF were filmed there, The War Lover (1962); 633 Squadron (1964) Battle of Britain (1969) and Mosquito Squadron (1969). and I also found out that during the Second World War in 1944, in the famous bandleader Glenn Miller departed from that airfield, never to be seen again.

The Americans had used it as a base for their Flying Fortress bombers, so the runway was concreted to take the weight of these huge aircrafts and their bombs. The runway still exists today, although now it's used as a Sunday market - and also as a racetrack for cars stolen by the local youngsters from Hemel Hempstead, allegedly.

Originally planned as a Category C training establishment, then the changing political situation meant that The Mount's role changed before it had even opened its gates in 1987 and it became HMYOI The Mount, designed to hold young offenders. Bloody great! The one type of prisoner I honestly didn't want to work with! I liked working with adults, but youngsters - jeez the only prisoners worse than them were women as far as I was concerned. Oh well, I'd wanted a challenge, and a challenge is what they would be.

When I arrived on my first day at my new establishment I was immediately impressed with my new governor and his deputy. I knew the deputy's wife, as she'd worked in the cashier's office at Pentonville and I remembered meeting her a few times. This governing governor turned out to be probably the best manager I'd ever served under throughout my whole career. He was the sort of man who went and made It his business to know all about you as a person and he never treated his staff or prisoners unfairly. On his weekend rounds, he would visit every part of the establishment, every unit and every spur on the unit and try to meet every prisoner and member of staff.

I remember one particular occasion when the governor came onto my unit to carry out his inspection and saw a lad doing his ironing. "What the hell are you doing?" he asked the lad.

"I'm ironing my shirt, boss. I've got a visit this afternoon from me mum and I wanna look me best," he said.

The governor looked at me, then at the lad and then at his ironing and commented, "Well, it's obvious that you don't know how to iron a shirt, so I'll show you."

He picked up the iron and started ironing the lad's shirt, explaining what he was doing as he went along. When he'd finished, the lad was beaming and his shirt looked in pristine condition.

"Thanks, boss," he said.

The governor answered, "That's all right, but in two weeks time when I come around again I want to see you iron a shirt as I've just shown you, or else."

And, just as he'd said, a fortnight later the governor visited this prisoner again and asked him to give a demonstration of how to iron a shirt. That was the sort of man he was - a real man's man and a great manager. Sadly, some years later he had a heart attack and took early retirement on medical grounds. What a bloody shame for the service. I'm sure he would've gone on to be an area manager at least.

The deputy was a like-minded man and he and the governor made a really strong management team - just what was needed when opening a new establishment. I believe the deputy eventually went on to manage his own prison establishment, but I don't know which one.

I was sent to work on Fowler, which was the second unit to open out of a total, I think, of six. Bristow, if I've remembered correctly, was the first and Fowler was situated on the other side of the corridor.

We would receive youth offenders from HMYOI Feltham, which had severe overcrowding problems at the time. Most of these prisoners were from the inner London boroughs, but I discovered that a large number of the new staff were actually from the northeast. I could see this leading to real culture problems, not to mention communication difficulties due to some of the new officers' strong Geordie accents, and occasionally even I had problems understanding them, so much so that on one occasion at the pub (of course, I only drank at Lyn and Dave's even though there were three pubs in the village), I'm sure I missed two offers of a drink as I failed to understand the question!

After my initial week of induction, I was called up to the governor's office. Bloody hell, I thought, what could I have done, or has somebody from the Ville informed the governor of some of the things I got up to there? Fortunately, it was nothing like that. The governor and deputy asked me how I would feel about taking on more responsibilities. They explained that they didn't have the number of senior officers needed to open more wings and that I'd been recommended as someone that could fill the role temporarily.

Fuck me! Temporary promotion? I've only been on the job for five minutes! Christ, when I left Pentonville there were still old officers that wouldn't talk to me because I hadn't put in enough time on the job, and yet here I am, being asked if I would like to be promoted, albeit temporarily. Of course, I bloody well would!

Promotion to senior officer meant more money, more responsibilities, more paperwork to contend with, together with less of being one of the boys, less outrageous behaviour and less time to mix with both colleagues and prisoners. Suddenly I'd become an icon of authority. I could no longer play the fool because I was now answerable to higher management and there was an expected code of behaviour. So the wind-ups and laughs diminished and the sit-downs over a cuppa for a chat slowly disappeared. When I walked into the mess or a tea room the rest of the staff curbed their behaviour. These are the same blokes that only yesterday were laughing and joking with me, but today it's different. Today I've got a pip on each shoulder. I'm their boss.

It was a strange feeling and my problem was how to approach this new-found authority. Yes, I wanted to be popular and, yes, I wanted my staff to like me, but I couldn't force them to do either. My dad's words came to the fore: "Son, in this life you earn respect by your behaviour towards others, not by the uniform you wear. Never hide behind that uniform." He was, of course, talking about his time in the army and the war, but they applied to any situation where you were in charge of others, be it staff or prisoners, and they certainly rang true in this case.

I made a conscious decision to try to be fair in my treatment of anybody that I supervised, irrespective of my personal feelings towards them or whether they were staff or prisoners, and also not to tell them what to do without being prepared to do it myself. I've often heard managers tell subordinates just to do what they're told, without question and without any explanation offered to them. That wasn't my style. I would always ask, not tell, and would try to explain why I required something to be done rather than just give an order and expect it to be carried out. I wanted to lead not just by example but also with respect. I was determined to continue to treat both my subordinates and my charges in the same manner throughout the rest of my career, and I believe or would like to think that I have done so.

I remained on Fowler and became one of the three SOs, working under a female PO boss for the first time in my service career. However, like the governor and the deputy, she was a diamond. She taught me to keep calm when inwardly everything was screaming, never to appear to be hurried into making decisions but rather think them through carefully, and not to forget that I was now responsible for my actions and therefore had to justify them. These were all good lessons and ones that I continued to work on.

Chapter 22

I'm a Character

It's funny that, when you look back on events and things that have happened over the years, you inevitably talk about the characters you met along the way, without realising that due to your antics other people view you as one of those characters, too.

I once attended a course at Newbold Revel, the national training college for the prison service located just outside Rugby, where new officers undertake residential courses that last around eight weeks. The college is a busy place, with many different members of staff present at any given time, although now several regional prisons also offer these courses. It must have been an important course that left a lasting impression, which is why I can't honestly remember what it was about! In fact, very few of the many courses I attended throughout my career stand out in my memories. I wonder if that's the same for most people.

I remember at that time you could walk from the college down an old farm track into the village, at the entrance to which was a pub called the British Flag. I spent many hours in that pub whilst attending various courses over the years, even though the college had its own bar. Maybe we preferred the village pub because it was more private and there was less danger of the wrong person hearing you ranting about the course or slagging off certain members of staff. Sadly, the village pub has gone, so if you want a bit of time away from the college you have to drive to somewhere else in the area. I bet that old pub could've told a few stories or two!

I'd driving to Rugby from my home in Bovingdon and arrived at the college in good time for the start of my course. I parked my car in the designated area walked to reception to check-in and produced my Home Office pass. I was told to go and wait in the games room, one of the three main rooms in the old building.

The two other rooms were conveniently named the green room and adjoining blue room. The games room had a free vending machine for hot and cold drinks, so those that were in the know always headed for this room anyway.

I walked into the games room and helped myself to a cup of tea, which was surprisingly good considering it came from a vending machine. A few new officers were sitting around with their folders, waiting to start their lessons for the day. Then the door opened and two men in suits entered.

One of the two men looked straight at me and said, "Bloody hell, it's Senior Officer Levy! I haven't seen you for some years. Do you remember me?"

Of course, I recognised him, but I just couldn't remember his name, so I muttered, "Oh hi, how are you doing?"

He turned to his colleague and said, "This is SO Levy. We used to work together at Pentonville before he went to The Mount and got a temporary promotion. He was one of the right characters there. Some of the things he got up to are legendary."

Shit, I wish I could recall this bloke's name, I thought. He knows all about me and yet I simply cannot remember his name.

He then turned back to me and said, "Do you remember when you and your mate Teflon did ...? And we all had such at laugh afterwards. Mind you, the chief went ballistic if I remember correctly."

The penny still hadn't dropped as to his identity, so I just stammered, "Well, I'd better get going or I'll be late for the start of my course. Maybe we'll catch up at lunchtime," and then I hurriedly left the room.

Was I honestly remembered as one of the 'right characters' at the Ville? It seemed a funny thought. Did I really do what he said, in the way he said it? Or was it an exaggeration? Was he actually there or did he hear about the incident and has just adopted it and embellished it a little? Me, a character? Nah, there were loads of officers at the Ville that I would describe as characters, but not me, I thought. But the more I thought about it, the more I came to suppose that maybe we were all characters in other people's eyes.

When my course broke for lunch I went to the staff canteen, where the food was pretty stodgy but nutritional. I sat at one of the long tables and up came my ex-colleague. Damn, what the hell's his bloody name?

"Do you remember the time that you and Keith started that water fight in the centre, while we all waited for the chief to say break off?" he asked. "We got soaked and you and Keith just carried on like you were playing cowboys and Indians, firing water at each other!"

I said, "Yes, he was up on the threes and I was on the twos. You know why it started?" Warming to my theme, I continued, "Some prisoner was ringing his bell and Keith told me to go and answer it, so I said, 'Nope, it's your turn, you lazy git', and with that, he walked up to the threes, answered the bell and then got the hose out of the box and soaked me, shouting. 'Who's a lazy git?' So I picked up the hose and started squirting the water back."

"Yes," he said, "but eventually you both started soaking the rest of us. That's when the chief walked out of his office straight into the firing line! Bloody hell, we laughed so much! He told us to break off and for you two to report to his office. What happened when you went in there?

"The first thing he said was, 'What the hell do you two think you're playing at? This is a prison, not a kindergarten! So Keith said to him,

'Well, chief, if you'd been your usual punctual self and come out of your office at the correct time, we wouldn't have got so bored that we thought we should check the fire equipment rather than waste our time waiting for your appearance.' I honestly don't think the chief believed a word of it, especially as we were both standing there soaking wet, but he then said, 'If you two gentlemen want to practise being fire officers, then tomorrow you can report to the fire officers for some training, because from what I saw you were both holding the hoses incorrectly. Now dismissed.' And, with that, we left."

My lunch colleague then commented, "It's those sorts of things that have always stayed in my memory about you. That's why I always regarded you as one of the characters, 'cause you never seemed worried when caught out."

Maybe that was how it appeared to him, but to me, it wasn't like that. I was always worried about being caught out, but I nearly always managed to talk my way out of it. Otherwise, I just took the bollocking like a man.

There were many other occasions throughout my post-Pentonville career when I was on a training course or at another establishment and old colleagues came up to me and reminded me of similar occurrences. So, on reflection, I suppose some of the things I got up to or said did indeed, make me become in others eyes, a character.

In fact, when I went back to Pentonville on detached duty with Teflon sometime after this, we were greeted by one of our original mentors, a senior officer, with the words, "Oh no, not you two characters back here again! Didn't we have enough of your antics when you worked here? Now you've come back to start all over again. What are you going to get up to this time?"

Chapter 23

Back to the Ville

On 2 August 1990, under the leadership of Saddam Hussein, Iraq invaded Kuwait. As a result, the then British government decided to round up any Iraqi undesirables that they saw fit to incarcerate. Most of those detained probably hadn't done anything more than speaking openly in favour of Saddam and his regime, but there were almost certainly one or two that, given the opportunity, would've caused a great deal of unrest within the Iraqi population and, in particular, in the London area. However, where to detain them was a major problem. Places such as Harmsworth detention centre and open prisons were deemed too low-security, yet places like Brixton and Wandsworth were considered too high-security for what was possibly just innocent people caught up in world politics.

So what to do with them? There were very few establishments in which these Iraqi detainees could be housed, but one place that was earmarked for them was Pentonville prison, in R wing, which usually held remand prisoners but was closed for timely refurbishment. The next question was how to get enough staff to oversee their detention in a potentially hostile environment, particularly as world events were unfolding at a fast pace. Generally, the prison service would instruct other prisons that they had to release a designated number of staff to the establishment that required assistance, due to a shortage of staff or in the case of disciplinary action. Prison officers were all employed as flexible grades, which made possible this sort of temporary transfer of staff, known as 'detached duty'. With detached duty came additional cash incentives for those who 'volunteered'.

At this time I was working with my good mate Teflon at The Mount, having both moved from Pentonville (in the future we would work together again at Woodhill), and we were attending a training session. Again, I don't remember the details of the course, but I do recall that I was sitting in the boardroom wishing it was dinnertime when the duty governor came in and started to explain the Iraqi detainee situation. He'd barely got onto the subject of the prison service looking for volunteers to go to Pentonville when both our hands shot up like a rocket launch. Yeah, I thought, back to the Ville on detached duty, I'll have some of that. I could stay at 'Taff's' quarter to save money on digs and would be able to make a nice tidy sum in subs. Taff was an ex Welsh Guardsman and had served in the Falklands War. He was stationed at Bluff Cove on either RFA *Sir Galahad* or RFA *Sir Tristram* when they were bombed by the Argentinean air force while anchored off Fitzroy in Port Pleasant. When Taff left the army he joined the prison service and starting working at Pentonville, where he'd been given a staff house to live in 'on the patch'.

Teflon and I were selected to go on detached duty to look after the Iraqi detainees at Pentonville the following week. We travelled from The Mount to Pentonville by coach, as there were so many of us starting work there on that very rainy Monday, as we reported to the detail office. Walking back into the Ville was very strange after leaving some time ago. That smell hit me, along with all my memories. Boy, did I have some good times here, I thought. But I wondered what impression some of the other lads had of the place, having only worked in a brand new prison and now on detached duty at one of the oldest prisons in the country. It must've felt like stepping into a century gone by. What would they make of the smells, the slopping out and the noise?

We were informed of our duties, shift patterns and what to expect, and then Teflon and I were immediately sent to C wing to help with the prisoner count while the others were given a quick induction tour of the place.

We arrived on C4 landing and helped with the counting and submission of the numbers. It's funny how you get back into the routine so quickly. Then the centre announced, "Recount, recount", indicating that the numbers were wrong. So Teflon and I went up to the fives and swapped places with the officers on that landing for the recount. Yet again, the tannoy announced that the numbers were wrong for C wing.

At this point, the wing senior officer exited his office and came out onto C2 landing, shouting, "What the bloody hell's wrong? Cant you two count since you went to The Mount?"

He was known to both of us, so I yelled back to him, "If you think we're wrong, then get up off your arse, come up here and risk a nose bleed (a reference to the days when POs and SOs never went higher than the threes landing), and count the bloody prisoners yourself! We're right with our numbers."

And that's exactly what he did.

One of the regular Pentonville staff said to us, "You really dare speak to a senior officer like that? Bloody hell!"

Teflon replied, "Senior officer? That wanker was never good enough even to make us a cup of tea when he was a sprog, so we'll speak to him any way we want. Oh, and by the way, we're senior officers as well, in case you hadn't noticed."

We're back!

The rest of the day passed all too quickly and before we knew where we were, after many reunions with colleagues of old and several cups of tea in various tea rooms, we were off to our digs. Taff's place was adequate and he was happy to get some money for allowing us to doss down there. This sort of arrangement is something you can't do anymore, as in order to be paid the full subsistence amount you have to produce official receipts. In our day, we were paid a fixed allowance and basically had to make the best of it. So the changes to the system, meaning that officers on detached duty now stay in much more costly official accommodation, certainly haven't saved the prison service any money in the long run.

From Taff's we went to the club for a few drinks, mulling over both old times and new. There's nothing better than prison officers getting together and slagging off their subordinates, bosses, governors and prisoners and then laughing about it all, or so I thought at that time. The camaraderie seemed to be unbreakable.

The next day we were sent to the remand wing to work with the Iraqi detainees. Yet another of my old senior officers was in charge of this wing and he invited me into his office, where a governor grade was present.

The SO said to me, "Tony, we've just heard that the Iraqis have sent Scud missiles into Israel. Will this affect how you deal with these detainees?"

What a bloody stupid question! I might be Jewish, but Israel is a country, not a religion. If the Iraqis want to send missiles into another country that's not my concern. It honestly showed just how people think when it comes to a person's religious beliefs. Having said that, this SO should've known from times past that I didn't follow my religion anyway and was always very forthright in declaring that I was English and British before anything else.

"I've no problem with that," I said. "But having to work with that prick," I continued, pointing directly towards the governor grade, "I'm not sure about."

The governor grade turned towards me and asked, "Do I know you?"

"You should," I responded, "'cause I'm the officer that's currently suing you for defamation of character for a staff report you endorsed about me. The Iraqis I don't have a problem with, but with you I certainly do. I'm Officer Levy."

The governor grade went bright red and then walked out of the office and out of the wing. I never saw him again during my time back at the Ville.

It was true that I was trying to sue this man, as he had indeed endorsed an annual staff report about me, stating he'd seen me working and could vouch for the reporting officer's accuracy. The reporting officer, a PO at the time had written a very derogatory report about me two years earlier because I'd reported him for being drunk on duty, and the case was still ongoing. The only prior dealing I'd had with this governor was when occasionally he'd come into the reception area where I was working at the time and pounce cigarettes off me. I'd never worked for him, he'd never been my boss, and yet he was the only one willing to endorse the report. I'm sure that he neither expected me to take on management over this in such a way nor thought we'd ever come face to face. How wrong could he be?

Some of the detainees under my charge were very religious and we had to ensure that every one of their requests was complied with and dealt with sympathetically, whilst also checking that these were indeed requisites of their religion. This meant a lot of contact with the local Imam, who had been appointed by the Home Office to deal with any such queries. I got on very well with this man. Although his role was to ensure that the religious needs of the detainees were being met, he also had great sympathy for the position of the prison authorities and, in particular, the officers working with the detainees.

On one particular morning my favourite POs, with whom I'd worked with many times previously came onto the wing. He took one look at Teflon and me and said, "Oh my God, you two characters are back to haunt me! Bloody hell, I thought we'd seen the last of you!" Funnily enough, a few years later he too came to The Mount, but this time as a governor grade.

I remember on one occasion when a local Labour MP was visiting the prison to ensure that the detainees were being treated well and with respect. I was escorting the detainees' visitors to the designated visiting area, which had been specially selected to ensure that these visitors were kept away from the main visiting area. After all, these people had committed no crime and were therefore not subject to the same rules and regulations as those convicted or being held on remand.

This MP was continually berating the prison staff and making general insinuations to the visitors that the staff were treating the Iraqi detainees inhumanely. I asked the man to please stop, as in my opinion, he was trying to agitate the visitors with his unfounded innuendos and told him that if he continued to do so I would have him removed from the establishment.

He responded, "Do you know who I am?"

"Yes," I replied, "but do you know who I am?"

He was dumbfounded. Under Home Office rules no MP can be refused entry to a prison establishment, but these rules also say that if there is overwhelming evidence to suggest that an MP is undermining the security of the establishment he can be asked to leave.

"Look," I said, "I understand what you're doing and it's not helpful in this delicate situation. These people want to visit their loved ones, not be used in some petty political point-scoring exercise. And if you continually undermine and indeed, in my opinion, continue to try to incite these people, then under the authority of the governor I will ask you to leave the establishment."

I could see that he wasn't going to drop this, but thankfully the visitors told the MP to stop trying to cause trouble between themselves and the prison staff, as they thought I'd been treating them in an extremely sensitive manner. They wrote to the governor of this prison complimenting me on my behaviour towards them. During their visiting period, the detainees also asked the MP to leave them alone and stop trying to cause a staff/detainee confrontation. Nice chap. I'm so glad I never voted for him. This MP eventually became the leader of his political party but never made Prime minister.

All too soon my month back at the Ville came to an end and so, with a heavy heart and a full wallet, I left Pentonville and returned to The Mount. I can't remember ever going back to the Ville again, and maybe it was just as well.

Chapter 24

Oh Shit, We Lost Two!

I was the SO on nights at The Mount and had two officers with me, one on patrol and the other running the radio network system. There were other officers on duty, but they were locked into their individually assigned wings and they didn't have keys.

As the night orderly officer (NOO) my job was to patrol around the units and sign the wing diary to show I'd visited that area, as well as managing any incidents or issues that might occur during the night-time lock-up period. We didn't have any medical staff on duty, so invariably if a prisoner was taken ill or swallowed something or needed emergency treatment then a trip to the hospital was required. Although working nights meant things were much quieter than during the daytime, the lack of staff could occasionally become a logistical nightmare. Imagine, for instance, what would happen if a prisoner needed to go to an outside hospital during this period - where would I get the staff from to escort him?

The other problem was that my assistants had to carry out several patrols of the prison exterior and I would also have to visit every outside area to unlock the gates, or 'doubles', meaning the double-locked gates that led into individual wings. The double lock was an extra lock below the main one and was used at night as additional security due to the reduced number of staff on duty. Doubles at The Mount were taken off at around 5.30 a.m., in preparation for the normal daily regime, and locked again by the evening duty manager at around 8 p.m., once the prison went into patrol mode at night. It's obvious due to security issues this is just a rough guide to the system, as every prison establishment operates differently and has its own unique requirements.

All modern prisons are designed by architects that have never worked in a prison environment, the layout and design aren't always the best in practical terms. For instance, the traditional radial design, where all the wings are attached to a central area, allows staff at that centre point to view each wing. Therefore, doubles would only be required at the farthest end of each of the wings, where emergency exit doors led outside. Modern prisons, on the other hand, tend to comprise of a series of separate accommodation blocks, each with its own entrance door and separate exit door, meaning that twice the number of double-locking gates is required. Every external gate has to be double locked and this procedure has to be done from the outside.

Unlocking the doubles in the early morning over the summer months was particularly enjoyable. Dawn would be breaking, so you could watch the sunrise and hear the world slowly coming to life. It was a wonderful spectacle.

Anyway, on this particular night, I came on duty and started the handover from the day shift to the night shift. Any events of importance or relevance to the night shift would be relayed at this point - security information, prisoner activities, and so on. The day PO informed me that they'd had a report that some industrial-strength hacksaw blades might be on the premises, but a search hadn't found anything. He also confirmed that they'd received the report I'd submitted the previous day stating that the concrete posts around the perimeter fence were, in my opinion, a security hazard and should be removed as a matter of urgency.

These small concrete slabs were about 18 inches high by 5 inches thick, with yellow plates on them informing the staff and the emergency services where the water hydrants were located. It would be possible for these to be removed and thrown at the joints of the security perimeter fence, thus allowing a prisoner to escape. The Mount didn't have a surrounding wall, just this single-skinned perimeter fence, which was about 18 feet high and had razor wire along the top. Most prisons with this type of outer security fence would have double-skinned ones, i.e., either an inner fence with an outer one set a few feet further back or a fence that was reinforced with a double layer, particularly at the joints. This wasn't the case at The Mount, however.

During our night shift I liked to share duties with my night staff. For instance, at some point, I would usually take over from the officer designated to be the controller of the radio net system, allowing him to go out on a patrol of the grounds with my other officer, and vice versa. This broke the boredom and the complacency that can often set in on nights and helped keep us all awake.

Sometimes you end up just going through the motions after walking around the outside area, a few times and can easily miss any subtle changes, so swapping duties meant that you always had a fresh pair of attentive eyes. It may seem like a small thing, but I wanted to make sure that my staff were as alert as possible at all times. Also, showing my staff that I was prepared to do the job I expected them to do hopefully helped to create a good team spirit.

At around 2 a.m. on this particular morning, I'd done just that. I'd taken over the radio net system and instructed my officers to carry out a perimeter check. Suddenly, I heard this noise. I looked out of the window to see if I could identify the source and, fucking hell, I spotted two prisoners legging it through the bloody fence right in front of me and as near to the gate as they could possibly get. I quickly got on the radio and directed my officers to go immediately to the relevant fence section, although I knew by this time they'd made good their escape.

Your professional training kicks in at this point. I couldn't leave the radio area unattended, but fortunately, each prison control room is equipped with an emergency direct telephone line to the nearest police station. I picked up the emergency red telephone, commonly known as the 'bat phone', supplied the relevant code word. These contingency plans are worked out and tested regularly in every prison throughout the country. I explained the incident and gave a description as best as I could. The police told me that a patrol would be sent out and that an officer would come to the prison to collect information on the escapees.

I then had to put our own contingency plans into operation, so I ordered a prison roll check to ascertain what wing the prisoners had fled and their identity. The trained radio controller relieved me from that duty, allowing me to carry out the necessary procedures.

By the time the police had arrived, I'd got the names of the prisoners and knew how they'd got out. What the bloody PO on the previous evening's changeover hadn't told me was that they'd previously intercepted a delivery of hacksaw blades and suspected that there were some more already in the establishment, most likely on the very wing from which these two had escaped.

Oh great, just bloody great! Well, thanks for the warning! Not that I could have prevented what had happened, but had I been informed I would've patrolled that area more frequently.

I sent my assistant over to the gate to escort the police into the prison and up to the operations room, where I'd gathered all the necessary information on the two escapees. He came back with a bloody chief inspector. "Blimey," I said, "it's not that important an event, is it?"

"No, I just happened to be carrying out a night visit when your call came through, so I thought it would break the monotony," he replied. "Do you know how they got out?"

Too bloody right I did!

Just as I'd predicted, these two had grabbed the piece of concrete and thrown it at the fence joint. This had caused the fence to split and - bingo! they were through and out free. They'd chosen that particular section of fencing as it was the nearest to the gate and also to the main road. Once through, they could either cut through the staff quarters and into the village of Bovingdon or go straight over the airfield and on towards Chesham.

The chief inspector asked if the duty governor would be attending. When I'd telephoned the duty governor, who was our new deputy governor, 'the twitcher' (more about him later) to inform him of the incident, he'd responded, "I'll see you in the morning. But how could you lose two in one go?" What a pratt! If they'd acted on my report, the bloody concrete post wouldn't have been there and these two wouldn't have been able to get out of the grounds. Here we go again, I thought. Let's look for a scapegoat. After all, shit rolls downhill in the prison service, doesn't it? I said to the chief inspector, "No, he'll get his report from me in the morning." I can't say the chief inspector was very impressed, and neither was I. I took him down to the escape point, where the concrete slab was lying on the ground in two pieces.

"How the hell did they get that thing?" he asked.

"Easy," I said. "We've got them all around the perimeter so we know where the water is in case of a fire. I submitted a report about them only yesterday."

I then showed him one of the hacksaw blades that we'd found outside the window of the wing from which the two had escaped. These hacksaws were very thin, but they would've cut through the bars on the prisoners' windows fairly easily.

The chief inspector had seen enough and didn't seem very impressed with our security, as he walked away muttering something like, "Why don't you just leave the gates open and save them damaging the fence?"

The next morning, after handing over to the day PO, I went to security to complain about the concrete posts not being removed as

I'd requested, and also about the handover information supplied to me. While I was there the deputy governor arrived.

"Well, what the hell happened?" he asked angrily.

In response I explained the events of the previous night, concluding with, "A chief Inspector turned up and he wasn't impressed that you didn't come in, so I thought I'd better warn you that he might telephone you today."

"So what?" he replied. "If he's stupid enough to give up his sleep, that's up to him. It's not my problem. But I can't believe you lost two in one go. There'll have to be an investigation."

"Yeah right," I said. "I assume this investigation will show that I had submitted a security report stating what could happen if those concrete posts were not removed? And I suppose your investigation will discover that the security department didn't carry out a lock-down search when they got the report of the blades being in the prison? So I agree that we should have an inquiry. It'll prove that I couldn't do anything about the escape but that others can be held culpable. Bring it on." And, with that, I left to go home and get some sleep.

The next night I felt vindicated by subsequent events. I'd decided during that cold, dark, wet night to go out on patrol with my assistant. As we walked around the perimeter, my glasses were getting covered with drizzle.

I said to my assistant, "Look. Have you noticed that bloody security have at last removed all those concrete posts I complained about? Too bloody late though."

Before she could reply I stopped dead in my tracks, staring at the farthest corner of our patrol area. I don't believe it, I thought. It looks like a prisoner sitting by the fence. It can't be. Not again, surely? But it was. He was just sitting there, soaking wet and looking very miserable. We approached and made ready to grab him, but he just sat there dejectedly. Stupidly, I asked him what he was doing, which was pretty obvious really.

"Trying to escape, guv," he admitted. "But you bastards went and moved all the concrete posts, so I couldn't find anything heavy enough to throw at the fence, and I can't get back into my cell either."

I had to laugh. "Come on, sunshine, let's get you back into the warm. I've got a nice cell waiting for you and nice blue and yellow striped clothing for you to put on, as you're now going to be regarded as an escapee and you'll be dealt with under those rules and regulations."

I also ordered a full roll check just in case. I took the lad into the segregation unit and made him a cup of tea. He told me everything: how the blades had got in, where they'd been hidden, how many were involved and how they'd planned it.

Having two escapees on your shift is bad enough, but having three? If this one had got away it would've finished my career there and then for sure, irrespective of where the fault lay. Fortunately, stopping this one and getting all the information meant that I was today's best thing since sliced bread. Oh well, that's the way it goes.

Chapter 25

The London Marathon

It was January 1991. I'd been at The Mount for a couple of years and had been temporarily promoted for most of this time, yet my life was just drifting. I lived on my own in the village of Bovingdon and went out occasionally for a drink in the local pub, but I generally avoided drinking in the officers' club or with groups of my colleagues. It seemed that whenever a group of prison officers got together all they talked about was the job. It had become boring and I was beginning to dislike everything. I was fast becoming a grumpy, intolerant old man. To be perfectly honest and although I didn't realise it at the time, I'd actually stopped liking myself and therefore everything and everybody else, and I was beginning to let myself go - a very dangerous position to be in.

One day a group of staff asked me if I wanted to go for a lunchtime run with them, just for three to four miles around the village. Thinking that I was pretty fit, despite being a smoker, as I still played football on non-working weekends and went training once or twice a week, I decided to go. Piece of piss, I thought. It'll be a doddle. Well, we set off and I could only get as far as the end of the drive, which was about half a mile, and I was struggling. Bloody hell, what's happened to me? One of my colleagues reassured me, saying that he felt the same when he first started running and that it would get easier with time and I'd be fine. Fine? I was bloody knackered.

I was smoking too much, not exercising sensibly or enough, eating crap and generally letting myself go, so I made a conscious decision at that point to sort myself out and get my life back on track. I'd lived alone for long enough without any really serious relationships and I was missing that closeness to another person. I'd already decided I wasn't going to find someone else, so I needed to find another interest instead. Football was out, as my knee wouldn't cope with anything more than the casual playing and a bit off training I was already doing. Also, I was fast approaching forty, so I wasn't exactly in my prime. I needed to pack up smoking and maybe this running lark was just what I needed?

Circumstances conspired to assist me. My father was rushed into hospital with yet another heart attack, after suffering from heart problems for some years by now. It was a Thursday, and I got home from work, put my pack of cigarettes on top of the television and as usual, went for a shower, changed and then rushed out to visit my dad in Chase Farm Hospital, Enfield, arriving back home pretty late.

In the morning I went off to work and, on arriving at my wing, I reached for my first cigarette of the day. At that point, I realised I'd left them on top of my TV at home. A colleague offered me one of his, but I declined. I decided I could manage without until lunchtime and then pop home and get them. However, that never happened. My new running mates said that they were going for a run that lunchtime, so I decided to join them instead. I never smoked again. Those cigarettes sat on top of my telly for several weeks as a reminder that I'd stopped smoking just like that. Well, I thought, if I can do that then I can master this running lark; in fact, I'm gonna run the London Marathon before I'm 41. This birthday was the following August.

I prepared for the London Marathon like some sort of military exercise, training every day and gradually increasing the miles covered. I just did a couple of miles per day at first, sometimes alternating between running and walking when I started feeling tired. I increased my run from five times a week to seven times a week, by which time I was doing five miles per day. The buzz I was getting from this exercise was indescribable; it was like taking drugs. I felt great when I went for a run and utterly depressed when I couldn't, which thankfully wasn't often. I would go out in the pouring rain and even bought a special waterproof and windproof running suit so that I could continue to train in bad weather. I also bought lots of books on running, and from reading these I devised my personal training schedule to ensure a good level of fitness for the London Marathon.

I completed my entry form, knowing that there was no guarantee that my application would be successful. The number of people that apply to run the London Marathon is phenomenal and getting selected is a difficult task unless you're being sponsored by one of the big charities or you've run it before. I wouldn't find out if I could participate until around Christmas time, but I still had to continue my training. It would be no good waiting until the end of December and then starting to train only if I was accepted, as I just wouldn't be able to get my fitness to an adequate level before the event if I did that. Come December, I was running around 30 miles during the week and around 15 miles in a single session at weekends.

By this time I'd been running seriously in preparation for the marathon for nearly nine months, I'd put my life on hold - no alcohol, no fatty fry-ups, no cigarettes, and basically watching what I was eating and trying to follow a healthy diet, comprising mainly chicken and pasta meals with jacket potatoes, etc. I was probably fitter than I'd ever been, and I certainly felt better about myself than I'd done for some time.

Then a letter of rejection arrived. All that bloody work for nothing, I thought, constantly pushing myself through the pain barrier to run further and faster than my previous effort. Oh shit. I'd run in my lunch breaks, in the evenings after work and even sometimes in the mornings before I went to work. I'd even got caught short running along the Grand Union Canal and had to squat over the side of the canal for a pooh and wipe my bottom with large dock leaves. And all this for what? To be rejected! Bloody hell, it just wasn't fair.

However, there was a slight glimmer of hope when I noticed a competition in my *Today's Runner* magazine, the prize was an entry into the London Marathon.

You had to write about your training experiences and why you wanted to run in the marathon, so I decided to enter it.

In the meantime, I continued with my running, but during January I was out in severe weather when something went in my ankle and I ended up limping home in real discomfort. I went to the doctor, who sent me to the local hospital for X-rays. It wasn't good news. I'd damaged my ankle ligaments and would have to rest up for some time. Double bollocks! Why did this have to happen now, when I'd been doing so well with my training? Never mind, I thought, it's not as if I'm going to be running in this year's marathon. It seemed as though my ambition to do it before my 41st birthday was now well and truly out of the window.

Then, completely out of the blue, I received a letter from *Today's Runner* magazine. Yep, I'd won the competition and an entry into the London Marathon and they wanted me to do an interview all about my training. Bloody well typical. I did the interview, omitting the part about my injury and my story was featured in a future issue of the magazine.

The inter-prison magazine decided to do a feature about all the staff throughout the country that had entered the London Marathon and, without any prior warning, a reporter turned up at The Mount to interview me. This interview proved quite interesting, as our PO PEI tried to claim that I was getting all the help I needed regarding my training schedule from his department! So I put the reporter straight and told him I hadn't received any help from the PE department and wouldn't have accepted any even if it had been offered, as I was determined to do this thing by myself. I didn't reveal my injury in this interview either.

I decided to seek the help and advice of a sports injury specialist, who carried out a course of intensive treatment on the ankle. When I explained that I needed to be fit enough to run in that year's (now 1992) London Marathon he just laughed at me and said, "No way."

However, I was determined to participate in that year's race. There was a clause in the marathon agreement that said that if competitors weren't able to run due to injury their applications would be held over for the following year's event, but as my entry was a competition prize this wasn't guaranteed in my case.

I was left with a choice. I either backed out of the event due to injury or I went ahead despite my ankle problems. I couldn't face putting my body through the pain barrier on long runs again, in preparation for the following year, so I decided it was going to be this year or never at all. And to me, never just wasn't an option. So I continued with the treatment, which was costing me £20 each session, and I strapped up my ankle whenever I went for a run. Somehow, I made it to Blackheath and the start of the race on 21 April 1992.

My training goal had been to get me fit enough to complete the race in a time of 3 hours and 30 minutes, which was a good standard for a 40-something to achieve. It was pretty ambitious, but I was gonna do it.

I'd run my first competitive race, Lincoln Half Marathon, before sustaining my ankle injury, and I'd managed to complete it in a respectable time of 89 minutes. This had put me in the top 100 finishers and I was really proud of myself.

On the evening before the London Marathon, I went to the famous pasta party that is held every year in London before the race, and I stayed in a hotel overnight so that I could be at Blackheath nice and early the next morning.

When the race began, I couldn't believe how long it took me to get from my position in the throng of runners to the official starting line. It was a huge distance, so much so that the organisers of the race officially knocked off nearly 20 minutes from my time so that it started when I crossed the actual start line. I clicked my stopwatch at this point, too, so that I could keep track of my own time.

The time I recorded was 20 seconds faster than the official one, but that's splitting hairs really. In the end, my finish time was 3 hours and 22 minutes, so I crossed the finish line 8 minutes inside my goal.

Something that amazed me was how many runners stopped within the first mile of the race and yet started in front of others that could run better. I guess it's just one of those quirks of having 35,000 runners in one race.

I did have one really bad moment during the race. I'd just run past the Tower of London, along with those awful cobbled stones that line The Embankment, and then through the gates and into the worst part of the race, surrounded by big, tall buildings and with the wind blowing straight into me. Then, as I came past Nelson's Column, on my approach to Admiralty Arch and The Mall, the dreaded wall hit me. Yes, it honestly does feel like a wall. My legs just wouldn't function properly. My brain said run, but my legs didn't listen. I struggled up to Admiralty Arch, where there was a water station, and for the first time in approximately 22 miles, I stopped running. I started to pour water over my head, my neck and my legs, as well as down my throat. Somehow I had to get my legs moving again. Come on, you're nearly there, I said to myself. If only my bloody legs would get going.

My legs started to respond and I set off towards The Mall. I was just going under the arch when a member of the public literally saved me. He'll never know it, but he really did. He shouted out, "Come on, number........

You can do it, mate." Bloody hell, I thought, somebody, is shouting out my number. I don't know who it is, but I could kiss him. He thinks I can do it, so I bloody well will. And at that point, my body came back to life, my legs started working, my head cleared and I was back to my race pace. Thanks a million, mate, whoever you are.

I continued along down The Mall, around past Buckingham Palace and up over Westminster Bridge. All the while I could see the finish line. Yes, I'm gonna do it. Come on legs, just keep going five more minutes, then you can rest. Is that Sebastian Coe standing at the finish line? It looks like him. Yes, it is, and he's waving at me. I always liked Seb Coe more than Steve Cram. I'm there, I've finished! I've just run 26 miles and 385 yards and then some prick sticks a gold medal that weighs a ton and half around my neck and says well done, while I practically collapse from the weight of the damn thing! Why can't they just hand it to you? Don't they realise I've just run a bloody marathon? I was then wrapped in silver foil and given more water, a Mars Bar and an apple. Good, 'cause I'm bloody hungry.

I was bent over, with my hand on my knees, taking deep breaths. My damaged ankle was throbbing and very sore and my legs were pretty shaky, but I was feeling on top of the world.

Then I heard a man's voice saying to me, "Well done. How do you feel?"

How do I feel? What a bloody stupid question, I thought. I was just about to tell him to fuck off when I looked up and - oh my God - it was Seb Coe. Thank God I'd checked who was speaking before I mouthed off! "Great," I replied sheepishly. "How about you?"

"Fucking knackered, but elated," he said, patting me on the back and walking off.

And that was that. I'd done it. I'd run the London Marathon. I'd finished in pretty poor condition, but considering the injury, I was carrying and the time I'd done it was undoubtedly one of my best achievements ever. Maybe I wasn't such a bad bloke after all? Maybe I was starting to like myself again? Yes, running had dragged me out of the doldrums and given me back a purpose.

Over the next few years, I really got into my running. I loved it. I lived for it. Running became my life. It helped me cope with the stresses and strains of working in a prison and in particular in a YOI.

There were several other enthusiastic runners at The Mount and we formed our own little running club. Every weekend we'd participate in local runs, competing in 5 or 10-kilometre races, 10-mile races. The Borehamwood Half Marathon, and even a charity run around Brands Hatch - my lap time was good, but not really in the same league as Lewis Hamilton! I also completed the Luton Half Marathon and the Great North Run twice, the second time finishing in the top 3,000 with a time of 90 minutes.

You may ask why this chapter is all about my running achievements and me and has nothing to do with the prison service. It may seem to have no relevance in this sense, but taking up running was a real turning point in my life. Had the prison service not brought me to Bovingdon, and had some of my colleagues did not ask me to go running on that particular day, the rest of my life would've turned out very differently. Anyway, it's my book, so I'm entitled to a little bit of self-indulgence, don't you think?

I've got to say, on a final note, that completing the marathon was easier than collecting the money from those that had sponsored me. However, in another one of those quirks of fate, getting sponsorship money and running for charities led me to another major life event: meeting my future wife.

Chapter 26

Falling in Love

This might not seem the sort of subject you would expect to find in this book either, but the prison service honestly did play a part in my meeting my present wife and therefore the story should be told.

I'd completed the London Marathon, and now came the even harder task of collecting the money that had been pledged to me by my sponsors: members of staff, family and friends. I was giving the proceeds to the National Heart Foundation and Alzheimer's.

The Prison Officers' Club decided to hold a charity night, where all the monies collected would be handed over to the respective charitable organisations. As I said earlier, due to my initial experiences I tended to avoid these clubs, except for occasional trips to the Holloway club on a Friday night, but I was asked several times to attend on this occasion, as I'd run the London Marathon for charity. I was further encouraged to go to this special evening by a subordinate colleague, who used the tack that he would be taking with him a female companion, who was nearer my age than his and so we'd probably have more in common.

I wondered what sort of game this officer was playing, but in the end, I thought, oh well, why not? I'd been training particularly hard and running half marathons virtually every other weekend, so it was about time I had a night off. I hadn't had any alcohol for several weeks.

I arrived at the club at around 9 p.m. and the usual crowd were there, including a couple of senior officers that I knew would be playing the slot machines all night, even during the presentations and the subsequent disco, but there was no sign of my persuasive colleague or his female escort. I had a couple of beers and some good chats with other colleagues, so the evening got off to a good start. I told a few people about my efforts during the marathon and nobody had started getting too drunk or abusive or relating heroic war stories. Whoops, I spoke too soon on that last one, as I spotted the usual culprit standing in the corner with his audience of young officers, telling them how he'd saved the prison service and ... hey, hold on a minute - there's my persuasive colleague but without any female company.

"Hey, Wingbolt," I shouted above the disco noise, "where's this girl you wanted me to meet, or was that a load of bull just to get me here?" "Nah," he said, "she's running late. In fact, I'm just going to get her now." Bloody hell, I thought, it's pretty late to be going to get her at this time. What does she do - work nights? It was nearly 11 o'clock and to be honest I was starting to think about going home, but I decided to wait. I was standing at the bar near the exit to the club when my colleague arrived back with a very slim, attractive woman.

He was right when he'd said she was more my age. She was much too old for him but was just my type. I looked her up and down: nice legs, nice body, a bit on the slim side but nice, lovely hair that looked ginger to me - a bit Rula Lenska, and an attractive face; in fact, she wasn't half bad.

We were introduced and seemed to hit it off immediately, although I did have a rival for her attention - one of the PE staff, who thought he was the king of chat-up. However, she seemed to like me, and I certainly liked her; I must've done because I stayed until the club closed that night just talking to her.

It was really weird, as we had so much in common. She was nine months younger than me almost to the day, and so she was conceived just as I was born. On leaving school she worked for the same company as me and at the same time, although she was in central London and I was in Tottenham. She went out with a Spurs footballer, who was someone I knew, and she was in Lloret de Mar in Spain at the same time as me. She lived in an area of London that I used to drive around when I was a driving instructor had gone to some of the same London nightclubs and liked similar things to me. Our paths had crossed several times over the years and now finally we'd met. It seemed like fate again.

I went home that night thinking about how well we'd got on. Over the subsequent weeks, my colleague would let me know if he was going to the club with her and would ask me to come along and keep her company while he was tied up with social club committee business. Keep her company? You bet! I fancied her and was beginning to think that she felt the same way. However, out of loyalty to my colleague, she wouldn't go out with me despite my asking her on several occasions.

We'd now become good friends, and I suppose the best way to a lasting, and a loving relationship is to be friends with your chosen one first.

After some time and around my birthday, my persuasive colleague was transferred to another establishment nearer to his home area and at this point, I started a serious relationship with this wonderful woman. I soon realised I'd fallen in love, and so had she.

In the September she accompanied me on a visit to my friends in Sheffield before going on to Newcastle, where I was to run in the Great North Run. We had a wonderful weekend and I realised I'd at last found my soulmate and someone that I wanted to spend the rest of my life with.

Later in the year, we went on a long weekend with my sister and her husband to Paris, and on the second morning there I proposed to her and she accepted. We were married on 10th December 1993.

I won't say that we've lived happily ever after because that only happens in fairy tales, but I think our marriage has been as happy as it could be. The good times have outweighed our sadder times and we still love each other. I couldn't imagine being without her; she's my soulmate and my best friend. We've shared some wonderful holidays together, seen many different countries of the world and had some amazing experiences. However, it's when you're facing the bad and sad times and receive a partner's support and kindness through them that you realise just how much you love that person.

We remain together and have a wonderful life. If it hadn't been for running the London Marathon we would never have met. Life has many strange twists and turns. I now really believe in fate, don't you?

Chapter 27

I Want My Promotion!

Well, I dunno what or how it happened but I'd met somebody I wished to spend the rest of my life with and we wanted to get married, but this also meant I really needed to get a permanent substantive SO promotion.

The original governor had called me to his office a while back and asked, "Are you going to take the promotion exam this year, Tony?" Take the promotion exam? A gang of us took it every year, didn't we? It was a great excuse to go to London and get pissed.

"Yes, I suppose I will be, governor," I answered.

He looked me straight in the eye and said, "Don't you think it's about time you either put up or shut up? I've watched you working here since I temporarily promoted you, and it's about time you took the job seriously. You'll make a good senior officer, I know you will, and I want you here permanently as one of my senior officers."

Bloody hell, I knew he was right. I'd always pissed around with the exam before, 'cause I'd wanted to be one of the lads, but now the lads were moving on; some had got married, some had moved to other prisons and the old gang had gone. Shit, when did that happen? What he said to me painfully struck home. And of course, he was right. The time had certainly arrived for me to take the exam seriously and go for it.

I studied for the exam and took it again, and when it was over I came straight home. I didn't go for the usual lunchtime piss-up and for once I finished the exam completing all parts of the exam. I felt I'd done very well, but you never knew. Was it a numbers game, where they passed so many each year or did you honestly pass on merit irrespective of how many reached the grade? I would just have to wait and see.

The original governor and the deputy had moved on to pastures new and we had a complete change of higher management, which is often the way when an old governor goes and a new one comes in: the whole managerial team seems to change as well.

The new deputy governor called me to his office and said, "Now, Mr Levy, the promotion exam results are in. How do think you did?

"Well, it's obvious I passed," I replied.

"What makes you think that?" he said

"I heard on the grapevine that an old colleague of mine passed, and if he did it must've been 'cause he was copying my answers," I joked. "Well, you have passed," the deputy confirmed rather grumpily. It was obvious, he had no sense of humour, but I'd passed. Perhaps they'll give me a promotion here? After all, I've been doing the job for two years, I thought, so why not? We're short of SOs, so it would make sense to give it to me, wouldn't it?

However, it wasn't to be. Although I'd passed, it seemed I needed to find a position somewhere else, but where? The only thing I could do was check around for vacancies.

I was aware that a new prison would be opening in Milton Keynes, HMP Woodhill, so I applied for a job there initially as an officer, but I also applied for the post for a substantive senior officer, thinking that two applications might give me a better chance of success.

In the meantime, I found out about an open day at HMP Woodhill, so I thought I'd take advantage of this opportunity and go along. I was surprised to come across several of my former colleagues from Pentonville there, who was transferring to Woodhill. Again, as Woodhill was a new prison it was operating an 'open trawl', meaning that unless you'd really blotted your copybook a transfer there was almost a given.

Such was the case in this instance, and I very quickly received confirmation that my transfer as an officer had been granted. I just had to await a release date from HMP The Mount. However, I'd also received notification of an interview for the senior officer post at Woodhill, which would be held at HMP Littlehey, Cambridgeshire.

I set out early for my formal interview, as I wasn't sure exactly where Littlehey was and didn't want to be late, and thankfully I arrived in good time. I remembered what some of the old-timers at Pentonville told me about their promotion boards and how they were put through the grinder, but I have to say I don't have much recollection of this one. I remembered the chair of the board, not only because he became my governor when I eventually moved to the special unit at Woodhill, or that he subsequently appeared in several television programmes regarding the criminal justice system, but also because of his huge personality. He was a doctor of some sort, but not a medical one. I think he was a doctor of criminology and he had what at that time could only be described as revolutionary ideas. He was a good talker and a good interviewee and he chaired the board in an honest manner.

When I left the interview I had no idea how I'd performed. It was a long drive back from Littlehey to Bovingdon and throughout the journey, I went over the interview in my head. I answered all the questions and didn't hesitate - well, not that often. I was honest, even when I said I didn't know. Bloody hell, I said that a few times. I bet that didn't go down too well with the good doctor. Oh shit. I talked a lot of drivel at times, too, nothing new there though. Oh, stop thinking about it. You can't change what you did now anyway, you prick.

The interview must've been satisfactory, as some time later I received a letter informing me that I'd passed the promotion board and would be transferred to HMP Woodhill as soon as HMP The Mount would release me. That's it, I thought, my first promotion on my first attempt. I've done it. I'm now a real senior officer and it's only taken me eight years. That's pretty good. All I can do now is wait for a formal date, but it won't be that long, will it?

As usual in the prison service, the pressure of overcrowding reared its increasingly regular head. You know, we lock up more people per head of population than virtually any other country in the world, and at the time I think we beat communist China in terms of percentage numbers. It's hardly surprising, then, that overcrowding in our prisons is a common and controversial occurrence. We can't keep pace with the number of people that need to be locked up and can't keep building new prisons to accommodate them. It will always be this way until we completely reform the criminal justice system of this country and stop locking away people for certain crimes. Don't get me wrong, I'm no do-gooder, but to put people in prison for non-payment of council tax? Come on it beggars belief. Our roads are in a terrible condition, our pavements are filthy and our parks are full of rubbish, used condoms and discarded needles, etc., so I say, put them to work for the good of the community instead of prison. Don't worry, I'm getting off my soapbox now!

Due to accommodation pressures and the types of people that were now being sent to prison, the powers-that-be decided to reassign The Mount back to its original designation as a category C training establishment so out went our young offenders and in came the cat C adults. Yeah, right! Most of the prisoners we received were in reality category B prisoners that had been re-categorised due to the accommodation problems. Basically, and to put it in a nutshell, prisons were giving their troublesome prisoners a lower-security category rating so that they could send them to us rather than deal with their own crap. We all did it and it still goes on today.

I recall, while at Pentonville, being told that we needed to send prisoners to one of the Isle of Wight prisons. Again, it was a category C prison. I used to call up any prisoner that had been particularly troublesome and ask them if they'd ever been abroad before.

"Why you asking that then, guv?" they'd say.

And I would reply, "'Cause you're going to the Isle of Wight. Don't forget to send me a stick of rock as a thank you."

And we would re-categorise them accordingly, just to reduce our numbers and enable us to take more prisoners direct from the courts. Many of the prisoners we eventually took at The Mount were heavily into drugs, be it as users or dealers, and The Mount very quickly gained the reputation of having a serious drug problem

I remember coming back to work after a two-week holiday. The weather was hot and I had to go from one side of the prison to the other to find a member of staff. All the prisoners were allowed out of their living blocks and were lazing around the grounds in the sunshine, totally unsupervised. It was honestly quite frightening, as I didn't see a single member of staff en-route. I thought then that, although I didn't like working with YOIs, having all these cat C prisoners who I knew should, in reality, be cat Bs wandering around without supervision was bloody scary and damned dangerous.

Then the bombshell was dropped on me. I was called up to the governor's office. "How long have you been acting up as senior officer, Mr Levy?" she asked me.

"You mean my temporary promotion, ma'am?" I said.

"There's no need to split hairs, Mr Levy," she snapped at me.

"Forgive me for saying so, ma'am, but it does make quite a difference to my pay and conditions, so I do feel it's important to clarify the difference between acting up and temporary promotion, ma'am," I responded.

"Not any more," she said.

Great, I thought, she's gonna offer me a substantive posting to be a senior officer here. But she continued, "We'll be getting your replacement here by the end of the month, so you will revert to an officer then. I'll give you an extra week at the higher grade so you can hand over to the new senior officer, then you can stay on Fowler as an officer, okay, until you move to Woodhill."

There wasn't much I could say at this point. She knew very well how long I'd acted up - for over two years.

The prison service has developed a way of saving money, whereby instead of replacing managerial staff with new ones they temporarily promote existing staff to the post, pay the extra money for the higher salary, but save their budget by not replacing at the lower grade. For example, an SO is paid £20,000 and an officer £18,000, so they would temporarily promote the officer and pay the additional £2,000, but they wouldn't put someone else in his former officer position, thus saving £18,000 on the wage bill. In a big establishment and with the current financial situation this practice could save the prison a fortune each year. One of the most important members of staff in a modern prison is the accountant, believe me.

Ah, you might say, but how is that a saving when somebody will have to do the work that the temporarily promoted officer was doing. This is where the service is clever. Nobody does it, or rather everybody else does it. That officer's former colleagues have to cover the work between them. Okay, but you still have to pay overtime to the rest of the officers for extending their shifts to cover the work, don't you? No! They will only be offered TOIL (time off in lieu). Of course, how they get that time off when they're now one member of staff short is a different matter. So, in that case, nobody will agree to cover the work then, you might think. Wrong again. You see, the vast majority of staff are too responsible for their own good. They would never refuse to cover the work, as that could leave their colleagues unable to cope with the additional work burden and could compromise their safety. No one would leave their colleagues in that position. We are all too conscientious to allow that to happen. I, as a duty manager, have found myself in that very position, and all we would do is put the prison into a patrol state and curb the usual regime, which is the politically correct way of saying that the prisoners would be locked up and not allowed out of their cells due to a lack of adequate staff numbers to ensure a safe environment. I'm starting to get the hang of this management lark now and am starting to see the bigger picture, although I'm not sure if I'm liking some of it.

After two years of having the temporary SO rank and the extra money, it was all about to end. This would leave me in a difficult position. As I was now in a relationship and it seemed to be getting serious, my social life had moved on and the extra money was very handy. I really didn't want to revert to an officer while I awaited my transfer to Woodhill as an SO.

In fact, to be honest, I'd forgotten how to be an officer after all that time, and I couldn't see the value in it either when I was due to move on. Bloody hell, I thought, I've gotta show, someone, how to do my job, then revert back to an officer and accept this new one as my boss. Fuck that! Why should I show him what to do? Couldn't he just learn the same way I did? But that's not my style.

In the event, when the new senior officer arrived I immediately liked him. He had a good sense of humour, told some great stories and got on with everybody. So how could I be nasty to him and not show him the ropes?

Thankfully I never did revert to an officer, however. As I'd passed my SOs exams and my promotion board interview, I was a substantive SO without a job, Why couldn't the old bitch have offered the promotion to me, or at least given me the chance there at The Mount? After all, she knew that technically I was a substantive senior officer, so she could've just appointed me there and then. But, of course, I knew the reason. As usual, my big mouth had got in the way. She didn't like my directness and the fact that I spoke my mind and held opinions that weren't necessarily in line with her policies. I suppose, in short, I was my father's son - a big-mouthed know-it-all, who spoke his mind irrespective of his position. I would always be my own person and would never be a yes man. It's strange really, but everything she didn't like about me was exactly what the previous governor did like. Oh well, you can't win 'em all.

When I'd finished my handover period and was ready to take off my pips, I was called up to the governor's office again. "Mr Levy, it occurred to me that as you've now passed your senior officer's exam and are awaiting your transfer, it would be silly for us to lose all the experience you've gained while temporarily promoted," she began.

Oh, I thought to myself so now she's saying 'temporarily promoted' and not 'acting up'. What's she after?

She continued, "We need to hold onto all our experienced officers and therefore I will continue to keep you temporarily promoted until I have all my substantive senior officers in post."

In other words, I was to continue as an SO until all her current vacancies had been filled. Well, she could've offered me one of those places, couldn't she? But no, as far as I was concerned she'd made it quite clear that she didn't want to promote me in situ. Well, that was fine by me, as I didn't want it there anymore working for her. I thanked her and returned to my office in Fowler House.

Over the next few months, I worked as an SO in the segregation unit, where I had daily contact with all the governors, especially the number one governor, who was a real hoot when acting as the adjudicating governor. She would come down to the seg unit and into the adjudication room and she would sit at the head of the table with me next to her. I had all the prisoners' personnel files and the relevant paperwork in a neat pile, as per the running order. We used to dread it down there if she was in charge, as all the cases took so long and she would very rarely make a decision.

I remember on one occasion at the end of an adjudication hearing, once the prisoner was locked away in a cell, she turned to me and said, "Well, Mr Levy, what do you think?"

"I think he's guilty, ma'am. The evidence is clear and he's pleaded guilty," I replied.

"No, I disagree. There is some doubt, so I'm going to adjourn the case for further investigations," she said.

What the hell? I didn't know how much more clear-cut the prisoner's guilt could be, but she still had doubts. Afterwards, the segregation staff and I were talking about it and we all reckoned that she hadn't had a drink that day and her mind was all fuzzy due to sobering up!

Our new deputy governor had a slight affliction, in that he had a muscular tic that turned into a head twitch combined with a wink when he got nervous or agitated. It was reminiscent of a comedian called Jack Douglas, who used to have a character in his act called Alf Ippititimus. Alf would throw one of his twitches and winks and say, "Phwaay," as he threw his head back, catapulting his cloth cap into the air in the process. I'm not sure if Jack got the idea for his character from our deputy governor or not.

I must admit that the deputy's affliction did give us some problems when he was the adjudicating governor. I used to warn any prisoner due to come before him that the deputy had a twitch and wasn't actually winking at him and that he mustn't laugh. I've got to say, however, that on some occasions, it was difficult to keep a straight face when the twitch got going. I can recall the proceedings of one particular adjudication with a pre-warned prisoner, which went as follows:

"What's your name and number," said the deputy governor, giving a little wink.

"Smith gn8784," responded the prisoner, winking back.

"How do you plead?" the deputy continued. Twitch, wink.

"Not guilty," replied the prisoner, who promptly twitched and winked back.

Oh no, I thought, here we go. Is this prisoner taking the mickey out of the Governor?

"The officer will read out his evidence and then you can give your version of events. Do you understand?" explained the deputy. Twitch, wink, wink.

"Yes," said the prisoner, with another twitch and wink.

The officer read out his evidence and the deputy asked, "What do you think about the officer's statement?" Twitch, wink, wink twitch. "It's all wrong," said the prisoner, giving a huge twitch and two winks.

"You may now give your version of events," stated the deputy governor, accompanied by a pronounced head jerk, another double wink, and a matching mouth twitch.

The prisoner explained his version of events and after every sentence gave the governor a wink, and after about half a dozen times I along and the escorting officer were both struggling to keep straight faces. At the same time, the governor was getting increasingly agitated, to the point that his twitches and winks were virtually continuous. How I managed not to burst out laughing I just don't know.

The prisoner finished giving his evidence and then treated everybody in the room to a stunning Alf Ippititimus impersonation. Then, as an aside, he said to the escorting officer standing next to him, "I'm gonna get a touch here, guv. That governor keeps winking at me, so he must be gonna make me not guilty."

The whole scenario looked like something straight out of a Carry On film. All we needed was for Matron to put in an appearance. What a great spectacle that would've been!

I can't honestly remember what the outcome of the adjudication was, but I do recall hearing some years later that this deputy governor was given early retirement on medical grounds after he lost the plot completely and had some sort of breakdown, poor man.

There were several other incidents involving both this deputy governor and also the governor. I remember one time when the governor was having her photograph taken just outside the prison gates for a feature in the local newspaper.

Contrary to prison regulations she still had her keys with her, although thankfully they were attached to her chain. The picture that appeared in the local paper was a classic shot, showing the governor holding her keys up for all the world to see, against a backdrop of the prison. How she got away with that one I'll never know.

For the remainder of my time at The Mount, I worked in the gate area and on the operations unit. I was being used as the general dogs body senior officer, filling in wherever I was needed. I'd been officially accepted at HMP Woodhill in Milton Keynes as a substantive senior officer and the delay in my transfer was making me get very frustrated.

The Mount wouldn't release me until they'd installed an officer to take my place, but I didn't expect there to be a problem, as the prison was getting new officers all the time.

As previously stated, my relationship was blossoming at this time, and although I'd initially been looking to move to Milton Keynes on my own, it soon became obvious that I would be getting married and what I desperately needed was to find was a home that would be suitable for my new wife and me.

As I said earlier we got married on 10 December 1993 at Hemel Hempstead Registry Office. It was a great day, even though I was suffering from a bad case of 'man flu' and felt awful even after a few whiskies and several paracetamols. We had a very boozy and most enjoyable reception at my sister's house and then went on honeymoon to Cyprus. On the flight, due to my 'man flu' symptoms, I went deaf in one ear and only regained my hearing three days later, at which point I realised that my lovely, quiet, new wife wasn't that quiet after all.

Despite the happiness of the wedding and honeymoon, I was becoming more and more agitated by the delay in getting my actual transfer date, and my temper was close to boiling point as I was offered each new excuse for the delay.

Chapter 28

“With Respect, I work with Shit”

I was called up to the governor’s office and thought at last my transfer date for moving to HMP Woodhill, Milton Keynes, had come through. I’d been temporarily promoted to a senior officer for several years now, had passed the annual promotion exam, was successful in the formal interview for a senior officer post at HMP Woodhill, which like Pentonville was a local prison and therefore familiar territory and my application to that establishment for level transfer as an officer had been granted, too. All I needed was that official date, but the wait had become extremely frustrating.

I was eager to move on, as I’d become disillusioned with HMP The Mount, especially since the change of management. I honestly thought that the previous governor and deputy had been the best management team I’d experienced in the service and, looking back now over my whole career, that is still true. It seems strange to think that a change of management could have such a dramatic effect on the running of a prison, but it really did.

Many of my Mount colleagues had also been accepted for transfer to HMP Woodhill and had already moved there, which simply added to my frustration. I’d made several complaints about the delay and I’d had several meetings with the governor and deputy governor, but still, no concrete transfer date had been forthcoming.

So I was somewhat expectant as I made my way from the unit where I was based to the governor’s office. When I arrived I knocked on her door and was told to enter, whereupon I was confronted by not only the governor but also her deputy and the area manager.

Bloody hell, I thought. Fancy the area manager coming to give little old me the good news of my impending transfer and presumably my promotion confirmation date as well. Oh goody.

I was invited to sit down and was then bombarded with a barrage of excuses as to why my transfer had so far not been granted, each in turn giving a different explanation for the delay. One of them - I can't remember who, but I think it was the governor - said that as I was an SO they had to wait for a senior officer to replace me before they could let me go to Woodhill. I asked, "Does this mean I'm going to Woodhill on promotion to SO then and not as an officer?"

"Well, no," said the area manager.

"So how come I have to wait for an SO replacement when I'm going as an officer?" I queried.

"Because," said the governor, "you're temporarily promoted to the senior officer post here and therefore we require a senior officer replacement." At this point, my anger got the better of me and I retorted, "With respect, ma'am, I work with shit all day, so I'm not gonna sit here and listen to it as well." I then got up and walked out of her office.

I was absolutely livid to have been called into her bloody office and told a load of what I perceived to be crap by all three of them. How dare they? What a bunch of bloody lame excuses! As far as I was concerned I was an officer until I was officially promoted and that would be at Woodhill, so how could they replace me with a senior officer rather than an officer? It just seemed like a crap excuse to hold on to me for their own convenience. Whatever happened to career development? It'd been binned, that's what. These thoughts were whizzing around my head as I walked back to my unit.

When I reached the unit I was greeted by an officer, who said to me, "Tony is it right that you said to the governor, 'With respect, ma'am, I work with shit. I don't have to sit here and listen to it as well'?" Bloody hell, I thought, how did that get back here to the wing so damn quick, and who told them? That's the prison life for you; it undeniably is a funny old game.

Incidentally, although that 'funny old game' comment has always been attributed to Jimmy Greaves, the ex-Spurs and England footballer, it was first said by comedian Harry Enfield in a spoof sketch of an interview with a *Spitting Image* Jimmy Greaves puppet for a football programme during the 1980 World Cup. Just a bit of trivia I picked up along the way.

So I continued to work at The Mount, but my heart was no longer in it. I just wanted to get away and start my new career, whether as an officer or senior officer at Woodhill. Still, my transfer date didn't come through. I can't understand why prisons insist on keeping staff that are awaiting transfer, as the productivity of those individuals, must surely go down quite dramatically, especially if they're awaiting promotion and a higher salary. After all, money is the motivation for working, is it not?

The governor eventually even asked me if I wanted to take the promotion in situ, which I declined immediately. I'd had enough of The Mount and I also felt that five years in any one prison was enough. You get stale and need new challenges. I've never believed in continuing up the promotion ladder in the same prison, as your colleagues will always see you as you were rather than what you've become. This must surely diminish your authority in any new rank you attain. However, the powers-that-be obviously disagreed with me, as many staff do get promoted several times within the same establishment.

Some weeks later a lunchtime get-together for the traditional farewell drink took place in one of the local pubs in Bovingdon village for one of my colleagues. Unfortunately, I had to go back to work in the afternoon, so I could only drink Coca-Cola. The speeches came and went and farewell gifts were exchanged - there was always a collection for the departing member of staff. While there, the governor approached me and said, "Mr Levy, I have some good news for you. Your transfer date has finally come through. You are to be transferred to HMP Woodhill on promotion to a senior officer on ..."

"Ma'am, thank you very much," I replied.

She then continued, "You can come to my office tomorrow and collect the official notification. But tell me, Mr Levy, why didn't you wish to take your promotion in situ? I wanted you to stay here, as I consider you an asset to the establishment."

I think at this point those of my colleagues that were still fairly sober and knew me sensed I would say something controversial, so the pub sort of lulled into silence.

"Well, ma'am," I said, "You've been about as honest with me as Saddam Hussein has been with the United Nations, so why would I want to work for you?"

Needless to say, my remaining time at HMP The Mount passed with very little contact with the governor or any of her management team, and not one of them bade me farewell when my final day came. Nor did I have the usual farewell drink in a local pub. Instead, I got together with a few of my close colleagues at the Prison Officers' Club at The Mount to say my goodbyes to them.

And so on to genuine promotion and a new prison.

Chapter 29

Woodhill & the Special Unit

HMP Woodhill was a brand new prison in Milton Keynes that served the local courts. It housed remand prisoners, young offenders, category A and B prisoners, E-list prisoners and sex offenders all under one roof but in separate units.

I'd been designated as one of the senior officers on a newly opened residential wing housing category B and C prisoners, who in general were serving five years or more. However, after only two weeks in this unit, there was a general trawl for staff to apply to work in the soon to be opened special unit. As I'd covered most of the usual SO jobs while on temporary promotion at The Mount, I felt that the special unit would present a new challenge and would also be a good career move, so I decided to apply.

I was interviewed by none other than the good doctor (now, I believe, a professor of criminology) who'd been the chairperson at my promotion board interview and was now one of the governors of the newly established special unit. My application was successful, although to be honest, I think they were desperate to get the special unit open and probably would've taken almost anybody. The new team for the unit comprised of myself, two other senior officers and ten staff. It had a nice ring to it - 'special unit'. Maybe because I'd been selected I felt pretty special about working there. But what sort of prisoners would I encounter at the new unit?

HMP Woodhill housed identified high-risk prisoners and these were to be held in the special unit, or CSC (Close Supervision Centre), as it was known.

There were other similar specialist units dotted around the country, most notably at HMP Hull, but this had closed down on the opening of the Woodhill unit. Prisoners were assessed by the CSC Committee, which usually sat at the prison head office in London, and it was they who decided which prisoners would be placed in the CSC system and to what prison they would be sent.

The idea was that prisoners that had been too disruptive and violent towards other prisoners could come to the CSCs and gradually be reintegrated into the mainstream prison system via a series of counselling and one-to-one therapy sessions and a more innovative regime.

The special unit comprised two different sections, aptly named Milton and Keynes, Milton being the assessment centre and Keynes the CSC proper. Also contained in this unit were three other wings, one of which housed supergrasses that had turned Queen's evidence (i.e., accused or convicted criminals who had testified as witnesses against former associates). These informants would eventually be given new identities and be relocated to safer environments. Each was allocated a police liaison officer, who dealt with their every whim and would be available for them on their release.

Another wing housed sex offenders while they underwent the sex offenders treatment programme (SOTP). The third wing housed any other prisoner that had been placed on a residential offender management course.

These three wings were originally known as the non-CSC units, but the staff working on them felt that this term had negative connotations, so we decided to change our 'corporate image'. We held a competition to rename the three wings and design a logo and, as a result, the wings became the DART (Development and Residential Training) unit, with its own dart logo. It was a motivational move that really worked and it gave the staff working in them a new sense of purpose.

Working in the special unit could at times be very stressful due to the types of prisoners we housed there. One of our concerns as managers were the potential scenario should the need arise to evacuate the building. There would be no logistical way to keep all the prisoners separate, and to have them mixing would be a disaster and extremely dangerous, particularly for the sex offenders. We never did solve this problem, but thankfully an evacuation was never needed.

In Milton and Keynes, the potential for violent incidents to erupt among the prisoners was ever-present, and not just fights with each other. I remember several instances of an individual prisoner grabbing hold of the wing television and threatening to throw both it and himself off the twos landing. On one of these occasions, this was accompanied by a second prisoner actively encouraging him to jump, while at the same time a third prisoner was threatening that if he didn't jump or smash the television he'd 'beat him to shit'.

I can recall another occasion when, while out on the exercise yard, a prisoner managed to climb up the perimeter fence and along the barbed razor wire. As a result, he sustained severe cuts to his hand and was bleeding profusely. We attempted to talk him down so that we could administer first aid, but he wasn't having any of it. The governor came onto the wing and took charge of the incident, with the rest of us in supporting roles. Then the telephone rang, and we could tell by the ring that it was an outside call. We assumed that it was head office enquiring about what was happening, so the governor took the call. All we could hear was the muffled voice of somebody sounding very agitated at the other end of the line.

The governor then very calmly handed the telephone to me, saying, "Mr Levy, it's your wife. Apparently, she's lost the cat."

"What do you want?" I hissed. "We're in the middle of a major incident here!"

“I don’t give a fuck about your major incident,” she retorted. “I can’t find the cat. What the hell are we gonna do?”

It seemed that one of our new kittens had managed to squeeze behind some units into what we later always referred to as their hidey-hole, but at that time we didn’t know about it. My wife thought that some workmen had inadvertently let the kitten out of the house.

The governor turned to me and asked, “Is everything all right, Mr Levy, or do we have to inform the head office of your major crisis and open the command suite until your bloody cat is found?”

Everybody fell about laughing, which relieved some of the tension we were all feeling.

The prisoner did eventually come down from the top of the fence and allowed our medical staff to treat his wounds, but I never did live down that day. Thereafter, whenever I bumped into the governor he would ask if our cats were all right.

This was the nature of the special unit. Incidents happened. Some were serious and some light-hearted. Some staff loved working there, but others struggled to handle the pressure.

There was one senior officer at Woodhill CSC who’d previously worked at the special unit at Hull prison before it closed, and he was so laid-back he was almost comatose. His ability to calm situations down was amazing. Even with the most irate prisoner nose to nose with him, he would turn around and utter his now-famous line, “And anyway …”. In fact, on some occasions, when we were completing wing paperwork, he was so laid-back that I wanted to grab hold of him and shake him, and all he would say was, “And anyway …’.

He was a great bloke to work with, and we had many incidents where his calmness under fire was so reassuring to us all.

The protected witness (supergrass) wing was something entirely different. The prisoners held there were known on their prison records under the pseudonym of 'Bloggs' (as in Joe Bloggs). All of them could have access to a telephone to contact their 'handlers' virtually whenever they wanted, and their visitors had to be kept apart from the rest of the visitors for security reasons.

One Thursday Bloggs One asked if he could telephone his police handler, so I asked if there was anything I could do to help. This man was a known bank robber, who used to go on a 'job' armed with a sawn-off shotgun and he'd been involved with some notorious criminals in the past. He answered, "Well, we want Sky telly and the governor told me we can't have it in this part of the prison 'cause of the cost of putting in the wiring, so I'm gonna get my handler to have it put in 'cause I wanna watch the footie at the weekend."

"Bloody hell," I said, "you honestly think the police are gonna pay for Sky to come and install that for you by the weekend?"

He replied, "Tony, you watch. One call from me and they'll be around tomorrow to fit it."

And he was right! He made his call and the next morning the Sky engineers turned up and fitted the cable so that the prisoner could have Sky TV. Some clout they had, that's for sure.

So that was the special unit. Due to a change of political will, it's now closed, but I really enjoyed my time working there. I did witness some terrifying incidents and dealt with prisoner of notoriety to the wider prison system this included one attack on a prisoner that resulted in the attacked prisoner eventually dying from his wound many months later. The perpetrator was charged with murder by the police. But despite the potential for explosive violence I really enjoyed my time working in this unique unit.

Chapter 30

Who the Hell's Wayne Gretski?

I'd been given the glorious title of 'Sex Offenders Treatment Programme Manager', which sounded very important but in reality, I was just the senior officer in charge of the uniformed staff. The real people in charge of this programme were, and quite rightly so, the psychologists. A team of staff from within the unit comprising of prison officers and probation officers (who were attached to the unit) made up our tutor/facilitator teams.

I had some wonderfully talented tutor/facilitator officers on the programme. Three of them, in particular, were very talented officers and are now high-ranking governors at other establishments and one has even featured in a TV documentary about her prison.

I was very lucky to have all three working for me in this unit, and I have nothing but admiration for the work they did. It was extremely draining emotionally, especially for those that had young children, to be subjected to hearing in graphic detail how these prisoners had committed their offences.

Together with an equally brilliant probation officer, they had been trained to facilitate the Sex Offenders Treatment Programme (SOTP), which was an eight-week residential course for sex offenders that had admitted to their offences, which was a condition of being accepted on the programme. The course formed part of their sentence plan, with the aim of reducing their risk of re-offending and thus allowing them to be released.

Don't forget that the term 'sex offender' covers a multitude of sins, from paedophilia to date rape. In fact, anybody over the age of 18 that had committed an offence against children or females was considered to be a sex offender. On release, they would be placed on the risk register and the local authorities in their release area would be informed before the release happened. A much more coordinated system exists today to keep some of the more serious offenders under surveillance. Basically, completing this course meant either an earlier release or a longer stay in prison, depending on the outcome.

Although this course was directed by a very senior psychologist at the Home Office, I'm not sure if there was any monitoring of the effect that this course had on the actual facilitators. It must've been extremely traumatic for some of them, especially if they'd experienced first-hand the types of abuse the course participants were describing in detail, and yet they never showed anything except the highest level of professionalism at all times. As I said earlier, I have great admiration for them and they deserved and earned their future successes.

After we'd completed a few courses some of us were offered the opportunity to be trained by one of the world's leading authorities in this field, Professor Robert Ross. He was from the University of Ottawa and was the founder of the original 'Reasoning and Rehabilitation' programme. He was one of the pioneers of the 'What Works' movement in criminal justice and remains a major influence in the field.

The Reasoning and Rehabilitation project comprised an experimental test of the efficacy of an unorthodox intervention programme in the rehabilitation of any high-risk adult probationers. The programme constituents were derived from a series of sequential studies of the principles of effective correctional programmes. These studies indicated that many offenders demonstrated deficits in the cognitive skills that are essential for prosocial adjustment and that training in these skills should be an essential ingredient of effective correctional programmes. Compared with regular probation and life skills training, cognitive training provided by probation officers led to a major reduction in re-arrest rates and incarceration rates among adult high-risk probationers.

It was considered that this programme could be successfully integrated into the SOTP, and I was one of those selected, at great expense to the prison service, and the taxpaying public, to become a 'Rossette' This course was sometimes quite simplistic and yet at other times it went way above my head due to the technical psychology jargon, but I soldiered on.

I remember at one point Professor Ross asked us, "Who is the richest sports star in the world?" Various names were bandied around:

"Gary Lineaker, Paul Gascoigne or that up-and-coming footballer, the one that married a Spice Girl … yeah, David Beckham."

"No, I reckon, it's got to be global. Maybe Michael Schumacher?" "I reckon it's a golfer. How about Nick Faldo?"

"This guy's Canadian so it's probably someone nearer to home. What about Greg Norman or Phil Mickelson?"

Professor Ross looked at us with a quizzical expression. "I've never heard of Gary Lineaker or Paul Gascoigne," he said. "The richest sports star in the world is … Wayne Gretzky."

"Wayne Gretzky?" I said. "Who the hell's Wayne Gretzky? I've never heard of him. What sport does he play then, professor?"

Looking directly at me, Professor Ross responded, "I can't believe you've never heard of Wayne Gretzky. He's the highest-paid sports star in the world and he's an ice hockey player."

We all looked at each other in bemusement. "Sorry, professor, but if you're gonna present this course in other UK locations then I'd suggest you don't use this analogy, as very few people here will have heard of Wayne Gretzky," I said.

I think I lost the whole purpose of the course, together with my concentration, at this point and I really can't remember much about the course apart from this particular incident. I believe the course lasted about three days and we all completed it, but I can honestly say that I never knowingly implemented any of it. I'm not sure how much of it was adapted to our own SOTP course in the end anyway, so taxpayers' money was largely wasted on this venture.

I suppose, like all things, this at the time was deemed to be innovative and forward-thinking, but I'm not convinced that any sort of treatment, whether based on cognitive thinking or anything else, has any great impact on those in society that wish to offend in this manner. However, that's just my opinion. I'm sure there are and always will be exceptions, but I can only base my conclusions on my own experiences, both within and outside the prison environment.

Chapter 31

You Didn't Ask If It Was Turned On!

I was off on another SOTP training course, this time to be held in the Grand Hotel, Leicester, a large hotel located on Granby Street in the city centre. Built between 1897-98 by Cecil Ogden and Amos Hall, it was owned by the Ramada Jarvis Group and was known simply as the Ramada Jarvis Hotel. The hotel was as grand as its name in the Victorian era and used to house a cinema, but it looked pretty run-down on my visit and has only a 3-star rating today.

All SOTP courses were difficult for the participants. As you can imagine, the subject matter was pretty depressing, but it also changed your innocent perspectives on life, putting what you perceived to be completely natural parental actions and feelings into a new and disturbing light. Anyone that has either facilitated or been involved in the SOTP will tell you that something as innocent as sitting in the bath with your own children, taking pictures of your children in public places, hugging your children and the tender and protective way you treat them - all activities that form part of a normal, loving family - take on a whole new meaning after the SOTP. This is why I have such great admiration for those who get actively involved in this course.

After attending a SOTP course it would usually take several days, sometimes longer, for me to return to my normal self. I would withdraw into myself and try to analyse what I was feeling. I would shut out my wife and she couldn't get close to me until I'd worked through it all and come out the other end.

It's not surprising, therefore, that participants on these courses, even when at the Prison Service College, tended to stick together and became a rather insular group. And on this particular occasion, it was no different. On the first night, we met at the hotel bar and I was introduced to a nice drink called Irish Mist, which was a whiskey-based liqueur. It was so lovely that on the third and last night of the course I got badly drunk on the stuff. I can't remember how many I drank, but I do remember that during the evening three of us left the confines of the hotel and walked around Leicester. However, we weren't that impressed and eventually ended up back at the hotel bar, at which point I discovered that my wife had telephoned me only to find I wasn't there. Not only did I have a bad head the next day due to the overindulgence, but I also had an even worse headache when I got home and had to try to convince my wife that this was the only night I'd got drunk and had been outside of the hotel. Incidentally, nowadays one Irish Mist is about my limit.

On another occasion, I was on a training course at the Prisoner Service Training College at Newbold Revel. I think this was another SOTP training course, too, and again the course members seemed to stick together and frequent the bar. By this time the old British Flag pub loved by all who had ever been to the training college before had gone, so the bar was the main choice.

I remember one night I was at the college bar when I heard this voice. "Hey, Yiddo, is that you?" Bloody hell, I thought, I haven't heard that nickname for some time. Then I realised it was an old Pentonville colleague, who had transferred to Gartree prison and was at the college for a 'pre-retirement' course. Later in my career, I, too, attended this course, which was supposed to offer staff that were approaching retirement age advice on how to spend their time and money once they'd given up work. For me, it seemed to come at the wrong end of your career and should've been at the beginning rather than the end, but that's a different story.

Anyway, we spent a very enjoyable evening putting the world and the prison service to rights. Just outside the bar was a public pay telephone. During the evening, armed with as much change as I could muster, I went to phone my wife to make sure that all at home was okay. Remember this was before most of us had mobile phones. "Thank goodness you phoned," she said. "Faye (our daughter) is here and we can't get the television to work. She was here last night and we had no problems with it."

The television was my pride and joy and it was linked to a surround-sound system. My wife has always struggled to remember which remote control operated which piece of equipment, as there's one for the Skybox, one for the TV, one for the surround sound, another for the DVD player, and so on. So I said to her, "I'll talk you through what to do, okay?"

"Yes, but take it slowly," she replied.

"Right," I began, "first press the button that looks like it's got a circle on it with a line running from the centre straight up through the arc of the circle. It's probably red."

"Tony, she said, "I know what the on/off standby switch looks like. I'm not an idiot, you know."

"Of course not, love," I responded, thinking to myself that this was going to be more difficult than I'd imagined, especially as I was struggling to remember what the different remote controls looked like, never mind trying to explain how to use them to someone that has absolutely no idea what each one does. "Have you made sure that you've switched all of them on? I'm trying to visualise this, so please bear with me even if you know, okay?"

"Yes," she answered. "We've definitely switched on the power for them all and the Skybox has come on, but we can't get any sound and can't get the telly to come on."

I said, "That's not a problem. The sound will only come on when all the boxes are talking to each other. I think you've just pressed the wrong button on the TV and lost the link to the Skybox. So look for the button on the TV remote that looks like …," and I talked her through it step by step.

By now a queue was forming for the telephone, and it was getting very hot inside the booth, so I opened the door and explained to the waiting queue my predicament.

"No," said my wife, "it's still not working. She must've touched some other button and changed all the settings. I'm fed up with having to go through all this every time. Why can't we have just one remote control instead of all these?"

This was a regular theme whenever she tried to turn on the system. I talked her through the set-up again, but still, nothing was working. 'Okay just describe to me what's happening," I said, by now getting a little desperate, not just because the queue was getting impatient but also because I was worried, they'd completely mucked up my very expensive surround sound, my drink was going flat and I was running out of cash for the telephone.

"It's the same as before. The lights on the Sky box and the surround sound are on, but not the television," she explained.

"Well, I haven't a clue what's been touched now, so I don't know what to suggest next," I sighed, feeling completely frustrated.

"Don't have a go at me," she retorted. "I told you this was too complicated. "Why we can't have just one that turns everything on and off?"

By this time, people were lending me change so I could continue my conversation and one chap in the queue said to me, "Go on, mate, you've got to sort this out, 'cause we're all on tenterhooks. It's better than an episode of *Brookside*."

"All right," I said. "Just one more thing. Is the red light on the front of the television on?"

“No,” she replied. “There’s no light on the television at all.” Bingo!

“Great,” I muttered, “the bloody television isn’t even turned on. I could be here a month of Sundays, but if the bloody thing has been turned off it’s never going to work, is it?”

I was furious. I’d just wasted all that time and money trying to explain to my wife how to get all the equipment working when the bloody telly wasn’t even turned on.

“Faye must’ve turned the TV off last night, but you didn’t ask if it was turned on anyway,” came the reply. “It’s working now.”

What could I say? My response was dripping with sarcasm. “Oh, I’m so glad. It just goes to show that if you turn the television off, one day you just have to turn the damn thing on again before it’ll work, brilliant. Why didn’t you just leave it on standby?”

My wife’s reply is not for publication, but it seemed she wasn’t sure why!

Following this incident, before ever going on any more courses I always made sure that my wife knew how to turn all the equipment on. Now if only I could get her to remember how to use a mobile phone …

Chapter 32

Tour of London

“Right, said my PO, “as I’m now responsible for the SOTP unit, I’d better come with you to the management meeting in London.” This trip to London was a nice little perk for me. The meetings took place roughly every three months in a lovely building in the heart of the capital. The meeting room overlooked Horse Guards Parade, and often proceedings would be halted while the bands paraded up and down. It was a wonderful viewing spot and I loved going to these meeting just for the chance to watch the Household Cavalry and the bands going through their repertoire.

The other good thing about these meetings was that I was certainly the most junior member of staff present and yet I was treated as an equal. But now my PO had decided to accompany me and I knew what would happen. He would make sure that everybody there knew that I was his subordinate, as he liked people to acknowledge his rank. What he didn’t realise was that the vast majority of those in attendance were governor grades or Home Office officials, and I made a point of not telling him this.

The other attendees, despite their high office, had always treated me as an equal and I doubted that would change. They had undergone most of the same training as me and fully understood my role, whereas my PO didn’t.

He just saw this as a chance of an away day to London and much better than a day in an office in the special unit, and I couldn’t honestly blame him for that.

We met up at Milton Keynes railway station. My PO was acting like a big kid, all excited and full of his own importance.

“Blimey, Tony, you’ve dressed smart,” remarked my PO, who was dressed in corduroy trousers and a denim shirt, with a red tie and suede boots. I, as usual for these meetings, was wearing a suit and expensive shoes, with an expensive watch to match. “Well, you’ve got to keep up appearances, haven’t you?” I responded. Our train journey to London went off without incident, except for those people that insist on using their mobile phones on a train and shouting down the phone so loudly that the whole carriage can hear them. I really didn’t want to know that a chap standing next to me had just taken his car into a garage, was running late and would ring his secretary when he arrived at Euston. This chap must’ve made five calls in the space of ten minutes, all about nothing. He must have a really important job in London - not, I thought to myself.

We arrived at Euston station and then took the underground train to reach our destination, from where we could walk to the meeting location. My PO was more interested in the buildings around us; it was obvious he had not been to London for some time, if at all.

Once we’d arrived in the meeting room and initial introductions had been completed, my PO turned to me and said, “You should’ve warned me that they would all be high-ranking governors.

I felt such a prick when I said I was a PO and they introduced themselves as governors, and there’s one I know from the island (a reference to the prison on the Isle of Wight) who’s the deputy governor. I would’ve worn my suit if I’d known. And they thought you were my boss, so I put them straight about that, I can tell you.”

The meeting was chaired on this occasion by a Home Office official, who reported to some very high-ranking civil servant at the Cabinet Office, so it was an extremely high-powered affair for a lowly senior officer to be there. However, they’d always treated me as one of their peers, so I felt quite at ease in their company. The same can’t be said for my PO, however, who seemed very nervous.

At around 11 o'clock the meeting had to stop, as the Horses Guards were passing by together with a military band. They were rehearsing for the annual Trooping of the Colour ceremony that was due to take place that weekend. The noise was such that it almost sounded as if they were in the room with us. My PO was like an awestruck little boy, shooting from window to window to get a bird's eye view of it all. A governor grade that I'd come to know quite well sidled up to me and said, "Who's that prick with you? Is he honestly your boss, Tony?" I replied, "Yes, and he'll be coming to the meetings instead of me from now on."

He responded, "Well, I can see he's going to be a real pain in the arse if this is the way he behaves when the horse guards come by."

As usual, the meeting finished at about 3 o'clock. The early finish was so that those who'd travelled quite some distance could get back to their respective establishments before their shifts finished. However, as our journey would only take about an hour, my PO suggested that we walk around some of the sights of London and then get a tube nearer to Euston. And that's what we did. I took him first to the Houses of Parliament, then to Buckingham Palace, along the Mall past the Queen Mother's house and then into Bond Street. He was so excited by all these sights; it was like taking a schoolboy on a tour of London. His enthusiasm was so infectious and he was great company to be with. It turned out to be a good afternoon, and it was well worth getting back home later than planned just to have had the opportunity to see all those places that for years as a Londoner I'd taken for granted. It was a shame that this would be the last time I'd tour around London while getting paid for it.

On another occasion, we were both due to attend a SOTP awareness course, designed for newly appointed managers and to be held in a lovely, plush 5-star hotel down in the west country, somewhere near the Welsh border. A new governor, under the job title of Head of Function, had just joined our unit, so he wanted to take part, together with my PO, another governor and me. Even though I'd completed this training before, he thought that it would be a good team-building exercise for all members of the management of our unit and a lot would be gained by going as a group. This suited me, as the programme had changed slightly and it would allow me to receive training in the new part of the SOTP course.

My PO told me he'd meet me at work and he'd give me a lift there, which was great. He'd got a nice new MX5 sports car and I'd always fancied a drive in one of those. Strangely enough I bought one of them in 1993 for my wife and we still have it and drive it around often.

Our new Head of Function, who drove a Skoda, left around the same time but got to the hotel a couple of hours before us. Boy, did my PO drive slowly - I reckoned I could've walked it quicker! We only just arrived in time for the start of the course. My PO never lived it down - beaten by a Skoda!

The hotel was wonderful, particularly as I'd been allocated a suite as opposed to a room. It had a king-size bed, a conference room adjacent to the bedroom, and a huge bathroom. My PO was incandescent with envy and kept going on about why I, as only the senior officer, should get the biggest and best room. He hated it! How the other half live, eh? It was such a step up from Leicester's not-so-grand Grand Hotel and the college accommodation. Travelling with governor grades obviously got you 5-star luxuries. It's about time I got some of the perks, I thought. A three-course restaurant meal with complimentary wine finished off a wonderful day, although the course subject matter left us all somewhat subdued by the end of the meal.

Hey, there's an indoor swimming pool here, too. I wonder if they hire out swimming trunks? I thought. They didn't, but I wasn't going to let that deter me. I just went swimming in my underpants instead. It was great. I swam, then a session in the sauna, followed by another dip in the pool. Then - oh shit - I realised I hadn't brought any spare pants down with me, so I ended up having to walk back to my room wrapped in a towel. To get to the pool area you had to go down a flight of stairs located near the reception desk, and on my return journey as I emerged at the top of these stairs, I got the shock of my life. It's a bloody mafia convention, I thought.

About 50 people were milling around, the men in tuxedos and the women in ball gowns, along with one chap in full mayoral regalia. So I had to weave my way through this throng to get to the stairs leading up to my room. Boy, was I red-faced and hot afterwards!

Once dressed, I joined the governor at the bar for a drink and related my embarrassing experience to him. "You've got some front, going for a swim in just your underpants and then running the gauntlet through that lot," he remarked, nodding his head in the direction of the official function.

"Yeah," I said. "Just as well I wasn't showing too much 'front' with that towel wrapped around me!"

Our return journey the next day back to Woodhill was marginally quicker than our outbound one, but by then I was knackered and just plain glad to get back home.

Chapter 33

We're Being Burgled!

According to all the experts, the most likely time your house will be burgled is between 2.30 and 5.00 a.m. on a Saturday morning, at the start of the weekend. More people have a drink and relax on a Friday night than at any other night of the week, and it's apparently at this time that you fall into your deepest sleep. If you don't have any sort of alarm or deterrent, you're more likely to be a victim of crime. I've worked with many offenders who've told me the same, so why was I living in the only house in the street that didn't have a burglar alarm? Even worse, my son-in-law worked for a bloody alarm company and installed the damn things! But you never consider that it'll happen to you, do you? Well, I'm living proof that it does.

We'd recently moved into a new home in a quiet, nice part of Milton Keynes, but we'd never got around to having an alarm fitted, unlike the majority of our neighbours. It was a new detached house with French doors leading into the back garden, and due to problems with the lock, we'd called a contractor to come and fix it. However, they didn't advise us how to lock these doors securely. Despite this, I always locked all the doors before going to bed each night

I was due to work over this April weekend. It was cold and there was snow still on the ground from a previous fall. I hadn't had a lot to drink on this Friday night, as I was conscious of being on duty the next morning. I'm a notoriously bad sleeper at the best of times, but my wife could sleep for Britain and could nod off anywhere: in a car, on a train, at an airport - you name it, she's slept there.

I was awoken by a noise, so I lay awake and listened. Silence. Then I heard a noise again, and this time I got up and went to the toilet. Once back in bed, I listened for any strange noises and was sure I heard something. So I got up, went into the third bedroom and took a look out of the window onto the street below. Nothing. However, I still had a feeling that something wasn't as it should be. I returned to my bedroom and my wife woke up and asked, "What's wrong?"

I answered, "Nothing. I just thought I heard a noise."

She said, "Well, so did I."

That's it, I thought, as something just hit me. It felt as if a draught was coming from downstairs, and I concluded that an outside door must be open. I turned on the upstairs lights and started to descend the stairs, trying to make as much noise as possible.

"Ring the police. I think we're being burgled," I shouted to my wife over my shoulder as I continued walking down the stairs. This is bloody silly, I thought to myself. I'm doing exactly what all my years of training have taught me not to do. But this was my house and my family, so all the usual reasoning went right out of the window. I was walking into an unknown danger with no backup and no resources to assist me. I just had to hope that, if I was right, the burglar was more frightened than me.

I got halfway down the stairs and saw that the lounge door was wide open. I always closed that before going to bed. And, yes, the French doors were wide open, too. Someone had gained access to the house.

I saw that all our electrical goods were stacked in a neat pile in the middle of the room. The noise I'd heard must've been the burglar wrenching my surround-sound speakers off the wall. There have to be two of them to be able to do that, I thought - the bastards. I looked outside and, sure enough, I could see two sets of footprints in the snow. Then I spotted something lying on the ground - the remote control for our television. The buggers had realised they didn't have enough time to take the TV after I'd disturbed them, so they'd thrown the unwanted remote control into the snow.

Yes, we'd been burgled. I don't know if this has ever happened to you, but it's incredibly distressing, especially when you're at home and in bed at the time, in what you believe to be a place of safety. Suddenly that safe world is violated, and it's one of the worst experiences that can happen to you and your family.

Some years later I used this personal experience when talking to the prisoners at HMP Grendon during their therapy sessions, explaining the effects of what they perceived to be a minor crime on the victims. In their eyes it was a victimless crime and the goods stolen could be replaced through an insurance claim, whereas for the victim it's, in reality, a major crime. You feel personally violated, traumatised, angry and guilty that you allowed it to happen and your family was put in danger. Your personal space has been invaded and you want to clean everywhere in order to erase all trace of what has occurred, but you can't get it out of your mind.

I'm aware of several instances where the victims of burglary have had to move house, as afterwards, they were never able to feel safe in their homes again, and others where certain members of the household couldn't even enter the room that had been burgled. In our case, even today, neither my wife nor I will go through the night without waking up several times. My wife went from sleeping for Britain to sleeping fitfully and waking up at the slightest noise. In fact, many times I've woken up to find her walking around the house listening for a noise she thought she heard. We loved our house, but it was never the same after this incident. I really believe the burglary trauma was the real cause of my wife's subsequent nervous breakdown some years later. No victims? Bullshit!

When I put it in these terms to some of the prisoners at Grendon they were gobsmacked and admitted that they'd never put themselves in the place of the victim before. After my talk, however, they fully understood how victims feel, so at least some good may have come out of it.

Eventually, after some hours, the police arrived and went through their normal procedures, advising us to get the locks fixed as soon as possible. However, they offered us not one bit of comfort and gave us no hope that either the perpetrators or our goods would be found. They informed us that the scenes of crime officers (SOCOs) would arrive later that day to check for fingerprints.

They looked at the French doors and said, "We've got five-year-old kids on our patch that would get through these doors in less than 30 seconds. That's how easy they are to break into. Your stuff will be at a boot sale later this morning, that's for sure." So much for NHBC standards relating to the quality of locks!

I telephoned work to explain what had happened and I was allowed to have that day off, but as I was the only manager assigned to work on that Sunday, I couldn't take that day off too I had to go into work the next day. The police took statements and asked what had been taken. They must've thought, we've got a right pair here, as we told them exactly what had gone and what hadn't. They did lots of prompting: what about your computer? They asked No, it's upstairs. Your camera? No, it's still here. Your jewellery? No, that's not been touched. Whether they were trying to ascertain whether we'd made up the burglary for an insurance claim or were just trying to ensure that we'd identified all the stolen goods I'm not sure.

Later that morning the crime prevention officer arrived to imbue us with even more confidence regarding the safety of our home, his opening remark being, "You'll probably be burgled again within six months."

Oh great, thanks for that. It's made us feel so much better now, you insensitive prick! That's just ain't what a burglary victim wants to here.

"Yes, what usually happens is they estimate it'll take around six months for you to get your insurance claim paid and replace what's been stolen, so then they come back for a second go," he continued. "However, if you put an alarm in and get some security lighting out the front and back, grow your hedges right up and get a dog, you should be okay."

He had certainly taken the police course in crime prevention diplomacy - very reassuring and comforting!

The SOCO team arrived a few hours later and dabbed several areas for fingerprints and that was that. We never heard from the police again, and thankfully, there was no repeat performance from our burglars either, although we very quickly installed security lighting and an alarm - we drew the line at getting a dog, however.

It proved very interesting when the insurance company loss assessor eventually came. He offered us some paltry sum of money to replace our stolen electrical goods and I wasn't amused.

"That's ridiculous!" I told him. "I can't replace what was stolen exactly, as some of the equipment isn't made anymore. So on what do you base your figures? The stuff cost more than that when I bought it."

He explained how it worked and then offered me a slightly higher sum. We were now haggling over what each piece of electrical equipment would cost to replace, bearing in mind that some were no longer manufactured, and he wouldn’t accept our estimates for alternative replacements. There was no budging him and eventually I had no option but to take the sum offered, but I wasn’t at all happy.

We’d also obtained quotes for cleaning our carpets and furniture, as the burglars had left muddy trainer footprints all over the place, so I presented those to him.

"What are these?" he queried. "No way. You can't get them cleaned. You'll have to replace the whole suite and the carpets. No, it's no good cleaning them, as they won't match up with the rest of the downstairs carpets. The whole lot needs replacing."

I honestly don't believe this, I thought. We'd gone for the cheapest option by getting quotes for cleaning everything, and yet he's now telling us to replace it all. He'd just been arguing over a measly £20 or so about the electrical goods, and yet now he was adding hundreds of pounds to the claim. I'll never understand these assessors, that's for sure.

We were now just another statistic, another burglary out of hundreds that happened every day. I'd lived in London for most of my life, followed by Cheshunt in Hertfordshire and then Bovingdon and had never been the victim of crime in all that time. Then I'd come to Milton Keynes and I'd been burgled.

Chapter 34

The Most Dangerous Prisoner in the System

Charles Bronson is regarded as one of the most dangerous prisoners in the prison system, but he's all about publicity; he loves it. It's the only thing in his life, he has now. You will notice that he's the only prisoner I mention by name and that's because he's known to most people both inside and outside the service and his notoriety has been well publicised. However, he really isn't the most dangerous prisoner in the British penal system. There are many more dangerous and scary prisoners and a lot of these passed through the Woodhill special unit during my time there.

Bronson had been to Woodhill on many occasions, and to be fair he'd also on one occasion taken our librarian as a hostage. It was certainly a frightening position for any member of staff to be in, but it also had its funny side.

I was on duty at the time of the incident, and our contingency plans had been put into place. Negotiators were on the scene and we'd opened the command suite, a purpose-built office equipped with telephone lines, radios, walkie-talkies, etc., to enable effective communication both up to Head Office and down to local commands.

I was sitting to the left of the governor, who was in charge of the command suite when over the public radio system a local news bulletin was broadcasting information relating to the current situation. How the press knew about it was a mystery to us all, but there it was. The radio newsreader stated that Charles Bronson had taken a member of staff hostage and was demanding a "blow-up doll and a helicopter". The governor and I looked at each other and just laughed. Then, just as this was being broadcast to the listening public, we received a piece of paper direct from the negotiators at Bronson's door informing us of exactly that demand. How the hell did the local radio station get hold of information that was happening right at that moment?

Thankfully the incident was resolved with no harm physically to the librarian who was taken hostage but it must have been very traumatic and left mental scars on the poor man forever.

I would say the prisoner that held the 'honour' of being the most dangerous prisoner, I encountered while at Woodhill was not Charles Bronson but a man that was called the Hannibal Lecter of the British penal system. When dealing with this prisoner he always made me feel quite apprehensive and a little scared. He will never be released from prison and is among only a few serving prisoners who fall into this category. This man had murdered a fellow inmate while in prison and, to date, and he's the only prisoner that has also killed a member of serving prison staff.

He came to the special unit to be assessed as a result of an MP's question at Westminster regarding the prison 'merry-go-round' system, whereby a prisoner would spend a month in one prison, then move on to another prison for a further month, then be transferred again, and so on. These prisoners were moved not only for their own protection in some cases, but also as it was deemed too dangerous to house them with other prisoners. After his time at Woodhill, however, he went straight back into the same system as before. What a waste of time and effort, not to mention the pressure that staff were put under while trying to assess this man.

Many other unsavoury characters came through the special unit - murderers, rapists, super grasses, drug dealers, we had them all. Other parts of the prison had to deal with some very nasty prisoners, too.

One evening I was on duty in the segregation unit, where prisoners were located if they'd been on a disciplinary charge and their punishment was removal from their usual place of accommodation, or if they'd been fighting and had been moved to this unit pending an adjudication. I received a telephone call from the orderly officer informing me that 'prisoner Z' was on his way to us from HMP Wakefield. This prisoner had been one of the main instigators of the Strangeways riots and was captured on national television on the roof of the building.

It had taken six PEIs to hold him down and place handcuffs on him just to get him into the vehicle that was bringing him to Woodhill, and the PEIs still had to sit on him for the duration of the journey.

Great, I thought. Normal staffing for my unit was one SO and two other officers, so I asked the orderly officer if we could have an additional member of staff just in case. This was agreed. Our prisoner arrived under full restraints, accompanied by the six officers, and he was placed in one of our segregation cells. The cell contained no furniture and no toilet or sink; it was purely and simply a place to hold a prisoner until he calmed down and was no longer considered a danger to himself or anyone else, and then he would be transferred to a normal cell.

Before leaving, the six officers filled us in about the fight this prisoner had put up, the injuries he'd inflicted on various members of staff and the damage he'd caused to prison property back at their establishment. They also handed over the prisoner's core record, so I had a look through it. It recommended that when this man was unlocked there should be an SO and six officers in attendance. You're having a laugh, I thought. I only had two other officers with me at the time, as the promised extra officer hadn't materialised.

I telephoned the orderly officer and told him what was written in the prisoner's records.

"Don't worry, he said, "you'll be all right. In any case, we won't be opening him up again tonight. He can stay in that cell until morning." Okay, mate, you're the boss, I thought, and I won't worry about it. Then I realised that I would be on duty the next morning for the unlocking and transfer to a regular cell.

As it turned out, the whole thing was a bit of an anticlimax. As with many of these sorts of cases, all the worry about what could potentially happen is worse than the way everything pans out in reality.

When I arrived on duty the next morning the night staff informed me that for several hours this prisoner had been doing exercises in the cell, ranging from sit-ups to press-ups, before going to sleep on his cell floor. Yet he had fought with six PEIs for a prolonged period and had then carried out a series of strenuous exercises for a further few hours, so he must be bloody fit. We went to the cell door and I looked in through the observation flap. He was just sitting there quietly, so I opened the door and then stood back. He peered around the door and asked, "Where am I?"

"HMP Woodhill, in the seg," I said.

"Thank fuck for that!" he responded. "It's where I want to be."

"Really? Well, what was all the fuss about back at the other place then?" I queried.

He looked at me and said, "What would you do if half a dozen hairy-arsed screws burst into your cell and tried to grab hold of you and bend you up? You'd fight, too. If they'd just come in and told me I was moving, I would've complied with all they asked. But they didn't, so I just started fighting to protect myself."

Another lesson learned. Maybe if we treated them with more respect it would be reciprocal and potentially volatile situations could be avoided.

However, although some prisoners were extremely violent and dangerous, they never really worried me. Sure, some incidents scared me, as you never knew what the outcome would be, but individual prisoners didn't. The only exception I can think of was when I was working at Pentonville and was sent to HMP Wormwood Scrubs to work for two days in a wing that was set aside for IRA terrorists. 'Terrorist' was a very apt name for them, as these individuals did terrorise you, not with threats of violence but by innuendo.

I remember walking into this wing, which had been separated from the rest of the prison. On entering you could feel the tension; it was different, oppressive, threatening and deadly quiet; none of the usual prison noises. Two individuals had been allowed out to walk around the landing, as heavy rain had prevented any outdoor exercise.

One of these men walked past me and commented, "You're new. First day here then." I didn't respond and he carried on walking.

When he passed me on his next circuit of the landing, he said, "By lunchtime, we'll know where you live."

Walking by me for the third time, he continued, "By teatime, we'll know how many kids you've got."

I was starting to feel extremely uncomfortable and I'd only been on the wing five minutes. When he came around again, he added,

"And by lock-up, we'll know their ages and what school they go to. Hope you like it here with us." This wasn't what I'd joined up for and I could feel the fear inside me building. The fact that at the time I wasn't married and had no children that I was aware of didn't make me feel any better. I can't imagine how I would've felt if I'd had a family.

The two days at the Scrubs were the longest of my career and I was relieved when they were over. I never went back to the place to work, not even for an hour. The prisoners in the special unit, whilst dangerous, had never made me feel that way.

Many other individuals come to mind from my time at Woodhill and in the special unit - super grasses, drug dealers murderers and sex offenders - but these are the ones that are ingrained in my memory.

Chapter 35

Life After the Special Unit

The special unit was to close for refurbishment, the powers-that-be had decided that in its present form the unit didn't function as was initially envisaged, and it would become a very special secure unit.

The unit staff were moved to other departments, and, for my sins, I was moved to the operations department and was put in charge of the staff carrying out the visits function. It was honestly a very boring job. My mornings were spent sorting out the staffing rota, dealing with paperwork, filling in attendance reports and other mundane desk jobs. Paperwork had never been my forte, but now it was a necessary evil that needed to be carried out daily and it was mounting up fast each day.

My afternoon duties were split between watching the visitors and prisoners during their domestic visits from the camera room and patrolling around the visits room, ready to pounce on any visitor caught on camera attempting to pass drugs or other contraband to a prisoner. These patrols did have their moments, from highly amusing situations to violent and downright dangerous confrontations between visitors and prisoners.

Part of my job was to review the video evidence of any incident that took place in order to ascertain whether an actual offence had occurred.

We had some excellent camera operators, and I must say that most of the time they captured quite clearly the passing of prohibited items between visitors and prisoners. Once we had the evidence, a visitor would always be prosecuted.

I was continually astounded by the lengths to which visitors would go in their efforts to smuggle in contraband, be it drugs the favourite currency in all prisons, or mobile phones - the up-and-coming new currency. There were sickening cases where visitors would use their babies and children to hide contraband. To me, for a parent to use an innocent baby in such a way was truly despicable, but that's life. Maybe they felt that the risks were worth it, or perhaps intimidation from their partners, pimps or relatives which forced them to take the chance.

I remember one incident that was both funny and disturbing. I'd pre-warned my staff that a wheelchair-bound man was coming to visit his son, who was on remand, and I'd advised them that they should be both professional and sensitive in terms of the visitor's condition and needs when carrying out a search of him. However, he arrived with all the other visitors and I went to the visits reception area to ensure a smooth passage through to the visits area. The search had just been completed, so I stopped the man and asked if everything was okay. He replied, "Yes, thank you. Your staff have been very helpful and very thorough, but I was a little concerned when they asked me to remove my colostomy bag, as I thought this could only be done by my hospital."

Thank goodness the staff realised in time, but, bloody hell, I couldn't believe they'd really thought of removing it!

One Saturday morning my cameraman picked out a female visitor that he thought was acting strangely. His instincts were usually infallible and, on this occasion, they proved correct once again. He'd caught her clearly on camera putting drugs concealed in her hand into the prisoner's cup of tea. Staff were alerted immediately by this cameraman and they responded so swiftly that the prisoner didn't have time to swallow the drugs. They got stuck in his throat, causing him to choke violently, and he coughed the drugs out. I thought I would have to perform the Heimlich manoeuvre on him but thankfully he coughed it up without help

So we had the video evidence, the physical evidence and the perpetrator and my job was to arrest the woman. I took out my warrant card and read the caution to her (the same one you hear said all the time on all British cop programmes), and then she was led away and placed in a separate room. The room wasn't locked, but I think she was so shocked at being arrested by prison staff that she didn't make any fuss. I then called the local police, only to be told that they only had two squad cars covering the whole of the Milton Keynes area and we would have to hold on to this woman until they could get somebody over to us. I said we could hold her until midday, but it would be difficult beyond that due to lunchtime staff shortages and shift finishes. Luckily, the police arrived in time and rearrested the woman.

In the end, she received a five-year prison sentence for passing the drugs Why do they do it? But I know why because some of their partners bully them into it.

During my time away from the special unit a new piece of equipment, incorporating an early form of thumbprint technology was made available to prisons for trial use in the visits area. As far as I can remember, the new system was never adopted by Woodhill, due to the high number of daily visits to remand prisoners the system wasn't designed to be able to cope with. However, I was invited to attend the daily morning management briefing in the boardroom, which was a first for me. I never really understood the purpose of the meeting, but it was supposed to be an opportunity for managers to discuss their dairies and any events due to take place that day. To me, it just seemed like a points-scoring exercise, with managers either slagging off other departments or telling everybody around the table just how great they were. Anyway, I'd been asked along to the meeting to explain how the implementation of this new thumbprint technology was going, which I thought would be pretty interesting seeing as I didn't honestly understand how the technology worked.

The governor took her place at the head of the table and explained what meetings she was to attend. Next came the deputy governor, who gave a wonderful diatribe directed at everybody and anybody, using such incomprehensible floral expressions and words that halfway through it I switched off completely. This particular man eventually went to work for the private sector prisons and made such a hash of it he was sacked. Next, it was the chaplain's turn and proceedings continued this way until it came to my big chance.

"First of all, I would like to ask how we go about getting the software company to come here and go through some of the faults with the system," I said.

At this point, the PO sitting next to me, whom I knew from my Pentonville days, kicked me and shook his head. "No point bringing up your problems here, she doesn't want to hear them," he said.

"But I need some guidance here as to how I take this further," I replied.

"Yeah well don't ask here. Nobody wants to hear problems. Just say everything's okay and throw in a few technical terms and they'll think you're the best thing since sliced bread," he said.

And that's exactly what I did. Nobody batted an eyelid, not that anybody was actually taking it in any way. So what the hell was the purpose of this very important daily briefing?

Sometime later we had a VIP visit from Ann Widdecombe MP the then-current Home Office minister, I believe she'd acquired the nickname The Rottweiler, and after meeting her I could understand why, as she was a formidable lady. She came to the visitors centre and was very interested in our fingerprint technology. I remember her asking all about it and the governor started trying to explain, at which point Ms Widdecombe said to her, "I was talking to the officer in charge, not you. Your understanding of it will only be what he's already told you." Bloody hell, talk about being put in your place. Well done, you, I thought. I'll vote for you in the next election, that's for sure.

Although interesting events happened during my time on operations, overall I was missing the special unit and the close contact with prisoners, especially those that were deemed to be dangerous. Strangely, I honestly felt that by interacting with them and treating them as equals I was doing my bit to help stop them re-offending and perhaps helping them go on to lead useful lives back in society. Naive or arrogant, I'm not sure which I was.

Just as a postscript, several of the staff that worked for me during my involvement with the SOTP at HMP Woodhill and the special unit went on to become high-ranking governors. One was at HMYOI Feltham, one became the governor of HMP Holloway and another eventually came back to Grendon as a governor grade and probably by now is at least a deputy governor somewhere in the system. I would like to think that perhaps I had something to do with their progress along the way

Chapter 36

Promotion to Principal Officer

I'd applied for a promotion to the rank of a principal officer at HMP Grendon and had been invited for an interview. I was aware that Grendon was a different type of establishment to the places I'd worked in so far, but I felt that the time I'd spent in Woodhill's special unit talking to the prisoners and facilitating the SOTP stood me in good stead and that I could adapt well to Grendon and its therapeutic environment.

I'd applied for two other PO promotions, one at Woodhill and one at another establishment, but I didn't feel that the interviews had gone well on either occasion. I never felt comfortable and no effort was made to make me feel relaxed at either of them. It seemed likely that the posts were already filled and I was just there to make up the numbers, which was the case with many vacancies. I'm afraid to say that nepotism runs rife in the service.

There was even an assessment board at Woodhill, which was a forerunner to the assessment centres that have now been established for all promotions. This was an all-day event and it had been designed by one of our psychologists. I knew my performance in the assessment had been going well, but when it came to the last exercise, nearly eight hours after the start of proceedings, my mind just closed down. A governor grade who was part of the role-play team confided to me afterwards that until that last exercise I'd been assured of promotion, but now it was touch and go.

There were 12 of us undergoing the assessment and Woodhill needed six POs. I found out later from someone that had been working nights that he'd seen the results lying on the governor's desk, so when they were announced officially, he was surprised that I'd come seventh, as according to his sneak preview, he had seen I'd come third. Whether that was true or not, I will never really know, but I was left with little faith in the whole process of promotion at Woodhill after that.

Around the same time as I was preparing for my Grendon interview, my family and I were preparing for the wedding of one of my stepdaughters. She'd moved to Leicester, so the amount of help my wife could give her was limited and a certain tension had developed between the two of them. On several occasions, I'd sat in bed in between my step-daughter on one end of the telephone and my wife on the other, both crying and at the same time arguing. My other step-daughter had gone to Canada to be with her biological dad for a while. My wife was therefore under extreme pressure and the stress was beginning to boil over. Not the best environment in which to prepare for promotion in a very competitive field.

The morning of my interview dawned, on a lovely, warm, sunny July day. I set off to Grendon in good time and arrived a little early. The interview would take the form of a ten-minute presentation followed by the formal interview.

The deputy governor, who immediately made me feel relaxed, met me at the interview room door. I have to say that it was the best opening to an interview I can ever remember. He told me his name and asked whether I preferred to be called Anthony or Tony, and then informed me that as it was so warm I could remove my jacket so that I was more comfortable, and as a gesture, he promptly took off his jacket, too. This really put me at ease, but what about my presentation? I hadn't done anything like that since my days at the training school. Then I thought, wait a minute, I'm pretty good at winging it, so sod what I've practised and I'm just gonna wing it.

I was invited to sit down at a round coffee-type table and was offered a glass of water. I was then introduced to the two other interviewers: the Head of Residence, 'Del', and a chap from Liverpool, who had his hair tied back in a long ponytail and looked like the stereotypical social worker, with his corduroy trousers, brightly coloured socks, suede shoes, shirt unbuttoned at the cuffs, and a tank top. He was, in fact, one of the senior therapists and a very highly qualified medical doctor and he managed D wing. Then the interview began.

"Okay," said the deputy, "before you do your presentation I'd just like to ask you something. It says on your CV that you work well under pressure. Can you give us an example of this?"

"Yes," I replied. "My daughter is getting married this Saturday and she and her mum has fallen out. In fact, just the other night I was sitting in bed with my daughter bawling down the phone to me in one ear and my wife bawling into my other ear." I was now getting some strange looks. They were wondering where this was going. So I continued. "My wife is so upset that she is currently off work sick with it all, so to cheer her up, and as Grendon is near Bicester village retail park, I've dropped her off there for some retail therapy and - oh shit - she's got my credit card … Sorry, what was the question again? Oh yes, pressure." At this point, there were laughs all round.

I knew at this interview I was going to get a fair crack at the whip, unlike some, I'd attended where it was obvious they'd already made up their minds before even interviewing me. I'd been to one such promotion interview back at HMP The Mount when I'd been told by an old colleague that still worked there that an in-house candidate was already lined up for the job. Throughout the interview, the chairperson, who happened to be the deputy governor, just sat there picking his fingernails and looking out of the window. At one point I answered a question with complete gobbledegook and then stopped talking mid-sentence. The deputy governor suddenly looked up and said, "Is there anything wrong?"

So I looked straight at him and replied, "Actually yes, you've just spent all this interview picking your fingernails and staring out of the window, which seems a really good example of how much interest you have in me as a candidate. Quite frankly I don't want to work for you anyway, so I'm ending this farce of an interview here and now." And I got up and walked out.

Needless to say, I didn't get the job, although funnily enough, they marked my performance as "fully meets the standard but not selected". The in-house candidate did indeed get the job. Talk about nepotism.

Meanwhile, back at my Grendon interview, it was now time for my presentation.

I took a card out of my shirt pocket, held it up and said, "This is my work bible. It's the booklet we were all issued with and I always keep it on me whenever I'm at work. It's our aims, goals and visions booklet. But first I need to tell you a story ..."

I sat on the corner of a desk behind me and related the story of my first day as a new officer at Pentonville after my initial training. I told them about getting there early, going to the mess for a cuppa, 'Nutty Freeman' and 'Slop-out McVicar', reporting to D wing, how I was treated and how I felt about the way I'd been spoken to, the ringing cell bell, the officer calling me 'sonny', the prisoner telling me he wanted a shit and my reply, and then how I was suddenly included in the gang. I then explained how it made me feel and how I vowed then and there that I would always treat prisoners the way I would want to be treated if I were in their place.

"What relevance has your story to the visions, values and goals?" asked the senior therapist looking at me suspiciously.

I answered, "Well if everyone followed the guidelines under each of the headings of visions, values and goals, I wouldn't have been treated the way I was, and neither would any of the staff have treated the prisoners that way, and it just seems a good philosophy to follow. You know, respect."

The deputy then asked if I honestly did always have the booklet with me when on duty and, unblinking, I looked him directly in the eye and responded, “Always, and if you give me this job you can check every day to see if I do.”

I thought the rest of the interview went well after this. I answered all the questions and there were no awkward moments where the conversation faltered and stopped. And that was just it - it seemed more like a nice chat with some colleagues rather than an interview.

On my drive home, as was the norm, I started to go over the interview in my mind. Yes, it went well. They seemed to like me as a person. They didn’t ask any questions I couldn’t answer and it all seemed to flow. Yeah, I reckon I did well. But by the time I got to the third roundabout on my way back to Milton Keynes, self-doubt was starting to creep in. Did they seem to like me ’cause they’d already made up their minds that I wasn’t suitable? There was that one question I hesitated on; oh shit, fuck it, I didn’t really answer it did I? And the bloody stupid presentation! What made me say, “I want to tell you a story”? They probably thought I was Max bloody Bygraves! And that dep asking me about the bloody card - he knew I was bullshitting and don’t always have it in my top pocket. And that long-haired scouser - I could tell he thought I was a cockney spiv bloke and he didn’t like cockneys .... By the time I arrived home I’d convinced myself that I’d failed. Why do we always do that to ourselves? Meanwhile, back at Woodhill, I was unexpectedly temporarily promoted to principal officer due to a PO going off on long-term sick. The governor of the operations group had specifically requested that I was given the post, and when they offered it I took it.

Working mainly from the operations PO office, I suddenly found myself having to put my money where my mouth was. It was a steep learning curve. Now it was me that had to take responsibility for mistakes or find a member of staff to cover the jobs even when there was nobody available. When a senior officer came to me with a problem, I was the one that had to sort it out. Well, I’d wanted to be a manager, I thought, so I’d better start managing.

I started to get my enthusiasm back and enjoy work again as I readily took on the additional responsibilities. When you arrived at work as the duty PO, even before you'd had your first cup of tea, you were in at the deep end and required to think on your feet. You could be called on to deal with a prisoner who's barricaded himself in his cell or taken a hostage, or you might have a bed watch going out (a prisoner needing to go to an external hospital) and had to sort out the relevant discharge paperwork and find the staff to cover it. You couldn't just order staff to go unless it was an emergency and then you had to sort out reliefs for them, as they were entitled to go home at their designated finish time. You couldn't demand that a member of staff extended their shift, they had to volunteer. In that respect, it was a different world to my early days at Pentonville. As operations PO I learned that the buck really did stop with me and it was up to me to make the correct decisions and be able to justify each and every one of them. But I loved it!

Then, late one afternoon, my governor called me to his office and said, "Tony, I've received this letter about your interview at Grendon." Bloody hell, I'd almost forgotten all about it, I thought to myself, as he handed me the letter.

"Oh, thanks," I responded, "I'll read it later. It's probably to tell me I didn't get the job. I heard it was going to somebody in-house anyway, but thanks."

"No, I think you'd better read it here," said the governor.

"Oh, all right then, but I'm pretty sure I didn't get it," I replied, and I opened the letter. Bloody hell, I'd got the job!

The governor, with a big grin on his face, said, "Congratulations, Tony, you deserve it. I would've liked you to be a PO here with me, but well done."

"Thanks," I stammered, still absolutely amazed and disbelieving that I'd passed.

It was the first promotion interview I'd attended where I'd felt it was being played fair - and I'd got the job! Yippee! I couldn't wait to get home and tell my wife the good news. I was due to start on 1 December. What a bloody good early Christmas present this was!

I was now married and had a mortgage to pay, so the PO salary was much needed. Ultimately, I would try to become a governor grade, as I was looking to the future and the higher the grade the better the pension I would receive when the time came.

So my time at Woodhill was coming to an end. Having just read back through these last few chapters, it has just occurred to me that, despite being at Woodhill for five years, I've got very few memories of my time there. It's not that I didn't get involved in wind-ups and jokes, but aside from my work in the special unit, I can't really recall anything worth putting down on paper – weird as there were many incidents and happenings during my time there, but none have stuck in my mind!

Maybe that is the way it happens when you're an officer you have the camaraderie and join in with the laughs and wind-ups but as you go up the promotion ladder your move on and your peer groups cannot get involved in the same things you could as an officer. More responsibility and less time for fun, but that was my choice.

Chapter 37

Grendon & Springhill

I was now Principal Officer Levy and was arriving for my first day at HMP Grendon & Springhill. I didn't know then that I would remain at Grendon for over ten years and finish my time in the service at this unique establishment. It is a complex of two separate but inextricably linked prisons. Grendon is a category B prison, holding around 240 prisoners, and Springhill, situated across the other side of the car park, is an open category D establishment. The two prisons share the same governor, staff change from one establishment to the other, and on occasion, certain prisoners are transferred from Grendon to Springhill on a progressive move.

From the outside, Grendon looks like any other category B prison in the UK, but behind the doors Grendon is unique. It is the only closed prison in the country that operates solely as a therapeutic prison and it contains the largest prison community living in these conditions. Prisoners qualify for acceptance at Grendon on the grounds of having both personality and psychological disorders. Half of them are serving life sentences and many are sex offenders, and most have been involved in extremely violent crimes.

HMP Grendon opened in 1962 as an experimental psychiatric prison to provide treatment for prisoners with antisocial personality disorders under the direction of a medical superintendent. In line with the rest of the prison estate, Grendon is now run by a prison service governor, but it continues to operate a unique, therapeutic regime for high-security offenders.

Each of HMP Grendon's six wings operates as autonomous therapeutic communities. The prison accepts category B and C male prisoners aged 21 and over from prisons throughout England and Wales, who are serving sentences of a length that will allow a stay of at least 24 months at Grendon. Prisoners have to choose to come to

Grendon and they must have a genuine desire to change and to work towards that goal.

The Grendon regime is unique in that the therapeutic programme is the core work of the establishment. The programme is based on therapeutic community principles, whereby a dedicated multidisciplinary team of staff work together with prisoners in an atmosphere where attitudes and expressions that would not normally be tolerated in a prison are accepted and used to give feedback to prisoners. This therapeutic dialogue leads to prisoners' increased understanding of their usual behaviour. At Grendon, the aim is to help prisoners develop more positive relationships, to change how they relate to others and to reduce their risk of re-offending, and statistics show that Grendon does succeed in its endeavours.

A commitment to abstain from drug misuse while in therapy is an important prerequisite for prisoners who go to Grendon. Drugs provide a way to hide, a crutch to lean on and an escape from the therapeutic process, so anyone taking drugs is unlikely to be successful in therapy. For this reason, Grendon's drug strategy is proactive and aimed at both prisoners and visitors. The incidence of drugs entering the establishment was much lower than in conventional prisons, and during my time there if prisoners were taking opiate-based medication they were usually not allowed to come to Grendon. Much has been written about Grendon and its work and, strangely, it appears to be held in much higher regard in the rest of the world than in England.

Springhill's primary aim is to reintegrate prisoners gradually into society after serving long sentences in higher-security establishments. The 334 prisoners housed there can walk freely around the site and, if assessments show that they no longer pose a risk to the public then they can work outside the prison. No sex offenders go to Springhill. It is believed that the less controlled environment and, where possible, work placements in the local community can play a crucial part in aiding prisoners to make a safe adjustment from life in a closed institution to a life lived outside. I say, cobblers!

From my experience, as soon as the prison service has an overcrowding problem the powers-that-be look for accommodation vacancies anywhere they can find them. If there are vacancies in a Cat D prison, then cat C prisoners will simply be re-categorised so that they can be accommodated there.

In a particularly difficult overcrowding period, when Springhill took in quite a lot of re-categorised prisoners, I remember Springhill being christened 'Club Ibiza' or 'The 18-50s Club'. The prison has no fence or wall and is surrounded by farmland, and prisoners would leave the prison on an evening, walk to the nearest village pub or shop, purchase copious amounts of alcohol, take it back to the prison, hide it in the grounds and then go back for it after the camp had been locked down for the night. In the lock-down period, the prisoners were supposed to be in the accommodation huts and not allowed outside them, but with only two members of uniformed staff and one operational support grade on night duty, it wasn't difficult for the prisoners to sneak out and retrieve their contraband. Hence the nickname. The wrong category of prisoner arriving at Springhill was a common practice, but of course, this wasn't made known to the public at large.

I can recall a particular occasion when a prisoner came to us as a cat D from another establishment. He arrived in a prison escort vehicle, whereas generally, they were allowed to make their own way there. It turned out that he'd been sentenced only two days earlier for a fairly minor crime. As such, cat D may have seemed suitable, but his record showed that this was not the first time he'd been in trouble with the law and, in fact, only 12 months previously he'd absconded from a similar establishment. (If a prisoner in an open prison walks out and doesn't return this is deemed an abscond and not an escape, as there are no physical barriers such as cells, fences or walls.) Unfortunately for us, we only found all this out after he'd absconded, as his prison record didn't arrive with him. He'd only been at Springhill for less than 24 hours and, as you can see, open conditions weren't suitable in his case. The cynic in me has to say that in terms of prison performance ratings an abscond doesn't count against the establishment, but an escape could get the governor sacked.

The history of Springhill is equally as fascinating as the Ville. Grendon Hall was built in 1880 and was used for various different functions. In 1939 the then government bought the house to train SOE agents who were to be dropped into Nazi-occupied Europe. Adorning the walls of the main boardroom are many pictures of British World War Two leaders meeting with newly trained spies who were about to leave the country on secret missions. Many of these SOE agents were captured and executed by the Nazis and some of them subsequently became the subject of Hollywood films. Refugees were given huts in the ground to live in, and the house was turned into a school for the children. Then, some years later, it became a firefighter training centre before finally being converted into Springhill Prison in 1953.

Most of my remaining service was carried out in Grendon, although I did have a brief spell working in Springhill.

My new appointment at Grendon was the butt of many a joke by my former colleagues at HMP Woodhill, with comments such as: "Grendon?! Blimey, Tony, you're a bit young to be put out to grass." "I thought the only officers who went there were due to retire or die." "Well, that's the end of your prison service. You'll have to forget all you've learned and put on some fluffy pink slippers to work there." But how wrong could they be?

Chapter 38

Grendon - My First Impressions

My initial reaction to Grendon was one of total horror. I'd previously worked at HMP Woodhill, which housed some of the most dangerous and violent prisoners in the system just like Grendon, but this place was at the other end of the spectrum completely.

There was a small population of 240 prisoners, all category B men, 60 per cent of whom were serving life sentences. Over half of the prisoners were sex offenders and nearly all their offences had involved severe violence. Yet here they were treated completely differently to the mainstream prisons.

For a start, Grendon was a therapeutic community prison, each wing forming a community in its own right. There were five main wings and an induction wing and each wing had a lead therapist, psychologist, probation officer, volunteer facilitators, and officers who also acted as facilitators during therapy sessions. The officers were mostly untrained, and how they carried out this specialist work and managed to keep sane was really beyond my comprehension. I have great admiration for all members of Grendon staff who got involved in the therapy, some of who did so to the detriment of their own health.

Each wing housed about 40 prisoners and these were divided into two or three therapy groups. Every week prisoners underwent a couple of morning therapy sessions and took part in two full community meetings. At the meetings, all the wing prisoners would congregate in the main room and discuss the running of the wing, and individuals guilty of antisocial behaviour would be taken to task.

Much has been written about Grendon's success in terms of reducing re-offending, but I feel that its success, in the end, may lead to its downfall. An increasing number of other prisons are now developing their own therapeutic wings to carry out the work that Grendon has pioneered and, if successful, politicians may review the costs involved in Grendon's operations and decide it's just too expensive to run. The current governor of Grendon is fighting a constant battle to keep politicians on his side, but ultimately the costs could outweigh all other arguments. That would be a real shame, as the work carried out at Grendon and the staff there are amongst the best, I've ever encountered in all my 25 years of service. That doesn't mean to say that I liked everything about the place - believe me, I honestly didn't, but my feelings on that score will remain private and are not for print.

As an aside, reading back through everything I've written over the last few chapters I realise just how much I changed throughout my years in the service. My attitude in more recent times has become much more about the big picture and running an effective prison system from a management perspective. I just hope that this change hasn't made me boring. No, I'm sure it hasn't; it's just the fact that I took on more responsibilities.

Anyway, I arrived at Grendon as the new PO of C wing and D wing, lovingly christened by staff as Beirut and Little Beirut respectively. Great! Well, I wanted a challenge, didn't I?

I was located, together with two colleagues, in the residential manager's office, which was located exactly opposite of the governor's office. In a strange quirk of fate, several years later this office was converted into the audit manager's office and I was based there for several years when I became the audit manager. I often wonder if it was a subtle way for governors to keep an eye on me - or was I just becoming paranoid?

My governor, 'Del', was an ex-PEI and a very fit man, and he loved to go to the gym each day and play sports with the staff during lunch breaks. He was honest and fair with me, allowing me to do my job and make my own mistakes and then pointing out how I could've handled certain situations differently. I had great respect for this man from day one.

My other office companion, 'Mr X', was the PO for A and B wings and was a character in his own right. Previously he'd worked in a London jail and he'd been a PO for a number of years. I worked with him for several years, until his retirement, and, although he really did exasperate and frustrate me from time to time, we had some great laughs along the way. Mr X never quite grasped the meaning of political correctness, but despite this many of the staff seemed to like him, and respect him and especially those that became the butt of many of his jokes, and most of us did.

Until recently the wing therapists were also the wing managers, and they ran the whole show. They were answerable directly to the governor for all that went on within the wing, including the management of the uniformed staff. My arrival signalled a change to this, however. The therapist would still be in charge of all therapy matters, but it became the PO's duty to oversee all matters pertaining to the prison service. This initially led to a certain amount of conflict between the lead therapist and myself, but gradually we both adapted to our new roles.

I had great respect for the lead therapist and his ability to perform such a difficult job at the same time as comprehending the prison officer role. He fully understood that in order for the therapy to work effectively there had to be a basic feeling of security for both staff and prisoners alike and therefore appreciated that security and therapy had to work hand in hand and in compliance with the requirements of the prison service.

The other part of my duties was to act as the orderly officer. I was detailed to this job, on average, two days per week and one complete weekend every three weeks. The duty involved carrying a radio with a unique call sign and being on-call throughout the whole of my shift, which usually started at 7.15 a.m. and finished at 9 p.m. The orderly officer was responsible for the day-to-day running of the prison, which meant ensuring that the correct number of staff were present on each wing before the prison could be unlocked; enough staff were available to run the individual therapy groups; that there was the cover for staff at lunchtimes and teatimes; that adequate staff were in place to run the prison during the evening and night lock-up periods; and that enough staff were available for emergencies, such as escorting a prisoner to an outside hospital and covering the escorting officer's shift duties within the prison. This role could be very stressful and busy, and if it had been a particularly hectic day I would go home absolutely knackered and wonder why I'd ever taken that bloody job.

During my 11 years at Grendon, I had to deal with many incidents as the orderly officer, such as attempted suicides, heart attacks, assaults, a hostage situation and even an escape, but my feeling was that this was what I was paid to do - manage, and do it efficiently whatever the difficult situation. I like to think that I dealt with all these difficult and challenging situations with both good professionalism and compassion, instilling confidence in the staff working alongside me.

I won't bore you with the details of such incidents, they could fill a whole new book and maybe one day I will write about them. As stated at the start of this book, I intend to share with the reader the more personal of my experiences I've had in the hope that they will entertain, rather than describe incidents that have probably been portrayed more dramatically and in greater detail by more accomplished writers. Not only that, it would be boring to hear how great I was in dealing with this or that incident and this book isn't just an excuse for going on a personal ego trip. At the end of the day, dealing with these incidents is what I was paid to do and I know how I performed, so that's all that needs to be said. I know many of my peers had a different approach but that says more about their needs and personality.

I have to say that during my years at Grendon I had some great times, but the work was stressful and it did take its toll on me and shape my feelings towards the prison service. It was during this time that I began to understand fully just how much politics are involved in running a modern penal establishment here in the UK.

Chapter 39

Punting on the River

"Okay," said Governor Del, "let's have a team-building day out somewhere This department has grown and there are more of us now so it's a good time for a team-building day out ."

"Yeah," agreed Mr X.

The residential team had now grown to four POs, plus one new PO who was on the accelerated promotion scheme, which would allow her to become a governor grade, plus an OSG (operational support grade). This OSG had made such a niche for himself that it seemed that the prison couldn't run without him. He seemed to be able to sort out every little thing, from needing a new office telephone to getting a new piece of computer equipment. The man had become quite indispensable to the prison and, apart from being a mad keen Manchester United supporter, he was a wonderful person to have to work with you - that was unless Man United lost, in which event he would get drunk and take a day off work. Thankfully for the prison, his team didn't lose very often; otherwise, I think the place would've come to a standstill.

Despite our work commitments, it was agreed that we should take an afternoon off work, have a team-building session and then all go out for a drink and a meal in the early evening.

Del asked us all what we thought we should do and where we should go. I won't bore you with all of the suggestions, but suffice to say it wasn't considered that doing a pub crawl around Soho in London fitted in with our responsible positions in society, and the idea of getting drunk and going to watch a live football match followed by a meal didn't get much support either.

It was decided by a majority vote that we would head for Oxford and have a go at punting down the River Cherwell, followed by a meal in the city centre. As I lived in Milton Keynes this meant quite a long drive for me and no alcohol, but the others all lived fairly locally and would be free of driving to enable them to enjoy themselves. I collected our new PO and Mr X en route and was pleasantly surprised by the city of Oxford. I wasn't sure that punting would be my scene but reckoned I could just sit in the boat and watch somebody else doing the hard work. Del assured me that punting was easy and anyone could do it, so I shouldn't worry.

As it turned out, our OSG couldn't make it due to other commitments, so it was just the six of us. We met up in a pub car park somewhere near the Cherwell. One of my fellow POs, 'Paul', was on his midweek rest day and had rather obviously taken advantage of not having to drive, as he'd already had a good drink. PO 'Eve' had been working with us for some time and had taken over the running of A and B wings, and I got on very well with her despite her allegiance to Arsenal FC.

We arrived at the punt station, or whatever it was called, and hired two boats. Del, Mr X and our new accelerated promotion PO teamed up in one boat, and Eve, Paul and I in the other. Paul explained that there was no way he could do the punting due to a bad knee, and Eve said she was scared of water and would be terrified to do anything but sit in the boat. This left a reluctant me to do the punting.

What a bloody silly thing to have to do, I thought, standing on the back of the boat on what I can only describe as a piece of decking that stretched the short width of the boat and holding a bloody great long pole. There were so many ways to end up overboard that it could've easily turned into a TV comedy sketch. It was a fine balancing act, trying to stand firm while dropping the end of the pole to the river bottom and pushing. If you overbalanced due to the movement of the boat or the weight of the pole, then you'd end up in the water; if the pole got stuck in the mud or you didn't pull it out quickly enough, you'd end up dangling from it before, yes, falling in the water; and if it wasn't you falling in the water, it was the pole!

However, I found that once I'd got into a rhythm the punting lark wasn't too bad. But Del, the super-fit ex-PEI, was faring even better and was fast disappearing into the distance. Paul started shouting, "Come on, Tony, faster, faster! We can't let him beat us." Beat us? For Christ's sake, I was only just managing to stay on the bloody thing and keep us moving, let alone get involved in a race! I don't know whether it was the effects of the alcohol or whether he was just trying to help me, but Paul then picked up a paddle, scrambled to the front of the boat and started doing a Hiawatha white-water rafting impression!

Rather than help, Paul was now making the boat rock badly, as he paddled first on one side and then on the other. The sorry outcome was inevitable. Paul rocked one way, I punted the other, and there was only one direction for me to go: yep, downwards, straight into the water! Bloody hell, it was cold, not to mention the fact that I was drowning, and all because of that drunken git! So much for a team-building exercise! And whose bloody idea was this punting lark anyway? Amid these thoughts, I hit the river bottom and at that point realised that the water was only about three feet deep. I stood up, completely soaked to the skin. Of course, everyone else thought this was hilarious, especially the part where all they could see was my hand raised above the water, holding my glasses and my wallet.

We limped back to our start point and I was soaked to the skin. Del told me he had some spare clothes in the car, so we walked back to the car park, with me leaving a trail of drips and wet footprints along the pavement as we went.

Once at the car I realised that Del, being 6ft 2in, wasn't going to have clothes to fit someone of 5ft 7in. He offered me a pair of oversized shoes and a pair of cream-coloured jeans, which, although two sizes too big, I reckoned I could hitch up with my brown belt and get away with it without looking too stupid. I grabbed a sweatshirt from the boot of my car to complete the outfit, and Mr X handed me a towel. Del and I then headed for the toilets so that I could get dry and complete my transformation. While I was trouserless and wiping myself and Del was stood holding my wet clothes, a man came into the toilets. He looked first at me, then at Del, and promptly bolted for the door and disappeared. I'm not sure what he thought was going on, but we never got the chance to explain.

Meanwhile, Mr X had then decided to change into his evening gear. However, brazen as he was, he was standing at the back of his car with the tailgate up, completely naked, with Eve stood there gobsmacked and passers-by staring at both of them incredulously. Somebody actually walked up to them to ask for directions before realising that Mr X wasn't wearing any trousers and, not surprisingly, also beat a hasty retreat. What a bunch we must've seemed!

We left the car park as soon as we could, by which time it had started to rain, and headed for a pub, where I laid out the contents of my wallet on a table to help dry them out. I was so pissed off with everything that all I wanted to do was go home, but as I was giving some of the others a lift back I had no choice but to stay.

Once back at the prison the story of our adventure went around the place like wildfire, each of us telling our own version of events, and it was the topic of conversation for several weeks. One of the officers drew a great cartoon depicting me falling into the river and it was displayed on the wall of our office. It moved offices with me and, in fact, I still have it today. The more I looked at it, the more I thought that maybe it wasn't quite as bad as I remember. After all, we did have some good laughs and a lovely meal in an Oxford restaurant later in the evening, as well as a very pleasant walk back to the car park when we were ready to make our way home. Thankfully, by then I'd dried out!

Unfortunately, Del's trousers had a slightly less fortunate fate, as the belt I'd used to hold up the jeans left an indelible brown stain on the waistband and belt loops. Oh well, call it a memory to treasure!

Suffice to say, I never again agreed to take part in another team-building exercise and I've never been punting since or ever intend to do so again.

Chapter 40

The Most Significant Change

I'd been at Grendon for several years and, as is always the case in the prison service, changes were on the horizon. The governor retired and just after that, a new deputy governor joined us. I'd already seen Del move on and deservedly become the governor of his own establishment nearer his northern roots and the residential office had been restructured several times.

It's one of the quirks of the prison service that changes occur all the time, and yet very frequently staff are told that they're inflexible. It's not that we're resistant to change, as we're well used to it, but we don't like the frequency at which it happens. However, those in the ivory towers of Head Office and the newly forming Ministry of Justice saw fit to spew out directives continually for one change or another. For Christ sake, why can't we just stop, take stock of where we are and give everyone a chance to adapt to the most recent changes before introducing new ones? They call it strategic planning, and all establishments must have a three-year plan, or was it a five-year plan? No, wait a minute, the last directive said that we had to have a ten-year plan. No, wrong again, that's also been revised, as somebody at HQ thought it would be better if we all had a three-year plan to run in conjunction with the prison service's five-year plan, or was it a ten-year plan to run alongside .... Oh, who gives a shit anyway? Things changed so quickly that the bloody ink never got the chance to dry.

These constant policy changes were beginning to make me realise that attaining the rank of PO was as far as I wished to go in terms of promotion. I was finding it hard enough to keep up to date with all the management changes within the establishment, let alone come to terms with all the national policy and strategic changes that were taking place.

Maybe, just maybe, this was my most significant change. I'd always thought that once I stepped onto the promotion ladder I would want to continue up it as far as I could go. After all, twice over a previous couple of years, I'd acted up to governor grade as temporary Head of Residence while Del was deployed to the area office for some reason or another. I'd enjoyed the experience - well, apart from suddenly realising, while sitting in the garden sipping a cool glass of Muscadet Sur Lie in the late evening sunshine after arriving home from work, that I was the duty governor and could be called back to work at any moment if required.

No, promotion isn't for me, I thought. It's gonna impinge on my private life too much. I liked my job, but it wasn't a vocation, it was just a means to an end. I wanted to finish work at the designated time, walk out of the gates and get back to the most important part of my life - my wife and family. I didn't want to have to worry about what might or might not happen in the prison and whether I might or might not have to go back to there. Nah, forget promotion. I just wanted to do my hours and get home.

The new governor arrived and he was a breath of fresh air. He was one of the most dedicated men I've ever had the privilege of working for, and he seemed to be interested in every member of staff as an individual. He got to know us all and earned our respect very quickly. However, this dedication came at a personal price for him. He took on board more than he could handle and cared too much, and as a result, his health suffered. Unfortunately, this man only lasted a very short time at Grendon and we were all sad to see him go, especially on health grounds. Had he received better support, I'm sure this man would have gone on to become one the best governors Grendon had ever had.

By the time a new governor had been appointed, the establishment had gone through several management changes. The new deputy governor was a whizz-kid and the youngest ever deputy in the service. It was difficult enough just coming to an establishment like Grendon without also being asked to take on the role of governor until a new one was appointed, so understandably he wished to surround himself with familiar faces for support. Consequently, many new staff of all grades arrived at Grendon. With the influx of new managers and staff, however, the existing Grendon managers suddenly found themselves down the pecking order, including me. I wasn't too bothered about it, as I'd already made my decision not to seek any further promotions, but a lot of the other staff were upset by it. By now non of the governors who had been there when I first started were left all had moved on or retired which meant that the complete management team except for the senior therapist who by then was also going through a lot of personal changes.

With this staff shake-up came a change in the way Grendon was run. Previously Grendon had seemed to be a 'bolt-on' to the prison service, with a greater emphasis on therapy and the therapeutic communities than on security. However, due to an escape by three prisoners, who managed to get through a wire fence in an area that was known to be below the required standard of a category B prison, the new managers decided that Grendon needed to be brought in line with the rest of the prison estate and security seemed to take higher priority than the therapy.

There is a very fine line in a therapeutic community between, on the one hand, ensuring a safe environment in which the therapy can be carried out effectively and, on the other, making the place so security-focused that this impacts on the prisoners' ability to engage in the therapeutic process.

And many, including the professional therapists and psychologist, felt that the balance had tipped too far in the security direction. As a result, it became obvious to both prisoners and staff that there was a conflict at the top of the management structure, which created an unpleasant atmosphere in which to work and it had a negative effect on morale.

The eventual arrival of the new governor just compounded the unease. Changes were made and several of my colleagues, who'd once been my subordinates were promoted above me. I didn't mind, as I was still the PO of my two wings and had contact with my senior officers, officers and prisoners, so as long as I was left alone I would continue to enjoy my job.

Then disaster struck.

The new deputy came into the Residential office, called me into the residential governor's office and said to me, "Right then. 'Eric', who was recently promoted to governor grade and sent over to Springhill, has been recalled over here to do a very important job for the new governor, so you're going to Springhill. How do you feel about that?"

I replied, "What does it matter how I feel about it? It's gonna happen anyway, so why bother to ask me?"

"Yep, you're right, but I had to consult with you," he responded.

I was livid and retorted, "You call this consulting with me? So much for career interviews!"

"Okay," he said. "You're going over there on Monday, so pack your things up."

Bloody hell, I thought, the last person I saw get moved from department to another department, this quick was a chap back at Pentonville who got caught shagging the governor's daughter and was moved within 48 hours of the governor finding out. It used to be a running joke that if you wanted a transfer you should go and shag the governor's daughter. I suppose I should count myself lucky seeing as I'm getting 72 hours notice to move from one prison to another.

So I moved from 'the dark side', as Grendon was known, to 'the light side', which, in addition to Camp Ibiza, was the term used for Springhill. I received no training for or explanation of my new role and, more importantly, I never understood it. Not surprisingly, I never settled there. Also, I had to go into hospital for a knee operation and was off work for some considerable time. I can honestly say that working in Springhill was probably one of my worst experiences in the service. Other staff loved it over there, however, so I suppose it's a case of horses for courses.

Then I was brought back to Grendon, again receiving no notice for or explanation of why the move. All I knew was that I would be taking over this new department called Audits. It sounded like my worst nightmare: bloody auditing, sitting behind a desk doing paperwork all day, and not working with other staff or prisoners.

I asked for a career interview with the governor and was granted a meeting with him in his office. It was coincidentally enough the day before the governor was due to go off on his annual holiday. When I entered his office I should've realised that this meeting wasn't going to be quite as it seemed, as I was confronted by a third person sitting at the desk - the deputy governor. In hindsight, I should've refused the interview, stating that this was supposed to be a one-to-one career interview with just the governor, rather than face a two-on-one scenario, but I didn't.

"We've noticed that you seem to be very unhappy here now, Tony," said the governor.

Too bloody right I was unhappy! Hardly surprising considering my two job changes without any consultation or notice and ending up with the crappiest job that a 'people' person such as myself could possibly be given!

I answered, "That's correct. I feel I'm being moved around and given jobs that nobody else wants rather than ones that will enhance my managerial skills."

"Well," said the deputy, "if you're not happy here at Grendon we can always arrange a transfer to another prison for you."

I'm being threatened, I thought. If you're not happy we won't bother to find out why we'll just get rid of you. The cheek of it! Nice, they care so much about their staff, isn't it? What a fine example of good management not! That was it there and then for me, and my heart went out of the job.

I'd never been made to feel that way throughout the whole of my career. Well, fuck them, I decided. From now on I'll do my job to the best of my ability, but when my shift ends so will my interest in the place until I'm back on duty. I responded, "We can't always be happy all the time, especially if we're given a job that we know other people are more qualified to do. So, no,

I'm not happy."

"We can't have unhappy staff here," said the deputy.

"Well, I can't walk around with a smile on my face just because you don't want to see the unhappy staff. Why don't you find out why staff are unhappy and try to help them?" I retorted.

Again, the deputy responded with, "If you're not happy we can move you to another establishment."

Angered by yet another transfer threat, I looked straight at the governor and stated, "I feel I've now been threatened twice, just because I dared to voice my own opinion. I am not and never will be a yes man, and if you don't like that then you'd better do what you think fit. But I'm not requesting a transfer, so please don't threaten me." After a short pause for breath, I continued, "Governor, thank you for your time, especially since you're going on your holidays. But I feel this interview has been totally unfair and I will leave your office now, thank you." And I got up and walked out.

I'd been threatened twice with a transfer because I was unhappy about how I'd been treated. What a terrible way to manage people, I thought. If this was a reflection of what was required of managers in the modern prison service, then it obviously wasn't for me anymore.

From that day onwards I lost my respect for management and my heart for my job, even though I took pride in doing it well and in treating both staff and prisoners with respect. It was obvious that, unless you were in their team, you were an outsider to be tolerated so long as you performed your allocated duties, but you would never be let into their inner circle. We'd got rid of the old ways of the Masons and replaced them with pure nepotism.

Maybe, then, the most significant change was in me. I no longer wanted to be in the prison service; I'd had enough. I was worn out, policy fatigued and disillusioned. I realised that my time was up and now I just wanted to get out. This wasn't the job I'd joined the service for, and nor was it a service that honestly cared about its staff or their careers. Oh, we all said the right things to the right people, but in our hearts of hearts - from the governor down to the lowest grade of staff - nobody cared about the prisoners, the staff or their jobs; or, even sadder, if they did care it had been completely suppressed. The main concern was ticking the right boxes and saying the right things in public. There was no longer any substance to what we were doing, and no one fully seemed to care what we were achieving or if we were reaching our goals.

It was said by some managers that the staff didn't care, but as I explained to some of my peers, "Morale is like shit - it rolls downhill." Lack of motivation and commitment stemmed from the top management. It was all about league tables - whoops, sorry, I mean 'performance indicators'. As long as we were in the top 25 on the performance table, no one honestly cared what we were seriously achieving. As long as our political masters were happy, then so were we.

I realised that I wasn't a valued member of the prison service, but just another number that could be dispensed with if need be, according to political and financial pressures and irrespective of how good or bad I performed as an individual. Care for our staff? That's the biggest laugh of all.

So the most significant change was my own realisation that I no longer wanted to be part of it all.

Chapter 41

Disillusionment

So there I was, sitting at my nice new desk, doing a job that I'd come to hate and that bore no resemblance to the job I'd started 25 years ago. I couldn't see the purpose anymore. I was no longer hands-on with the prisoners or with my staff and peers. All the interpersonal skills I'd learned and all the experience I'd gained over 25 years were now not needed. I was a dinosaur! I was surplus to the requirements of the modern prison service, out of touch with reality and had no further ambition to move up the promotion ladder.

I was regarded as something of a renegade, a rebel, as I didn't follow blindly the party line. I had my own opinions and voiced them, much to the annoyance of higher management. Yet I still had the respect of the staff and prisoners alike. If I had to ask a member of staff to change their shift or work extra, most would do it, not because they'd been ordered to do so, but because I'd asked them respectfully and they in return held me in respect. This applied to the prisoners, too. If I told a prisoner that I would find something out and get back to him, he knew that I'd do exactly that and in turn, he would accept the information I provided.

However, the modern prison service doesn't want this from their staff. Blind obedience is demanded. You mustn't tell either prisoners or staff the absolute truth unless required. You must be politically correct at all times and ensure that your staff follow suit. You should avoid conflict, keep the peace and never give a straight answer. You mustn't be a character or an individualist.

On one particular annual staff report the reporting officer a governor grade that used to be one of my peers wrote that 'Tony's problem was that he cared to much' well if that was a problem then I'm glad I cared too much because it meant I was a professional and not a yes man for the sake of being a yes man. He saw that as a weakness yet I saw it as my strength.

The modern service requires its staff to display total professionalism, as it must prove that it is a professional organisation that has no signs of institutional racism, prejudice or political incorrectness within its structure. Staff must know the rules and apply them at all times, ensuring that the prisoners under their care are given every courtesy expected and everything to which they are entitled (and that applies to staff to a lesser degree). The prison service will act against anybody within the organisation that doesn't follow the laid-down procedures.

Yet when the chips are down and the prisoners refuse to comply with the rules and become disruptive, where do the authorities turn? Why to the old dinosaurs of course; the ones that know how to talk to prisoners and can use their experience to calm down potentially dangerous situations and keep their staff cool, and if that means setting aside political correctness for a moment in order to resolve the crisis, then so be it.

But now I was the audit manager and felt like a square peg in a round hole and the governor and deputy knew I would hate it. What sort of management threatens staff with the boot if they're not happy? Is that the way to motivate staff and deal with their worries? I'd do my new job to the best of my ability and try to make the audit department the best in the prison service, but if management expected any respect after treating me like that, they could stuff it! My father always taught me that you had to earn respect. It can't be bought with threats.

So fuck them, I decided. I'd do a bloody good job and earn the right to be an individual, to speak my mind and to have my own opinions and views. I would never toe the party line if I felt it was wrong. But my heart had gone out of it and it would be just a job now until I retired. I'd make them regret giving me this job, not because I'd be rubbish at it (although I suspect that might have been behind someone's motive for putting me in that position), but because I'd do it so well that they wouldn't be able to criticise me for criticising them when I thought it was deserved.

Nepotism runs rife in the prison service, although the service takes great pains to prove publicly that this is not the case. Everyone within the service knows it goes on. If you socialise with the right crowd, crawl to the right people, always agree with them and toe the line, then you stand a good chance of being promoted. But if you stand up for yourself as an individual and have your own mind and views, then you're out on a limb big-time. Your peers do not want to be associated with you as you are a renegade, but the important thing for me was that I was being honest to my principles and I could look at myself in the mirror and know I had always been honest to my staff and the prisoner population and that was enough for me. I did not join the job to be liked by everybody but having the respect from my staff and the prisoners was the most important thing.

There were so many things changing in the job; some I didn't like, but others I could see would be changes for the better. I could accept that in life nothing was forever. But this was the final nail in the coffin for me.....disillusionment!

My job was now to ensure that the establishment was complying with all the laid-down procedures, completing all the paperwork correctly, ticking all the boxes, and basically ensuring that the establishment could prove that we were doing what we claimed we were doing. So I had to identify the areas where this wasn't the case and make sure that they were put right. Why? What was the purpose?

Well, for a start, if I were good at my new job then the governor would keep his, as his establishment would come high up in the internal league table you know that league table that officially doesn't exist.

The really daft thing, however, was that the audit job was the 'whim of the day'. At the next budget review, it could get the chop and all that hard work and effort would be wasted. Someone could simply look at the audits and say, "We're expending too much time and money here. There's a much cheaper option …".

And that would be it. Audits would no longer be important and resources wouldn't be allocated to carrying them out. Governors wouldn't need to incorporate them in the running of their establishment, and I would've wasted five years of effort for nothing.

That's what the service has become. Today's priorities are tomorrow's budget savings.

Complete disillusionment.

Chapter 42

My Decision to Take Early Retirement

My decision had almost certainly been made for me. As I explained in the previous chapter, disillusionment had set in and I had no ambition to go for promotion. I had acted up to governor grade on several occasions, but I'd found that it intruded into my home life, which was something I wasn't prepared to allow.

My life with my family was sacrosanct. And as a governor grade, I would always be on call in the case of an emergency, day or night. This wasn't what I wanted. Once my shift was over, I just wanted to go home, forget about work and enjoy my time with the most important part of my life - my family.

There were strong rumours that my present rank was to be scrapped and that pay could be frozen until the lower level of a senior officer caught up with you, at which point you would revert to that lower rank. This would affect my pension and was a no-brainer as far as I was concerned. Besides, it would also mean that I'd wasted 11 years being a PO.

My only other alternative would be to jump through hoops to gain promotion to governor grade. Great, just what I didn't want. Many of the serving POs thought that, because of this change to the ranking system, there would be an easy way into the governor grade rank. What were they thinking? Bloody hell, the governors weren't prepared to let POs into their little club that easily! The usual process for promotion to that rank would have to be completed and there would be no free ride for POs to upgrade, that's for sure.

And, even if a PO did go for promotion, what the hell was the prison service going to do with all these new governor grades when they already had more in that rank than positions available? Once again, really good joined-up thinking from my peers at the Ministry of Justice.

The more I looked into it, the more I concluded that there was no future for someone like me in the modern prison service. They didn't want the old-style, pre-fresh-start man managers; they only wanted yes men, who wouldn't air opinions different to their own and who would treat the staff with disdain while giving the impression to those outside that they sincerely cared. In other words, they only really wanted those that could talk the talk and it was irrelevant whether they could physically walk the walk.

I had been to several seminars in my role as an audit manager, and one of the benefits of attending them were that also present were governors and other senior grades. and they were happy to speak quite openly about what they envisaged would happen to the service in the future. During breaks, this always seemed to be the topic of conversation, and it seemed that the removal of the PO rank would be an inevitable consequence of the future modernisation of the service. One Head Office representative even went so far as to say that, once the new ranking plans had been made official, the existing POs would be given two years to attain the higher rank, otherwise they would be downgraded automatically to SO. If that were so, then my decision had been made for me.

I also made frequent contact with other pre-fresh-start POs and governor grades and they all seemed to have similar thoughts about getting out of the service or they wished they were in a position where they could. They all felt that, over the next few years, our final salary pensions would come under increasing attack. 'Bloody hell, let's just take the money and run' seemed to be the overall view.

I considered the option of leaving, taking my lump sum and pension with me and joining some other establishment as an OSG (operational support grade). Although the salary would be lower, with my pension I would still be on the same money as my current position, but I wouldn't have any of the associated hassle or responsibilities. What a bloody good idea, I thought.

My wife and I had already discussed the idea of retirement and a move to warmer climes. I couldn't foresee spending my retirement in England, as we both loved the sun. What would we do all day in England, given the unreliable weather? We could move to the coast, but even then it could be pouring with rain or dull and cold. God forbid I ever took up indoor bowls, or spent every day in a shopping centre just to keep warm and dry, or joined old codgers at the bingo. No way. Yes, a move to the sun was what we both wanted.

So the possibility of early retirement was on the cards, but when? That was easy. My contract stated that once I'd reached the age of 55 I could take early retirement and draw my final salary pension, provided I'd completed at least 20 years in the service. Brilliant! I'd planned for a long retirement, so I'd get my money's worth out of the service and go early. I could even take an increased lump sum.

So our decision was made. I would retire at the age of 57 and we'd go and bloody enjoy ourselves while we were still fit and able. If it should all go wrong, well, we were both still young enough to be able to go back to work. It was a risk, but we felt it was one worth taking all in all.

It worked out that on 4 July 2008 I would complete exactly 25 years in the service. I planned to retire officially on 14 August 2008, but I could take any leave and TOIL (time off in lieu) hours due to me and bring that date forward. I then meticulously worked around that retirement date, two years hence, gaining TOIL hours here and there. When I needed to work additional hours for an audit I did so, not for the love of the job but because the extra hours would bring my retirement date forward.

Initially, I decided that I wouldn't inform anyone of my retirement plans and at the appointed time would simply hand in my notice and walk, as the time owed to me would cover the notice period I had to give. However, I realised that such action would only serve to confirm to some managers that I was indeed a stroppy, selfish person rather than a dedicated and conscientious member of staff. I couldn't let that happen. I was determined to leave with my head held high, as someone that had given 25 years of professional service, despite my cynicism regarding the modern approach to management and staff. No, I would give the proper six months' notice of my intentions.

After this rethink, I duly handed in my notice at the appropriate time. I never expected to be talked out of my decision, and nobody tried. In fact, I think some of the governors were relieved to see me going early. They certainly wouldn't want a renegade joining their ranks, that's for sure. I was called up to the governor's office for the formal resignation interview and we went through the motions. I could tell his attitude wasn't sincere. I expected people on every level to be honest with me at all times. Very naïve, I know, but that's me.

I continued to work to the best of my ability, so much so that my audit department became recognised as one of the best departments in the whole prison system, which comprised 146 establishments. My prison attained a top ten placement in the national league table. Not bad for a cynical, bitter and twisted bastard like me to achieve.

I'm sure that, a few years down the line, audits will become yesterday's big idea and today's unsustainable and unjustifiable cost, due to the changing economic and political situation. Budgets have to be managed, cuts have to be made, and audits will be gone and forgotten.

I can just hear someone at that point saying, "What was the name of that stroppy geezer? You know, that little jumped-up PO who thought his department was really important? Bloody hell, it wasn't as if it was security or anything, was it? Can anyone remember him? Oh, who cares anyway. We've got more important things to consider, like how we can save another £50,000 ..."

And I'll look back at those five years spent in a job I hated but did well in and wonder - for what? My pride that's what. I was going to walk away from a job I had loved with my head still held high and with pride at what I had achieved during my time. Oh well, that's life I suppose.

Chapter 43

My Farewell Piss-up

As farewell drinks go, this was one of the best I can ever remember, although by the end of it my memory had become a little hazy. So thanks to my wife for reminding me of what subsequently happened and how I felt when she finally drove me home from the pub.

One of my colleagues, 'Ched', came up to me and asked, "So are you going to have a piss-up for your leaving do?"

"Nah," I replied, "I won't be able to find a telephone box small enough for all my friends to fit in."

"Seriously," he continued, "both prisoners and staff have a lot of respect for you and there's a lot of the staff that would like the opportunity to say goodbye."

I responded, "That's a load of cobblers and you know it. They'll hold the usual farewell in the boardroom, get the catering managers to do the usual cheapo buffet and then order all the managers to attend even though most won't want to, especially seeing as it's for me. Then you'll get the staff and the officers only attending 'cause of the free grub. I'll get the usual cheap Bicester Crystal that's been in the governor's safe for the last 20 years 'cause they bought it as a job lot and never knew what to do with it. The governor will ask somebody that has known me for the last 11 years to give him some background information for his farewell speech and it'll be full of the usual crap about what a great bloke I am and funny little anecdotes that are supposed to embarrass me. Then it'll be all over and by Monday I'll be erased from everyone's memory or remembered as 'that grumpy old PO who was never happy and made loads of mistakes while he was here'. And the members of staff that genuinely want to say goodbye won't be able to 'cause there's no cover on the wings for them to get their lunch breaks. No thanks, mate. On my last day, I'm just gonna walk around, say goodbye and fuck off

Ched remarked, "You're a cynical bastard, even at the end."

"Yup," I replied, "but I'm still right even at the end, so no farewell and definitely no surprise farewell in the boardroom, 'cause if there is I won't be turning up, and you'll all look pretty silly. If you don't believe me, ask my wife."

He knew I meant every word, as I'd said them many times before when I'd been the one asked by the governor to write down some little anecdotes about a member of staff who was leaving or retiring and I'd been present in the morning meetings when the governor had told us all to turn up for the farewells. This was not my scene and it never would be.

However, once I got home from work and told my wife about this, she talked me into having a farewell do. She knew very well that I wouldn't attend any function in the boardroom, as she was well aware how I felt about these little presentations, so she suggested that I hold a farewell drink in a local pub. That way, anyone that honestly wanted to say goodbye would have to make the effort to leave work and attend the pub event in their own lunch break.

I had to agree that this was a very good idea. At least then it would prove that the usual farewell crowd wouldn't attend if there was no free food and they hadn't been ordered to do so. So a farewell drink in the pub it would be, and I would let my colleagues know.

So the date was set and staff were informed. My immediate governor grade, whom I always referred to as Doctor Death or the Obergruppenführer had asked me several times if I would consider a formal farewell in the boardroom and each time I'd told him that the answer was a definite no. When he first made the suggestion I remember explaining my reasons to him, just as I had done with Ched. I really don't know what happened after this, but many colleagues subsequently came up to me and assured me that they would be going to the pub for my farewell, do.

Bloody hell, I'd only reckoned on a dozen people turning up, but judging by this response it seemed that there would be far more than that. I hope they don't think I'm gonna buy them all a drink, I thought to myself. My name's Levy, not bloody Rothschild!

Doctor Death asked if I would be embarrassed to be presented with the usual farewell gift at the pub, so I told him I didn't want either the glass decanter or the rose bowl and explained my reasons. He seemed to agree. But now I got the feeling that the governor was going to attend my little party and he was supposed to be in London that day. Bloody hell, even more people coming, I thought. I didn't expect that. They must be really glad to be seeing the back of me!

So my final day in Her Majesty's Prison Service arrived. The deputy governor no less, who lived quite near me, offered to pick me up and take me to work. My wife would be meeting up with me at the pub and would take me home afterwards. It was a very strange feeling getting up on this final working day.

As I looked in the mirror while shaving, I thought to myself: jeez, this is the last time I'll ever have to do this getting up early, shaving and going to work routine. Never again will I have to put on my uniform and a smart, newly ironed shirt. Incidentally, I always ironed my shirts, except when I first met my wife and paid my eldest stepdaughter to do them, so she had some money to go out with her friends and we could have the house to ourselves and some undisturbed peace. From now on I could get up whenever I wanted, dress how I liked and not be dictated to by time or routine. It was a weird feeling, I can tell you.

I arrived at work, handed in my tally, number 13, at the gate and was given my bunch of keys of the corresponding number - and today 13 honestly felt like my lucky number. I went to the locker room to get my stave, emergency medical kit and all the other paraphernalia that POs were required to carry. I then made my way into the reception area, through the wooden door and metal gate and into the prison proper, and headed down the M1 corridor to my office. I was the first one in, as usual. I switched on the kettle to make my first cuppa of the day, turned on my computer, checked my e-mails to find out what had happened overnight and settled down to drink my tea. That was the routine, day in, day out, but never again. I thought, after today I'm not going to wear a watch ever again, as time isn't important. To this day I still have not worn a watch.

From around 7.45 a.m., as usual, the prison started coming to life. The staff were on their designated wings, ready to unlock the prisoners and serve breakfast. My own staff had arrived: one officer, a young lad, who had been assigned temporarily to the audit department and had been a great source of entertainment for me over the previous few months and had certainly helped me to cope with the job I'd come to hate, and another administrative officer, who had listened attentively (even though she must've been bored silly) to my constant reminiscences of past events and was the very person who convinced me to write this book. Doctor Death, who was located further up the admin corridor and opposite the governor's office came down to our office for a cup of tea. He kept telling me that I was a "lucky bastard" to be getting out. He, along with a lot of other managers were becoming disillusioned with the service and wanted to take early retirement, but he had about five more years to go. I think, like many of those at governor grade, he to really missed the daily rapport with both prisoners and staff. It's a difficult transition to make and, as I said before, one that I wasn't prepared to consider at the sacrifice of my home life. So I had some sympathy with my boss, who'd always been good to me and very supportive.

I went to the 9 a.m. meeting in the boardroom, which today was chaired by the deputy governor, as the governor was still in London. Oh good, I thought, maybe he won't be at the pub after all. No more morning meetings with all the heads of function, governors and manager grades; no more watching people crawling to the No. 1; no more listening to those that loved the sound of their own voice; no more being told to toe the party line; no more hearing the 'schoolboy banter' that took place and often upset others even though they weren't allowed to say so; and, most importantly, no more stomaching the bullshit that pervaded these meetings each and every day of the working week in every prison establishment. Hmmm, maybe I really was just a cynical bastard after all!

I'd narrowed down to the exact minute what time I was due to leave the prison service, and although my official retirement date was 4 July, precisely 25 years after my first day with TOIL and annual leave, it worked out that my last working day would be Friday 5 May at exactly 12.15 p.m. I'd ensured that working the extra hours carrying out audits would bring my retirement to this date, as it suited my plans to move to warmer climes.

What was I going to do until 12.15 p.m.? Well, one thing was for certain: I wasn't going to do any work! After the morning meeting, Ched stuck with me, as he was going to give me a lift to the pub, so we went back to my office and just chatted. Another PO 'Eve' came over from Springhill to join us. I'd worked with her for over eight years, so we knew each other pretty well. She was doing the exact same auditing job as me over at Springhill and we'd recently amalgamated the two audit departments. It was planned that she would move into my present office and run both departments from there. I doubted this would ever come to fruition, however, as things changed so quickly in the modern service that nothing was ever certain until it had already happened, and then it would change again anyway. Yes, it's official I really am a cynical bastard!

Although I'd originally planned to go round every department and say my goodbyes personally, at this time of the morning it wasn't convenient to visit the working wings, as all prisoners and staff were engaged in therapy. So Ched and I decided to go and get some bacon butties from the Springhill canteen and charge them to my boss's account. What a good idea! We sent my young lad over to get bacon butties for all of us, including my boss. I then telephoned to tell him that some butties and a cup of tea were about to be served if he would like to come and join us.

We all sat there eating our butties, drinking our tea and reminiscing about the good old days: the characters we'd come across during our time in the service; the incidents that had happened to us; and the notorious prisoners we'd encountered.

After this, I started my farewell walk around the prison. I wasn't feeling sentimental about it, but I was very surprised by some of the nice things many of the staff said about me. Mind you, it's easy to talk like that when someone is leaving and you're never gonna see them again. Ever the cynic! However, I was a little taken aback when one of the prisoners serving life gave me a handmade retirement card. I'd also received several e-mails from staff that had wanted to come to the pub but were unable to do so and wanted to wish me well. Bloody hell, I thought, I must be more popular than I realised. I even received e-mails from the staff at the area office and national audit department, so they must've been impressed by the way I carried out my job.

Finally, it was 12.15 and time to leave. Together with Ched and my two admin officers, I walked up the M1 corridor for the last time, through the metal gate and wooden door, through the centre and out through the wooden door to the gate. I handed in my equipment for the very last time and reminded the gate officer to log my time of departure. I was then allowed through the final gate and was now out of the prison service forever. Shit, I thought, I forgot to hand in my PO epaulettes. Oh well, a souvenir.

Once at the pub, I was determined not to drink too much, but I was very taken aback by the sheer number of staff and colleagues that had turned up. This really was like the piss-ups of old. Even previously retired former colleagues and staff that were off-duty that day came along to say goodbye. Luckily, my minder (my wife) arrived in good time to ensure that I didn't make too much of a fool of myself. I started by just having one glass of wine and sipping it slowly. Anticipating that my farewell drink would only last around an hour, I reckoned I could remain reasonably sober. Boy, how wrong was I? It lasted several hours and even incorporated staff changeovers to allow others to come to the pub.

This was either a genuine show of affection and respect or the biggest excuse in ages that staff had found for a lunchtime drink. I would like to think that it was the former, but will never know.

It's a shame that you only realise just how much respect you've gained when it's too late. Several of the staff told me that they wouldn't have attended a farewell do in the boardroom, as they shared my sentiments about that tradition.

The governor did arrive, having left London early so he that could come and say his farewells. I discovered that my young admin officer had done a collection for me and so, much to my surprise, the governor presented me with a Tom-Tom navigation system, which was greatly appreciated and will always remind me of that day when I use it.

The governor, who had obviously been pre-warned about my feelings, made a short, quick speech. I thanked him and said, "Actually, governor, I've got something for you, too," at which point I removed my epaulettes and handed them over to him for all to see, a final gesture that confirmed that, yes, I really had retired.

The rest of the event is a bit of a blur, as my good intentions not to drink too much evaporated when several glasses of wine turned up at the same time. Well, you can't appear to be ungrateful, can you? So I felt forced to indulge and drank them all, followed by the Scotch and Cokes, and before I knew it I was pissed. But it was a great do, chatting about the old days and catching up with former colleagues. I barely remember my wife driving me home and vaguely recall going straight to bed, then getting up some time later feeling hungry and hung-over.

So that was that. I'd said my farewells, I'd had my drink, and I would now be forgotten - or at least until the following week when somebody would complain about something in the prison and someone else would say, "It's that bloody old git's fault. You know, the one that retired a while back. What's his name now? Yeah, that's right, Tony Levy. He always was pretty useless anyway"!

Chapter 44

Reflections and New Beginnings

I suppose now I can look back after serving 25 years in the prison service, which incidentally is the equivalent of a murderer serving two life sentences back-to-back, and I can be a little more circumspect.

I was never the conventional, archetypal prison officer - at 5ft 7in I didn't have the build. So I knew early on that my approach would have to be different from what most people thought a prison officer should look and act like. What I didn't know at the time was most prison officers came into the same category as me and it was only a public perception that all screws were built like brick shithouses and wanted to take on the world at every opportunity. But I was a bit different. I always kept my hair longer than the regulations. In fact, in my later career, I was one of the few members of staff that sported long hair rather than having it cut extremely short, as was the modern fashion, to try to look as hard as the prisoners themselves. That wasn't my style.

I could have written about many more incidents and bad situation that I had to deal with during my time at all my establishments and my irreverent comments and attitude to some managers who I had little respect for but it would only be a form of self-indulgence and feed my ego which is not my style so I have not included them in this book

My first five years in the service were probably my most enjoyable ones, despite the appalling conditions; or maybe it was because of those conditions, I don't honestly know. Then, as you take on more responsibilities and get promoted, you have to curb your behaviour, as you're no longer one of the boys and you have to set an example and be a mentor to your peers and subordinates alike. That doesn't mean you can't have a bit of fun and a joke, but your additional responsibilities mean that you've got to be aware of the repercussions of every decision and action.

When the much-vaunted fresh start was introduced in 1988 it signalled the biggest change in how the prison service would function. Gone were the days of overtime and Spanish practices, weekly pay in cash and Paul Childs. In came regular, predictable hours, monthly pay, legislation, and more accountability. The change wasn't a bad thing in itself, but we all knew that there would always be a requirement to work more than the stipulated hours.

Like today, we were always short of staff and the hours had to be covered by someone somehow. So in came TOIL - time off in lieu - or overtime without pay, as we called it. It meant that even if you didn't want to do extra hours you could be ordered to do them if it was deemed a local emergency and you would be given TOIL instead of overtime. However, as we were so short of staff, actually fitting in these awarded TOIL hours was difficult and often staff accumulated masses of owed, unclaimed hours that they'd basically worked for free.

Over the years, successive government policies gradually introduced more legislation, requiring increased accountability, social awareness and political correctness, together with an obsession with paperwork and directives regarding anti-racism, mixed staffing, GALIPS (gay and lesbians in prison service), RESPECT (racial equality for staff), and many, many more. We became bogged down by new initiatives, new ideas and new directives, and at the same time, our finances were cut, cut and then cut again, with the same message each year about efficiency savings. New measures relating to staffing will lead to fewer staff and less money to pay those staff, combined with an expectation that the hours and jobs will still be covered by the remaining staff. The morale of the service has suffered beyond belief. The fun has been legislated out of the service, and it's now just a job.

The prison service has become so obsessed with political correctness that you can't ask colleagues if they want their coffee black or white, as this is deemed racist; you have to ask, "With or without?" Neither can you use the term 'brainstorming', as it's deemed offensive to people who suffer from epilepsy; you must use the term 'collective thought processing'. My old nickname from the Ville is now a huge no-no, and anyone that dared to call me Yiddo to my face or even behind my back could end up losing their job, their pension and any prospect of obtaining further employment, as uttering this name would be deemed racist. In addition, if I didn't report a member of staff for doing this I, too, would be placed on a disciplinary charge and deemed a racist.

Yet all this has happened without anybody fully realising it. We've accepted all that has been thrown at us, taken it on board and got on with it. The element of fun has been lost in the process. I don't mean that you can't tell a joke, but it must be politically correct and not racist, sexist, religious, ageist or offensive towards any person or anything. Carefree remarks that mean no harm can land you in a lot of trouble. The characters that were around in my early days of the service have all gone: Steve, Nasher, Ray, Jock, George, Mr X, Joe, Del, Teflon and Taff. They've been driven out and have either taken early retirement like me or have gone underground and now resent the service and what it has become. All that remains are the anecdotal stories that the older staff can relate when they talk of the old days. In fact, new officer recruits are told not to take any notice of the older staff, as they're all old dinosaurs. Mind you, I was referred to as an old dinosaur when I'd only been in the job for four years, so that's nothing new.

Yes, there were bad old days, too, but overall most days were good despite the conditions and pressures we worked under, and despite the long hours we worked to enable us to earn a good wage, and despite the overall institutional atmosphere. And my most memorable and enjoyable time will always be the Pentonville days.

So I'd reached the end of it all. I'd completed my last shift and said goodbye to the prisoners, many of whom thanked me for just being me over the years they'd spent in my charge and wished me good luck. I'd said my goodbyes to my colleagues, some sad to see me go as I'd earned their respect, and others glad to see me go, as they didn't like the fact that I told it like it was (from my perspective) or that I was still popular with the prisoners and staff and they weren't for whatever reason. I'd handed in my keys for the last time and had walked through the gates to start the next chapter of my life.

What will I do? How will I cope? The service is a very protected place not just for the prisoners but also for the prison officers. What goes on in the real world is a long way from a life working in a prison and the prison way of life can make you quite insular.

I knew I would find it difficult to get another job at my age even if I wanted to, so I would have to survive on my prison pension alone until I reached state pension age. Having to live on a third of my salary was a frightening prospect, but I was my own person again and my family and my wife were the most important things now.

I was no longer ruled by time and routine. I could sleep and eat when I wanted, I could go unshaven, I could wear what I liked and I could plan my social events and holidays without worrying about shift patterns. Yes, there would be many changes and I would have to adapt to them. The old prison rulebook had been thrown away, and no guidebook existed for what was now running through my mind.

This was not the end of the game but the start of the next and most important part of my life. To quote from the great Winston Churchill:

Now, this is not the end, It's not even the beginning of the end, But it is, perhaps, the end of the beginning.

This was now the beginning of the rest of my life and I intended to enjoy it.

Epilogue

Looking back now that I've completed my story, which travels through my 25 years as a serving prison officer in Her Majesty's Prison Service, it seems strange how the memories came flooding back into my mind as I wrote. I didn't have to think hard as I started each chapter, as the words just seemed to flow. I could recall in vivid detail all that is contained in this book, and as I wrote I could see the characters I met along the way clearly inside my head. Other incidents and events that are not included in this book appeared crystal clear in my thoughts, too, and those memories occasionally stopped me in my tracks, as I needed to replay them in my mind.

As I wrote, I could even recall the smells, particularly of Pentonville: the stink of stale tobacco and human body odours that emanated from every orifice; the smell of sweat and fear when an incident erupted; the aromas in the tea rooms; the mustiness of the courtrooms on prisoner escorts. I also remembered the smells at Grendon, with a chicken farm on one side and a waste disposal landfill site on the other, which became overpowering on a warm, sunny evening.

These memories will never go away and can never be replaced. They are my personal and individual record of those events, and I'm so pleased to have them.

Truly, dear reader, if you're reading this then some very clever person will have corrected my poor grammar and spelling and transformed my words into a readable book that makes sense, but the stories are just as they appeared in my mind and as I wrote them down.

It has been said that we all have a book inside of us, and now, having completed mine, I have to agree. We all have stories to tell. I thought I'd lived a pretty mundane and boring life, but I discovered it was filled with colourful incidents, events and people. I hope that you've found them interesting, enjoyable and maybe sometimes unbelievable, although I can assure you that everything is true. There are many more tales that I could've recounted, but this will be my one and only (I have subsequently written three more books that I never planned to write at the time of this book) book, and I've got to say that writing it has been a most rewarding experience.

All the characters mentioned in my book honestly existed and all the stories mentioned happened. As stated at the beginning of the book, I have changed the names of all individuals for obvious reasons, although in some cases I must admit that I've forgotten their real names anyway, as my memory is getting old. If I've inadvertently offended or upset any individual in relating my stories, please accept my humble apologies, as this was certainly never intended.

During the time covered in this book, I can honestly put my hand on my heart and state that I've encountered only one or two individuals, whether prisoners, staff or visitors, that I honestly didn't like as human beings. My philosophy while in the service was to treat other people as I would wish to be treated if I were in their position.

All men are born equal and all should be treated as equals. This is how I've tried to live in both my working and personal life.

My thanks go to all the staff and prisoners I've met during my 25-year career in all the prison establishments I've worked in or visited, as well as the professionals I've had dealings with at police stations and criminal justice courts. Without all of you, this book would never have been written. Despite my changing feelings towards the prison service as I moved towards retirement, overall, it was an enlightening experience.

Many thanks, too, for the most valuable commodity any human being can be given: **memories.**

Lightning Source UK Ltd.
Milton Keynes UK
UKHW020833270223
417728UK00016B/1373